Poverty, Gender and Health in the Slums of Bangladesh

Poverty, Gender and Health in the Slums of Bangladesh provides comprehensive ethnographic accounts that depict the daily life experiences and health hardships encountered by young women and their families living in the slums of Dhaka city and the injustices they face.

The analysis focuses on two specific historical eras: 2002–2003 and 2020–2022 and shows that despite recent improvements in employment opportunities and greater mobility for young women, their lives reflect ongoing challenges reminiscent of those faced two decades earlier. While national and global organizations acknowledge the nation's economic and social progress, those on the outskirts of society continue to grapple with enduring poverty. They are excluded from the advantages of economic growth, oppressed by unjust local, national, and global systems, discriminatory laws, and policies. Their struggles go unnoticed as they confront a slew of challenges, including slum evictions, enforced lockdowns, income losses, food insecurity, and ongoing crises related to health, injuries, fatalities, and exploitation and harassment by law enforcement and influential individuals within the slum and the city. After two decades, these obstacles persist, and life remains tenuous, with health severely compromised.

This book will appeal to students, academics, and researchers in the fields of Public Health, Medical Anthropology, Gender Studies, Urban Studies, Development Studies, Social Sciences, as well as professionals engaged in urban health and poverty-related work.

Sabina Faiz Rashid, PhD, who previously served as the Dean and Professor of BRAC James P Grant School of Public Health at BRAC University from 2013 to 2023, is Professor in the Mushtaque Chowdhury Chair in Health and Poverty endowed by the BRAC Founder, Late Sir F.H. Abed in 2015. Her background is in medical anthropology and public health from The Australian National University. She has two decades of experience in ethnographic research, focusing on the intersections between poverty, gender and health, which significantly compromise the lives, health and overall well being of disadvantaged communities in Bangladesh.

Routledge Research on Gender in Asia Series

18. Literature, Gender and the Trauma of Partition
The Paradox of Independence
Debali Mookerjea-Leonard

19. Sexuality and Public Space in India
Reading the Visible
Carmel Christy

20. HIV/AIDS in India
Voices from the Margins
Sunita Manian

21. Sexuality in a Changing China
Young Women, Sex and Intimate Relations in the Reform Period
Nicole Zarafonetis

22. Gender, Development and the State in India
Carole Spary

23. Female Chinese Bankers in the Asia Pacific
Gender, Mobility and Opportunity
Wai-wan Vivien Chan

24. New Muslim Women of Bangladesh
Nazia Hussein

25. War, Violence and Women's Agency in Pakistan
The Case of Swat
Rehana Wagha

26. Poverty, Gender and Health in the Slums of Bangladesh
Children of Crows
Sabina Faiz Rashid

Poverty, Gender and Health in the Slums of Bangladesh

Children of Crows

Sabina Faiz Rashid

Routledge
Taylor & Francis Group

LONDON AND NEW YORK

First published 2024
by Routledge
4 Park Square, Milton Park, Abingdon, Oxon OX14 4RN

and by Routledge
605 Third Avenue, New York, NY 10158

Routledge is an imprint of the Taylor & Francis Group, an informa business

© 2024 Sabina Faiz Rashid

British Library Cataloguing-in-Publication Data
A catalogue record for this book is available from the British Library

ISBN: 978-1-032-74060-7 (hbk)
ISBN: 978-1-032-74061-4 (pbk)
ISBN: 978-1-003-46747-2 (ebk)

DOI: 10.4324/9781003467472

Typeset in Times New Roman
by Taylor & Francis Books

To Abbu and Mom – For teaching me the values that I still hold dear to me.

Thank you for your unconditional love and for being my champion.

Contents

Acknowledgements   viii
Foreword   xi

1 The Tyranny of Poverty and Health   1

2 The Tyranny of Everyday Life for Young Women and their Families in Slums   7

3 Life on the Margins   28

4 Social Position, Relationships and Strategies to Survive in 2002   43

5 Relationships, Networks and Survival during Covid 19, 2020 and After   57

6 Police, Gang Fights and Insecurity in 2002   75

7 Arrests and Resistance, 2020 to 2022   84

8 Battered Bodies, Minds, and Hearts in 2002   97

9 Health is a Battlefield, 2020–2022   111

10 Displaced Lives in 2002: Eviction and Instability   123

11 What Lies Ahead in 2022?   135

12 Dead End   146

Index   172

Acknowledgements

This journey of writing *Children of Crows* has been both a personal and professional odyssey, and I am deeply grateful to all those who supported, encouraged, and pushed me along the way.

This journey, which has led to the completion of this book, was born out of a promise I made to my beloved father, before he passed away on January 13, 2020. He always wanted me to write and believed in the value of scholarship and was always there for counsel and support. Following my Mom's passing and after his retirement, he became a prolific writer on international affairs, foreign policy, peace and conflict. To him, I owe my inspiration and unwavering commitment.

I initiated the process of reviewing my data and commencing writing in 2021, but it was characterized by sporadic periods of activity. Toby (Safi) was my rock, motivating me to persist in writing even during moments of self-doubt. He consistently encouraged me, even during moments of insecurity, and supported me tirelessly throughout the writing process which I properly embarked on in 2021 and continued well into early 2023. It was Toby who ingeniously derived the subtitle *Children of Crows* from a transcript, and he selflessly reviewed final chapters, even after long, exhausting days at work.

Meeting Lenore Manderson, Distinguished Professor of Public Health and Medical Anthropology in the School of Public Health, University of the Witwatersrand, Johannesburg, South Africa, was divine intervention, and I am forever indebted to her. Although I had known her for some time, given her role as my supervisor's supervisor, Lenore's immediate and enthusiastic response when I expressed my interest in writing this book was a pivotal moment. She graciously volunteered to read, review, and edit and provided invaluable feedback on the entire manuscript in 2022 and early 2023.

My deep gratitude extends to my two wonderful and loving brothers, Amin and Mamun, and their beautiful families, as well as my aunt, Zarina Khalammi. They have been a constant pillar of support and love for me, since my mother's passing on October 3, 1997. I am also thankful for the support of my wonderful in-laws – Ammi (Toby's mom) for her love and care, Aunty Hameeda, Speedy, Riaz Bhai, Amala, Dina and Sara for their support.

To the cherished group who supported me in this endeavour and, who I am grateful to have in my life: dearest Samia, who often chided me about my writing, as I had a tendency to start and stop, even going as far as to threaten to sever ties due to my procrastination; Bonnie (Bonlet), who patiently edited my first chapter and has been a source of unwavering encouragement and care; Monami (Put..) was a wellspring of reassurance during the trials of COVID-19 with her regular WhatsApp texts, maintaining her enduring belief in my writing; Kudsia, with her 'carrot cake fixes' spurred me to hold on to faith when I lost motivation and Kate (Vindaloo), my bestie from college and beyond, who was overjoyed to see me finally embark on this writing journey during Covid-19 and after. Additionally, Minnat bhabi, my spiritual elder sister, and dear Fariha and Tamara, who encouraged me during this period and celebrated the completion of my manuscript. Thank you to Keya (NJ) for your silly jokes and encouragement.

The overwhelming enthusiasm of my family and close friends when I was awarded the Andelot Fellowship at Harvard as a Visiting Scholar from May to July 2022 was heartwarming. I received calls and WhatsApp messages from the 'usual suspects', and one of my friends, Mahboob, continually sent me simple cooking recipes and words of encouragement, as I navigated my culinary challenges and continued my writing.

My deepest appreciation and affection go to my most favourite couple, Richard Cash and Stella Depuis, who graciously opened their home to me in Cambridge, Massachusetts for writing, with both of them checking in on my progress, motivating me to 'keep at it', and Richard who readily agreed to review the entire manuscript in early 2023. I am also grateful to Marcia Castro, Chair of the Department of Global Health and Population at the Harvard T.H. Chan School of Public Health, for offering me the fellowship that made my time in Boston possible. I would like to thank Amanullah Khan, who told me that we need to create the change we want to see in our lives, which inspired me to apply for the Andelot Fellowship. I extend my thanks to Malabika Di, (didi) for her support and agreeing to be Acting Dean at BRAC James P Grant School of Public Health, which allowed me the opportunity to take time off for three months in 2022.

Special thanks to aka mini-monsters at JPGSPH: Selima, who continuously encouraged me to write, and assisted with formatting the final document; Wafa and Ishrat, who were most excited when I shared my details of publishing this manuscript, and all of them put in extra hours to assist me in the final stretch. I extend my sincere appreciation to Lamisa, who helped me with final formatting of references and to Mahmud, our ever-reliable IT colleague. I want to give a big shout-out to my other awesome cheerleaders at the school – you know who you are, and I'm so grateful for your support and belief in me. Thanks a million!

I must acknowledge Mushtaque Bhai, my first boss at RED, BRAC who reminded me that perfection is not a requirement for submission and encouraged me to take that step when I was struggling to submit the manuscript in 2023. I want to acknowledge Hilary Standing, Emeritus Professor and Emeritus Fellow of the Institute of Development Studies (IDS), University of Sussex, who shared creative writing resources.

I want to express my appreciation to Sally Theobald, friend and colleague and acknowledge the ARISE project, which focused on communities and accountability in urban slums, making my ethnographic research on young women in Dhaka during COVID-19 possible.

My heartfelt thanks go to Nipu and Sumona, my lifelines throughout the fieldwork, who were always pleasant, helpful, and insightful. Their support was invaluable on this journey.

I want to express my profound gratitude to the remarkable young women and their families who generously shared their stories for this book. Their openness, vulnerability, and courage have brought these pages to life, adding depth and diversity. Thank you for making time, and trusting me to tell your stories, and for the inspiration and learning they will provide to others. It's an honour to have been a part of capturing and sharing your narratives.

The motivation behind my decision to focus on writing about individuals living on the fringes of society is closely linked to late Sir Fazle Hasan Abed, founder of BRAC, and his lifelong dedication to effecting change for the most disadvantaged. It was he who provided me with my initial opportunity at BRAC in 1993 and introduced me to the realms of development and health, enlightening me about the critical importance of addressing the welfare of impoverished communities.

Finally, I would not be where I am today, without the mercy of God. I am grateful for His guidance, strength, and blessings throughout my life. His guidance helped me overcome challenges and reach the completion of this book. I am thankful for His grace and for the faith that sustains me. My belief is due to the profound influence of my mother in shaping my spiritual journey. She not only taught me the importance of faith and staying true to myself but also enriched my life with her vibrant spirit. Her fun-loving, silly, and vivacious nature served as a constant reminder to embrace the joy in life's moments and to remember to have gratitude.

Foreword

An individual's health is the portrait of many factors: a person's genetic profile biology, exposure to pathogens, exposure to other risk factors, which themselves are influenced by a person's physical and emotional environment. This latter set of factors, often passed over when assessing an individual's health, are often the most important. Nothing could make this clearer than the book, *Children of Crows*, by Sabina Rashid, former dean (2013–2023) of the James P. Grant School of Public Health at BRAC University in Dhaka, Bangladesh.

This is an engaging book that explores the ethnographic narratives of young women, shedding light on their susceptibility, daily life hurdles, and overall welfare. Professor Rashid adeptly crafts a vivid depiction of the non-biological factors that impact their physical health and quality of life. She employs specific case studies that mirror the life paths of 84 young women and their families, from two different time periods, 2002–2003 and 2020–2022. These instances unveil the disruptions, fragility, and day-to-day difficulties encountered by some of the most disadvantaged families residing in the slums of Dhaka, offering insights into what lives must be like for similarly vulnerable populations in low- and middle-income countries (LMICs) and in the United States, where numerous families continually grapple with life at the bottom of the socioeconomic ladder.

Professor Rashid takes readers on a journey through the intricate realities of living on the brink, dealing with irregular income, cash and job insecurity, food scarcity, harassment, and exclusion from various sectors. These challenges not only impact their health but also perpetuate a cycle of intergenerational deprivation. She effectively demonstrates how a major or minor crisis in the lives of impoverished households can push them further towards disaster. The life stories of these young women make a compelling case for the necessity of a morally just and equitable approach to public health. Health disparities cannot be adequately addressed without recognizing and addressing the broader social and systemic factors that contribute to them.

Through the stories of these young women in Dhaka's slums, Professor Rashid exposes the flaws in the traditional disease-centric model of public health, emphasizing the importance of considering the conditions in which people live, get sick, and pass away. She argues that the experiences of these women and their families challenge our existing understanding of health and development, demanding a critical and ongoing examination of health and development strategies and interventions. This entails acknowledging the multitude of actors, both global and local, who perpetuate these injustices.

I would like to extend my congratulations to Professor Rashid for highlighting the pivotal role played by the environment in shaping people's lives. These individual stories contribute to our efforts to create environments where people can flourish. Furthermore, social science research in the fields of public health and development in Bangladesh provide an opportunity to generate new evidence regarding the intricacies of structural and social systems that lead to exclusion, poverty, and health disparities, not only in Bangladesh but also in other societies.

Richard A. Cash, MD, MPH
Senior Lecturer, Department of Global Health and Population.
Harvard Chan School of Public Health, Boston, Massachusetts, USA
Recipient of the Prince Mahidol Award 2006

Credit: Asif Faisal, 2023, BRAC James P Grant School of Public Health, BRAC University, Dhaka, Bangladesh

1   The Tyranny of Poverty and Health

25 July 2002

In a single night, thousands of people were abruptly uprooted from the Phulbari slum, leading to profound and disastrous impacts on the lives, health, and overall well-being of young women and their families. It plunged their existence into a state of complete turmoil.

It was 3 pm. The residents of Phulbari slum had just been evicted. I was there the previous day when the entire place was in total and utter pandemonium as residents frantically ran around dismantling tin and cardboard homes, removing fans, bedding, and kitchen utensils. I returned to an empty site the next day. Except for the mosque and clinic, which were made of brick, most of the dwellings had been removed. I ran into some of the residents who despite the demolition by bulldozers, were hopeful they would be able to reclaim their space in Phulbari. They were emotional and angry. The mother of one young woman, Roshonara, her eyes swollen from crying, shared, 'We are children of crows, with no respite … forced to fly from one place to another, looking for a place to live!' A man standing next to her said angrily, 'The government and the rich should just kill all the poor people in the country.' Then he looked at me, with a scowl on his face: 'You don't have our kinds of worries, do you?' I was ashamed and had no response. Even though I was in shock, I knew that I would be returning to a comfortable bed and home. The newly evicted residents of Phulbari would never have the same privileges and opportunities.

I had completed seven months of fieldwork in Phulbari and had become close to several families. For 3,500 households and their families, this had been their home for close to 20 years. What would happen to the residents and others I had met during this period? Where would they go? In my ten years of rural field experience, I had never witnessed a community and locality completely removed and the place demolished, as if the residents and Phulbari had never existed.

Overnight, thousands were forcibly displaced, with devastating consequences for their lives, their health, and their well-being, along with familial and social relationships. As I followed many of these families for several months post

DOI: 10.4324/9781003467472-1

eviction, I witnessed first-hand families struggling to survive. Tensions and fights increased within households and with others. I saw up close how precarious and fragile their circumstances were, as wages were lost, and debts began to mount. As personal relationships began to crumble, and previous informal networks of support disappeared, emotional and mental anguish increased. Five months post eviction, Monsura, one of the residents I had become close to, rang me. It was late evening in December 2001:

> Monsura whispered that she had fallen pregnant again and had an abortion. She was terrified as she was bleeding nonstop. With the Phulbari eviction, she had lost contact with the health providers. She did not have any of their contact details, or their phone numbers. Like many other families who were grappling with severe cash shortages and the sudden loss of familiarity of networks following the demolition, Monsura took matters into her own hands. She and her husband were plunged into a nightmare of cash shortages and a cycle of debts accrued from three consecutive relocations, from slum to slum. Rental money was owed to the current landlady. Desperate, and fearful of having another baby during the worst period in their lives, she and her husband opted for an unsafe abortion. It was cheaper and for them their only option, given their uncertain future.

Fast forward 20 years

It was March 2020, and Coronavirus Disease (Covid-19) was declared a global pandemic. A national lockdown in Bangladesh left millions of poor people in the country, particularly the residents in Dhaka's slums, struggling to survive. A Covid-19 lockdown, announced by the government on March 25, 2020, was declared a "holiday" to avoid panic. All factories, schools, retail and hospitality industries, and transportation were forced to shut down indefinitely. No one could leave their homes, whether they lived in a well-to-do suburb or in a slum or in a rural area. The army and police were deployed on the streets to enforce the lockdown, and the entire country came to a standstill. The situation continued for two months, extended every few weeks by the government.

By April 2020, I was receiving frantic calls from poor young women who I had known for a while. They lived in slums and worked as informal workers. They were frightened. Most were in limbo, confused and scared of the virus, but mostly they worried about starvation as a direct result of the lockdown. Meena, 19 years old, called me in late April 2020, a month after the lockdown began:

> It has already been a long time with this lockdown *Apa* (sister). What will we do? I keep hearing that the government is calling it a holiday and it will continue ... there are police on the streets and the army ... they won't let us leave the slum and there are stories of beatings and fines from

the police … what will I do? How will we survive? Everyone is talking about a virus, but my children are hungry. How will we manage? Do you know when the lockdown will end?

Meena began to cry and the fear in her voice was palpable. I did not know how long the lockdown would be extended. I had no words of comfort. The sheer horror of impending starvation was discernible in Meena's scared voice. This fear was mirrored amongst the millions of informal workers living in slums, who were abruptly left without the means to earn cash. Many slum residents rely on daily wages to survive. A lockdown meant no income; no income meant no cash; no cash meant no food. How would they eat, pay rent? And if they were to fall sick with the virus, how would they pay for treatment? As income options dried up and without any social security system to fall back on, many had very real anxieties about what lay ahead.

In this book, I present unique and rich evidence on Dhaka's slums by drawing on ethnographic historical fieldwork data, following two different groups of young women and their families 20 years apart. Very few detailed ethnographies exist, documenting everyday lives over time and capturing the effects of crisis periods, be it an eviction from a slum or a pandemic, on urban poor young women and their families living in Dhaka city. The narratives reveal the complex realities of how health unfolds and manifests for these women and their families, living in contexts of deprivation, persistent poverty, excluded from economies of scale, and oppressed by unjust local and national structures and systems. These combine to reproduce intergenerational poverty and a bleak future for many of them.

In the chapters that follow, I share the experiences of young women and their families living in 'their' slum and the immediate aftermath of their eviction (2002 until early 2003); and a second group of young women living through the pandemic lockdowns and beyond (from 2020 until 2022). The main aim of the book is to enable readers to, at the very least, gain some understanding of how structural violence, systematic exclusion, and environments of marginalization, discrimination, and exploitation are interconnected, create suffering, and impact poor people's everyday lives, health, and wellbeing. The chapters chronologically document how life unfolds in expected and unexpected ways for these women, and in turn how these have a domino effect on their daily lives and health. The main argument of this book is that health is much broader and enmeshed in the structural, social, economic, and political. These driving factors create endless struggles, strife and suffering for those who are vulnerable.

By drawing on selected case studies of six young women and their families, I document how structural and social inequalities and top-down state policies wreak havoc on them. Any major or minor crisis, an eviction, a pandemic related lockdown, erratic income sources, an abrupt job loss, an illness in the family, breakdown in networks of support, an accident or death, push many of these already fragile households to the brink of catastrophe. Some of them remain persistent in trying to break even. Being unable to afford necessities such as food, rent and other basic services leads to a constant state of stress and anxiety. Their lives endlessly fluctuate between hope, fear, and despair. They try to survive by leveraging income sources, social relationships, frantically drawing on any stable and temporary networks of family, friends, neighbours, and more powerful intermediaries, local political affiliated leaders, and various gatekeepers, employers and even strangers to cope.

Some social relationships are strong while others are temporary; some were simply accidental. Depending on the strengths of these relationships, young women and their families managed to pull through. The narratives in the chapters reveal the importance of paying attention to non-quantifiable concerns, such as powerlessness, discrimination, harassment and insecurity, which leaves many families stuck on the margins. The young women's narratives reveal the many different layers and faces of poverty. Deprivations are not only economic. Life is one of continual precarity, with few options for a dignified life. Health itself is severely compromised.

The experiences of the six young women illustrated in this book, while diverse, are largely representative of the 84 case studies I documented – 50 repeated in-depth interviews and case studies between 2002 to early 2003 and 34 case studies from 2020 until 2022. Although many of their lives unravelled in diverse yet predictable ways, it varied depending on individual circumstances and strength of relationships and support. Overall, the fear of not having enough cash to manage and falling back into poverty was an underlying anxiety shared by all. The young women and their families in Dhaka slums not only occupy the lower rungs of the social scale socially, economically, and politically, but one can argue that some of them are simply off such a scale (Perlman, 2016:131). As marginal people, they have no position in the dominant social system but are 'exploited and repressed' and excluded and stigmatised from a 'closed social system' (Perlman, 2016:131).

Despite all the gains and achievements occurring in Bangladesh, poverty and widening inequalities affect millions who live on the margins. Structural and social inequalities continue with little substantial change for those who remain vulnerable, before the pandemic, and the situation considerably worsened with Covid-19. Any crisis is disastrous for many vulnerable households, who already live life on the edge. Banks argues that poverty is more than simply lack of income and assets (Banks, 2016). Political and social inequalities in the slums and the city more widely, maintain and exacerbate poverty and inequality by more powerful groups at all levels. Being excluded from formal systems of power, and having to mediate multiple oppressive structures, creates environments of exploitation. Local and national policies and laws remain disconnected from poor peoples' realities. The multitude of intersecting factors remove any possibility of sustained incremental improvements. Their daily lives remain in a constant state of flux, wavering between uncertainty, hope and fear, and at times in limbo, while they fight to remain out of the poverty trap. All of these are major drivers of *bad health*.

One of the challenges is the narrow way in which urban poverty is conceived, defined and measured, leading to its misrepresentation and underestimation (Sen, Amartya, 1976, Mitlin & Satterthwaite, 2012; Satterthwaite & Mitlin, 2013). Banks argues that this leaves our understanding of urban poverty incomplete, with little detailed documentation on the challenges of living extremely deprived lives and the effects of being excluded which continue to create and reproduce urban poverty (Banks, 2016). The heterogeneity of those living in slums, including poorer temporary migrants and more vulnerable households, can remain undercounted in large-scale surveys or become aggregated, homogenised and generalised. This neglects the multifaceted nature of everyday life, diversity of poverty experiences, which lends itself to messy and insecure lives. Social science research can contribute critical evidence on understanding the urban poor, an incredibly complex, wide and varied group (William, 2022). Drawing on ethnographic data, the chapters in this book provide a deeper understanding of the continual vulnerabilities, maladies and risks experienced by these young women and their families. Sadly, it shows not much has changed in the past two decades for those who are vulnerable in the slums of Dhaka.

The writing of this book is prompted by the narratives of the young women, which challenges the long-standing focus of public health and development, which tends to silo and compartmentalise individuals into disease states in public health, or assess individuals and households mainly on economic indicators, where income is the dominant criteria to understand improved circumstances. However, it is critical to understand why chronic social disadvantage persists even for people who are not otherwise rated among the income poorest; to what Gayatri Spivak defined as "the chronic marginality", where multiple and overlapping vulnerabilities happen in hugely determinantal ways, due to both income and non-income deprivations (Sen et al, 2004:77).

Good health is key to living a full and optimal life. Many of these young women, like billions of marginalised populations around the world, continue to live in extreme hardship. All human beings have the right to a safe environment, access to decent housing, clean water and sanitation, education, nutritious food, a stable income and access to basic material, social and political resources. Or do some lives matter more than others? More than ever, there is a moral urgency to interrogate power, politics, privilege, and vested interests, deeply embedded in national economic, social and political systems, and the multitude of agencies, corporations and global actors, who perpetuate poverty and inequalities. Young women and their families in Dhaka's slums lead greatly diminished and undignified lives, which is a reminder of the unevenness of development with the consequence of their lives being unfairly cut short. The burdens placed on them provide ample evidence of the need for a socially just model in public health. Unless there is a pursuit of the ideal, a vision embedded in a just world and health for all, we will continue to reproduce poverty, and damaging health outcomes will persist well into the next century and beyond.

References

Banks, N. (2016). Livelihoods limitations: The political economy of urban poverty in Dhaka, Bangladesh. *Development and Change*, 47(2), 266–292.

Mitlin, D., & Satterthwaite, D. (2012). *Urban Poverty in the Global South: Scale and Nature*. Routledge.

Perlman, J. E. (2016). Rio's Favelas and the Myth of Marginality. *Politics & Society*, 5(2), 131–160. HYPERLINK "https://doi.org/10.1177/003232927500500201 "https://doi.org/10.1177/003232927500500201 (reprinted from 1975)

Satterthwaite, D., & Mitlin, D. (2013). *Reducing Urban Poverty in the Global South*. Routledge.

Sen, B., Hulme, D., Ahmad, I., Kabeer, N., Ali, Z., Khan, I., Begum, S., Matin, I., Haider, O., Sen, C., & Shahabuddin, Q. (2004). *Chronic Poverty in Bangladesh: Tales of Ascent, Descent, Marginality and Persistence: The State of the Poorest 2004/2005*. Bangladesh: Bangladesh Institute of Development Studies Dhaka.

Sen, Amartya (1976), Poverty: An Ordinal Approach to Measurement Econometrica, Vol. 44, No. 2 (Mar., 1976), pp. 219–231 (13 pages)

William, S. K. (2022). We need to recognise the diversity of the urban poor. *The Daily Star*. www.thedailystar.net/opinion/views/news/we-need-recognise-the-diversity-the-urban-poor-3121506.

2 The Tyranny of Everyday Life for Young Women and their Families in Slums

On January 26, 2023, I received information about the imminent eviction of residents from two significant slum settlements within Dhaka city. This narrative of loss and displacement was sadly not unfamiliar, as Dhaka city has been stuck in a recurring cycle of destruction of slums. Once more, families find themselves subjected to harassment and mistreatment as they strive to rebuild their lives in new surroundings. This brought back memories of my time conducting fieldwork in Phulbari, where the demolitions in 2002 served as a poignant reminder of how many individuals felt 'worse off than dogs.' They believed they had been abandoned by the government and the more affluent population of Dhaka, who appeared indifferent to their fate. A few shared that they would forever be 'children of crows,' with no respite.

The capital city hosts the largest number of slums in the country. My colleagues and I had been conducting research since 2019 in one of these threatened slums. The settlement is government owned and is in the south of Dhaka city, with a population of approximately 20,000, including government street cleaners. Rumours were that some government employees may be rehabilitated, but other residents would have to leave immediately. Many began to desperately search for a new slum to rent, and established residents were anxious about losing trusted social connections – the neighbours and the local shopkeepers they relied on for goods and occasional cash, and the health clinics and pharmacies (unlicensed drug shops) they visited for various illnesses and received medication on credit. Many had informal jobs close to this slum and the sudden displacement would impact on their livelihoods, which in turn would affect their ability to generate enough cash to maintain their households.

As urbanization rapidly expands to all parts of the city, with investments and financial interests tied up in developing high-rise commercial buildings, apartment complexes, gated communities, shopping malls and further gentrification of the city. For instance, the government inaugurated the well-known Hatirjheel project, which comprises of a recreational and landscaping part, including a water court, floating walkway and so on, including lakeside landing steps and an Amphitheatre, which cost TK1,971 crore (almost US $200,000). Poorer residents who used to live in the area for decades, were

DOI: 10.4324/9781003467472-2

forcibly pushed out to other places, particularly the peripheries of the city (Hossain, 2006). This will be a continuing saga, a repeated tragedy with thousands of residents of slums, shoved out of their homes, suffering silently and living in a city, which has no place for them.

A Supreme Court ruling in 2000 requires that the government find evicted residents of a slum a new location to live, as a basic human right of all citizens. This law is not usually followed.[1] This ruling set a precedent for protecting similar claims and became a crucial tool for slum residents and activists in their ongoing fight against forced evictions. Though eviction drives have decreased in frequency, the government has made no long-term efforts towards a housing policy for the urban poor. As a result, despite progressive rulings, legal solutions only serve to maintain status quo. Through strict interpretation of the law, the government can evict slums as it chooses, provided there is a rehabilitation plan. This means that successful responses to eviction threats, however important, tend to be reactive and stopgap measures only (Farid, 2013).

Bangladesh has one of the fastest-growing urban populations in the world, with estimates that by 2050, more than half of its population will be living in cities, of whom around half will live in slums (World Bank, 2015). Several pull and push factors from poverty lead rural migrants to the city: the desperate need and opportunities to earn cash, the promise of better economic options, and increasingly now climate affected migrants. At least 1,500 new migrants arrive each day in Dhaka city, making it one of the fastest growing megacities in the world. Being the capital, it is the political centre of the country – housing the Parliament, ministries and it is the financial and commercial capital, accounting for the 35% of the country's economy (Ahsan, 2019). It is predicted that by 2030, the city will become the world's fourth most populous megacity, according to the UN (World Bank, 2015; Streatfield & Karar, 2008).

What is happening in Bangladesh and other rapidly urbanizing LMICs is the great urban dilemma. This is exemplified by the contradictory effects of urbanization in the twenty first century 'as a force for unparalleled development on the one hand, and as a risk for insecurity amongst the urban poor on the other – the double-edged character of urbanization' (Muggah, 2012). Bangladesh is a densely populated country with a population of 161 million as of 2018. The rate of population growth has been slowing, reaching around 1% in 2018 and as per UN projection, the population size is estimated to reach around 173 million by 2025. The country has successful garments and pharmaceutical industries, and various manufacturing sectors have embraced an exports-led growth model. A decade of consistently recording over 7% GDP growth has resulted in significant gains in the reduction of absolute poverty levels. In over a decade, extreme poverty fell from 18% to 10.5 % in the country (Chattopadhyay, 2021). Bangladesh graduated from being one of the poorest countries to attaining lower-middle income classification in 2015 and is reportedly on track to attain middle income status around 2040 (Giménez et al., 2014).

Bangladesh has made significant progress. Maternal mortality rate has come down by almost two-thirds, infant and child mortality rates were reduced by 44% and 35% respectively. The country's total fertility rate is currently approaching replacement level and is the lowest in South Asia (exception is Sri Lanka). Several diseases have either been eradicated or brought under control, and the mainstreaming of nutrition interventions in the public sector, increasing agricultural self-sufficiency and supportive policies, wasting among children is down by half, while stunting and underweight prevalence have come down to some extent (Centre for Policy Dialogue, 2023). In the past, Bangladesh met many of the health related MDG targets including in areas of water and sanitation. In 2013, the prestigious journal, *The Lancet*, singled out Bangladesh as a South Asian model. Despite the challenges of poverty, the country achieved remarkable progress in areas such as health, opportunities for disadvantaged populations, women's empowerment, increased enrolment in education, and effective mitigation of natural disasters. Several factors contributed to this, such as timely policies, low-cost solutions, large scale and innovative public health interventions, with a productive partnership between government, private sector and non-governmental agencies (Chowdhury et al., 2013; Centre for Policy Dialogue, 2023).

Notable contributors from the non-governmental sector are visionaries: the late Sir Fazle Hasan Abed, founder of BRAC, one of the largest southern-led non-governmental organisations in the world, who was a recipient of multiple global awards, and was knighted by the Queen in 2010 for BRAC's work on reducing poverty (MacMillan, 2022); Professor Muhammed Yunus, founder of Grameen Bank, was awarded the Nobel Peace Prize in 2006 for his work on microcredit for the poor (Yunus, 2023),[2] and Gonoshashto founder, the late Dr. Zfarullah Chowdhury (for their outstanding record of promotion of health and human development, 2023),[3] a leading public health activist, who worked tirelessly to improve community-based health and services, including pioneering a national drug policy in the country. Their life-long passion, dedication and commitment has been to improve the lives of disadvantaged populations, pushing forward innovations and locally led solutions in microfinance, health, education, and other sectors.

While Bangladesh has made impressive progress in various areas, income inequality remains a persistent issue. Widespread inequality continues to affect the population, with at least 10.5% living below the global poverty line of $1.90 per day. This percentage has reportedly increased by 14% due to the impact of the pandemic. According to the 2016 Household Income and Expenditure Survey (HIES), the Gini coefficient of income stands at 0.48, indicating an even worse income distribution compared to previous assessments. The country's 8th five-year plan identifies policy shortcomings, particularly the failure to achieve a more equitable wealth distribution. One glaring problem is the low Tax to GDP ratio, which currently stands at just 9%, and tax evasion is rampant. The Chairman of the National Board of Revenue (NBR) has reported that less than one-third of eligible taxpayers in the country actually pay taxes. This is concerning, especially considering the large number of people living in poverty, and it negatively impacts public infrastructure, service delivery, and social protection programs. Another critical concern is the state of the country's environment. Bangladesh ranks 162nd out of 180 countries on the Yale Environmental Protection Index (EPI) (Chattopadhyay, 2021). Dhaka faces severe traffic congestion, costing the city an estimated $3 billion annually, and approximately 40% of solid waste in the city is inadequately managed. Open spaces, parks, and water bodies are rapidly disappearing, further limiting future land use planning possibilities (Roy et al., 2018).

Bangladesh's position in the Human Development Index report is 133rd out of 189 countries. The income distribution reveals a stark disparity, with the bottom 40% of the population holding a meagre 21% share, while the wealthiest 10% possess 27% (Financial Express, 2021). The country appears to be moving in conflicting directions. Despite substantial GDP growth since 2013, income inequalities have surged. Job creation has slowed, and real wage growth has stagnated, leaving the less fortunate with insufficient income opportunities. Moreover, public spending on education and healthcare as a percentage of GDP has dwindled, contributing to heightened inequalities in access to essential services, including healthcare, education, financial resources, and social protection. Individuals in poverty have limited access to benefits typically reserved for businesses and special interest groups, such as bailouts, loan restructuring, tax exemptions, subsidies, and licenses. Social protection programs, though available, are inadequate to significantly alleviate poverty. Compounded by governance weaknesses, expenditures intended for the poor often fail to deliver the promised benefits (Financial Express, 2021).

While the country's projections suggest it could become a 'trillion-dollar economy by 2040,' there is a concern that an excessive focus on GDP growth may overshadow other vital social indicators necessary for achieving sustainable development and addressing the persistent issue of growing inequalities (Shibli, 2023). The emphasis on GDP growth alone can hinder efforts to reduce inequality and promote economic growth that benefits everyone. The assessment of whether the country is truly 'on track' often occurs at an aggregate level, sometimes overlooking the specific challenges faced by various groups of impoverished individuals within the nation (Sen et al, 2004). Inequality remains a significant barrier to both economic progress and poverty reduction, and it is crucial to consider these disparities in any comprehensive evaluation of the country's development trajectory. For instance, while there is improved availability of food due to increased production, 40 million people, one quarter of the population remain food insecure, and 11 million suffer from acute hunger. These figures have worsened with the impact of Covid-19, which has descended into continued risks and deepening poverty for those who live on the margins (World Food Programme, 2020).

In 2019, the World Bank highlighted two contrasting narratives of progress in rural and urban Bangladesh. Surprisingly, urbanization, rather than being a sign of economic advancement, has become entwined with the challenges of underdevelopment (World Bank, 2019). The statistics tell a concerning story, as urban poverty increased from 36.1% to 41.4% between 2010 and 2016. This surge is closely tied to the country's rapid urbanization rate, which stands at a significant 3.9% annual growth. Historically, both the government and the development sector have predominantly concentrated their efforts on addressing rural poverty. However, this focus has inadvertently resulted in the neglect of the urban poor, leading to a lack of systemic planning and coordination between government and non-governmental entities. The consequence is that critical aspects like housing, healthcare, education, and social services remain inaccessible for the thousands of urban poor residing in slums. A comprehensive strategy for addressing urban poverty is essential, particularly to align with the country's national target of reducing overall poverty to 15.6% by 2025 (William, 2022). While Bangladesh has yet to endorse a single, overarching national plan for urbanization, existing and future government policies and plans provide a foundational regulatory framework to guide urban development in Bangladesh (Sowgat & Roy, 2013).

Urban Slum Settlements

Dhaka has emerged as a bustling economic centre, characterised by chaotic and unplanned urbanization, struggling to accommodate its vast population of 20 million residents (Hossain et al., 2015). A study in 2010 projected 17.6 million people living in Dhaka city, with up to 60% residing in some 3394 slums (Islam et al., 2006; Khan, 2010). Newer data reports that between 1997 and 2014, about 11,000 slums emerged in urban areas (Bangladesh Bureau of Statistics, 2015). Many are spaces of deprivations located on the periphery of the city and in satellite towns built for workers in garment factories (Banks, 2016). The city businesses, schools and other industries feed on the constant flow of migrants fleeing scarcity or climate disasters and are in desperate need of work (Ahmed & Islam, 2021). Slums vary in size and temporality, so certain areas have slums which have existed for decades; others, including those along railroads and riverbeds, fluctuate and function as temporary homes for newer migrants, with the varying presence of non-governmental organisations and other actors providing services (Haque et al., 2020). Some of the older slums exist alongside office complexes; others are part of dense suburbs, spilling over into fancier locations, with rows of usually crude makeshift rooms, cramped together, with waste lying around and dirt paths leading to people's tiny homes. The newer slums on the periphery of the city tend to be smaller and even more rudimentary.

In Dhaka, the availability of services in slum areas varies significantly. Established slums tend to have a higher presence of non-governmental and other organizations providing essential services, whereas newer or more isolated slums often have limited to no access. Unfortunately, evidence highlights the shortcomings of urban poverty alleviation programs in reaching these smaller, harder-to-reach communities. These difficulties stem from social marginalization and the precarious living conditions of households in these areas, which expose them to high eviction risks and a constant turnover of residents. Consequently, this situation leads to a loss of program participants and investments (Baker, 2005; William, 2022). Investment on development programs requires resources and in the event of an eviction, these stake-holders stand to lose much, having paid for latrines, tube-wells and taps, schools, health campaigns and the provision of micro-credit loans (Baker, 2005). Although large scale urban poverty projects have focused on 'commu-nity-level' interventions, mobilising residents on infrastructural slum-upgrad-ing projects, livelihood activities and building capacity of women for local level advocacy, these interventions remain out of reach for some of the more vulnerable communities living in neglected slums, and remain left out of programmes and its benefits (William, 2022).

Rising demand for land and housing, because of rapid urbanization results in the price for land and cost of housing extremely unaffordable for the poor. Studies report the average costs for $1000ft^2$ housing unit ($50/ ft2) is more than the average monthly income of the citizens ($45) in Khulna city, a dis-trict in Bangladesh, which is far beyond the reach of the urban poor who can earn as low as US$1 a day. A very small section of the poor in slums are engaged in formal services, earning a regular individual income of over US $1.67 a day (Roy et al., 2018), whereas most work in the informal sector. Bashar (2022) found that rent in slums differs across cities, with monthly rent in Dhaka and Chittagong (the second largest city) slums are BDT 2042 (US $18.52) and BDT 2017 (US$18.29) respectively (Bashar, 2022). Around 88% of homes in slums of Dhaka and 79% in Chittagong are single-room dwell-ings, with the rest comprising of two or three-room housing units. Usually, a unit comprises of a room or a few rooms, and a small space for cooking, washing, latrine for better off households. Ironically, the urban poor pay more per square feet of housing in slums compared with other areas, across all cities. Given the situation, incoming rural poor migrants who arrive in cities are forced to move into established slums or periphery slums or construct new informal housing.

In these congested slums, on average four to five or more family members live in one small room, on average no larger than $45ft^2$. These families share a communal kitchen, toilet, and bathing space with many other tenants and their family members. Most slums have access to piped water (set up illegal), and water taps may be shared between 20 to 40 households, with water available for a few hours at certain times of the day or night. Sanitation facilities are shared by 91% of households; one toilet, often decrepit and dirty, may be used by around 70 people (Haque et al., 2020). Given the absence of formal recognition and formal governance structures, residents pay inflated prices to powerful local leaders, and government employees (i.e., government cleaners) charge residents to have access to a room and basic services. Lining up in the morning or afternoon, waiting for water to be supplied for a few hours, or queuing early or late at night to bathe, wash clothes, cook and use latrines, is everyday life. There is little to no drainage, and during the monsoon season, alleyways and paths overflow with waste and sewage.

Residents of slums with little education and formal skills rely on finding work in the informal economy. Income opportunities in these areas are unpredictable, with residents sometimes earning a decent income on one day and, on other occasions, bringing home very little or even nothing at all. Work is temporary and unpredictable, but cash is required to pay for rent, food, and the basic costs of living in a settlement. According to Bangladesh Bureau Statistics (Bangladesh Bureau of Statistics, 2015), 85.1% of the workforce or 51.7 million people are employed in the informal sector in the country, working in hospitality, retail, trade, and transport, in low paid, menial and laborious jobs. These workers are the masses responsible for keeping Dhaka city and other cities functioning, ensuring the roads are swept, the local transport system operates; they clean apartments and buildings, cook in people's homes, work as sweepers and cleaners, and weave and sew in informal businesses. They guard homes, work as low-level assistants in hospitals and shops, and provide labour for the service industry in both the public and private sector, in informal and formal economies. Jobs in the informal sector tend to be insecure and there are no safety nets or pension, and workers have no legal recourse mechanisms, should they be fired, injured or mistreated. With little to no social insurance, minimal savings, and limited access to loans from banks, the impacts of changes in the economy and global and local macro and micro-policies severely impact on them Heinrich Boll Stifthung (2020).

Due to the lack of legal status of slums and ambiguity surrounding their rights, there has been a proliferation of local slum leaders, referred to as *mastaans*, and other gatekeepers who control these spaces. Banks writes that these leaders can push for development by connecting settlements to the wider city, managing community resources, and bringing in informal services, opportunities and resources (Banks, 2016). Thus, these leaders are not simply villains who take advantage of new and longer-term residents by extorting money; but also, secure tenure and fight off evictions and broker services. Rival factions and opposing interests complicate the power and politics within slums and in the city. These leaders provide a source of social control to politicians, profits to police and service providers, and informal labour to businessmen outside the settlements, contributing to an urban informal economy.

Local *mastaans* positions can also be destabilised depending on various factors, for instance, a change in national political leadership can affect local level political factions, or an eviction of the slum can disrupt local political networks and loss of power. For most residents, the environment in the slum and in the city is insecure, with extortion and bribes given to a hierarchy of gatekeepers: local leaders, police, legal representatives, mediators, and various other powerful actors. This is accepted as a *natural* reality in the absence of formal power and voice, and access to powerful people at different levels, and building relationships is key to survival. The greater a resident's networks with these different levels of powerful actors, the stronger their support and access to material gains (Rashid, 2004). Temporary and newer residents without influential social relationships, and residents from very poor households, tend to be positioned at the bottom of the social and power hierarchy. The reliance and relationships with *mastaans* and other powerful individuals is similar to patron-client relationships, which help more vulnerable residents survive (Wood, 2005).

This culture of 'Mastanocracy' refers to an urban political economic culture, an informal system to assist residents in slums manage risk and insecurity, critical when there is an absence of sufficient formal rights offered by the government. In this space, emerges the role of intermediaries – *mastaans*, 'who operate between people and their imperfect institutions' (Sen et al, 2004:98). The nature of governance means that even *mastaans* can remain vulnerable to volatile political situations and can lose powerful support. This depends on pressure groups, local-level politics, wider business interests and competition to control the informal economy of drug trade and other illicit activities, which is widely prevalent in slums. This is a 'subaltern economy of survival, areas of resistance and creative agency' of the poor who remain stuck 'at the outskirts of the visible macroeconomy' (Sen et al, 2004:4). Any change in government can undermine and disrupt relationships, networks and the lucrative businesses of drugs and even small arms that flourish in these spaces. Most of the trade is illegal and *mastaans* and *shontrashis* (thugs) do most of the groundwork and face the territorial battles and wars over controlling these money-making operations. However, it requires the 'blessing of the police, ruling party members and the administration' to operate (Sen et al, 2004:109). As such, any regime change at the ward level and national level, can turn violent, as money and control shifts to a new set of gatekeepers and local leaders and actors (Sen et al., 2004).

Others living in the city – the middle class and the well-to-do – tend to view slum residents as a 'blot' on a thriving cosmopolitan city; others see them as a nuisance to be managed or avoided, or as criminals (Hossain, 2006). They are the 'not so hidden' underbelly of the capital city, a reminder of the stark disparities which exist. They live marginal lives in a modern city, in the shadows of high-rise apartments, wide roads, gated communities, thriving businesses, banks, trendy cafes with cappuccinos and lattes, and fancy restaurants. Residents living in these informal settlements live as second-class citizens. Kees Koonings and Dirk Kruijt, writing on the global urban marginalised poor speak of separated cities to describe the dichotomy between elites and well-to-do middle classes and neglected residents living in slums (Koonings & Kruijt, 2007). They argue that urban segregation is not simply about the geographical distribution of the usual indicators of poverty (i.e., congested settlements, houses of corrugated tin and cardboard, lack of services) but also the territorial and social division of urban landscapes – places or sites to avoid, for example, from the perspective of wealthy and middle-class citizens and administration. However, these spaces overlap as slum residents inhabit public and richer areas and spaces, as they are part of the informal work economy, and remain clearly visible. As Perlman argues, slums around the world have come to be viewed as dangerous and dirty spaces, with their own conduct and rules, thereby blaming residents for their own conditions of life (Perlman, 2016). The stigma of living in such spaces continues to be a powerful force, contributing to continued marginality and exclusion. Dehumanised and relegated to a lower status, their daily struggles and plight remains invisible.

Etzold and authors argue that due to party politics in the country and weak governance systems, slum residents' rights and responsibilities exist only in theory (Etzold et al., 2013). Residents of slums who live on government land live in perpetual anxiety of eviction and for those who live on private land, they remain dependent on the mercy of landowners who may choose suddenly to develop the plot, or hike up rental prices, and they are forced to leave. According to Center for Urban Studies (CUS), 42% of slums are located on privately-owned land, and approximately 35% are under multiple private ownership, with 21.4% living on government or semi-government owned land (Hossain, 2006).

Urban Health

To increase governance and ensure adequate planning and services, Dhaka was divided into two large areas: Dhaka North and Dhaka South (Ahmed, 2013). Despite this, the coordination between the 16 to 40 different decision-making bodies in urban planning – transportation, traffic, waste, electricity and so on – remains inconsistent and they are often sites of political battle between party factions (Baker, 2005). Ambiguity in roles and responsibilities, lack of planning, and an absence of coordination between relevant ministries has resulted in a fragmented health care delivery in urban Dhaka. As a result, in the urban space, private health care services and non-governmental organisations play a major role in the largely unregulated urban health care delivery system. There are stark inequities in the quality of care provided – with the rich accessing high quality private health care facilities and the poor left with receiving low standard services from public health care providers. While non-governmental organisations provide health care services geared toward the poor, they are mostly location and service-specific (i.e., maternal care, antenatal care, vaccination, etc.), with varied access and services across locations, making it difficult to provide wide coverage to all the urban poor. There are gaps in public health coverage – especially for the urban poor and those residing in urban slums. The urban health system in Dhaka is dominated by private hospitals and clinics, where out-of-pocket expenses are high (72.68% in 2019); and very costly for the urban poor (World Bank, 2022; Misha et al., 2023).

Partnerships among government, development partners, and non-governmental organisations in the past 20 years to improve the provision of primary health care in urban areas, remains grossly inadequate (Ahmad, 2007).

Evidence points to the urban poor primarily relying on local (unlicensed) pharmacies (drug shops), homeopaths, and traditional healers, due to a lack of equitable access to quality health care (Misha et al., 2023).

Covid-19: A Cascading Risk for the Poor

In a World Bank press release from 2020, which was based on an upcoming report, it was forecasted that the Covid-19 pandemic would have a significant impact, pushing an additional 88 million to 115 million individuals worldwide into extreme poverty (World Bank, 2020). This figure was projected to potentially rise to as many as 150 million by 2021. The surge in extreme poverty was particularly pronounced in low-income countries, erasing approximately eight to nine years of progress. In upper-middle-income countries, the setback was estimated to be around five to six years (World Bank , 2020).

The shutdown of the entire country, closure of all businesses in Bangladesh for two full months in early 2020, led to substantial income losses. Hardships continue, with debts, reduced salaries and less work available, even after many businesses partially resumed operating post lockdown. A survey by PPRC[4] and BIGD[5] during Covid-19, covering 4,872 households, 54% from urban slums across city corporations and municipalities in districts, 45% from rural areas, and 1% from the Chittagong Hill Tracts region, found that households in slums experienced a more drastic 'income shock' due to both Covid-19 lockdowns – two months in March 2020 and shorter partial lockdown in 2021 (Rahman et al., 2022). There were severe job losses, with households having little to no income. The lockdown impacted 30 million slum residents who are dependent on cash from the informal economy (Heinrich Boll Stifthung, 2020), and between March and August 2021, household income in slums had dropped by 18% (Rahman et al., 2022). Residents in slums desperately need cash to pay rent, buy food, and other services. Cash was critical to their survival. Amis and Satterthwaite argue that the more vulnerable a household is to becoming poor or 'more' poor in the face of price rises, income shocks or fluctuations, other large scale or smaller crises have disastrous effects on their lives (Amis, 1995; Satterthwaite, 1997).

The situation was further exacerbated by global responses to the pandemic. National and international organizations rely on aid from a global pool of donors to sustain their programs. However, during the Covid-19 pandemic, several key players, including funders, abruptly cancelled long-term commitments, resulting in program closures or reductions in funds for urban slums and various sectors. Some donors redirected their resources internally, citing national priorities and pandemic-related needs in 2020, diverting aid money back into their own economies that were affected by the pandemic (International Development Committee, 2022). The impact of the pandemic also reverberated through the garments sector, which employs millions of workers. Over 1,900 global brands postponed or cancelled orders worth $3.7 billion from factories, leading to income losses and job cuts in these facilities (Preetha & Islam, 2020).

In response to the pandemic, the government implemented a policy to close schools for nearly two years, from March 17, 2020, to September 11, 2021 (Ahmed, 2022). As a consequence of these prolonged school closures, it was reported that there was a 13% increase in marriages, driven by deepening poverty and social insecurities (Hossain et al., 2021).

The Covid-19 pandemic only exacerbated the preexisting deep-seated disparities, resulting in those who were relatively better off in the slums becoming worse off, while those who were already living in poverty found themselves in dire circumstances (Rahman et al., 2022). The government rolled out an economic stimulus package to address the severe economic and business fallout from the pandemic. This package aimed to provide support to farmers, who play a crucial role in ensuring the stability of the food supply chain. However, the relief efforts in urban areas were less structured and more ad hoc. Numerous reports cited mismanagement, irregularities, and a lack of coordination among various entities responsible for distributing cash and food relief across the country (Rashid et al., 2020).

Fieldwork

Wahlberg, Burke and Manderson (2021) write that anthropologists have a responsibility to share knowledge of infections and disasters, structures, and systems; document lived experiences; and provide evidence of the social impacts on the health and lives of people affected (Wahlberg et al., 2021). Standard surveys and RCTs have certain methodological approaches and an enumerated list of determinants, and while this is useful, the data does not capture the messiness and diverse realities of peoples' lives enmeshed in poverty. Nicola Banks argues that analyses need to give sufficient attention to the influence of local power and politics and how these shape and constrains livelihood opportunities for low-income households (Banks, 2013). In addition, the influence of broader economic, political, and social systems at the community, city, and national levels, as noted by Scoones, plays a significant role in determining the extent of discrimination, the nature of networks and support structures, and, most importantly, who can avail themselves of these resources (Scoones, 2013).

This book offers unique ethnographic evidence collected 20 years apart, from 2002 to early 2003 and more recently from 2020 to 2022, to understand the everyday lives and experiences of health of urban poor young women and their families who live in slums in Dhaka City. Very few detailed ethnographies exist that document crisis periods (such as, slum evictions or the recent Covid-19 disaster) and their effect on the lives of urban poor young women and their families. An approach that decontextualises the individual from their environment not only ignores the complexities of how health is experienced, but also neglects the broader dimensions of health experiences.

These dimensions include personal and communal contexts, social and cultural environments, and the impact of historical, political, and economic factors (Adams et al., 2016).

I, thus, draw on a range of theoretical and conceptual approaches, including critical medical anthropology, syndemics and development literature, intersectionality, social suffering, and structural violence to inform my analysis and writing. Through these young women's case studies I demonstrate how unequal structures and systems, as well as social, economic and political factors, discrimination and exclusion, all work to keep young women and their families perpetually stuck in a cycle of precarity.

Fieldwork in Phulbari Slum: January to July 2002 and Post-eviction until early 2003

From January 2002 to early 2003, I spent time interviewing young women and sometimes their husbands and other family members who were living in Phulbari. I conducted longitudinal case studies of 50 young women and their families for seven months, from January to July 2002, until the place was violently demolished by tons of armed policemen and several bulldozers. Post-eviction, I was unable to locate some of these young women – but from this group of 50, I continued to visit ten young women until early 2003, visiting them in their new rented homes across the city. Some of the young women who had left for their husband's village or maternal villages returned within a month or two. Others had remained in the city, moving to neighbouring slums, if they could afford the rent. Some of the young women who moved to slums in the outskirts of the city, were especially difficult to locate. Phone numbers provided were incorrect, or they didn't pick up the phone. Sometimes the relocations were temporary, and more often than not, the young women struggled to provide clear instructions and were hard to find in the maze of rows of tiny look-alike dwellings with no numbers to indicate who lived where.

During my fieldwork and post-eviction, I kept a daily journal and spent most of my time spending time with young women in their tiny dwellings/homes, or following them around as they cooked, cleaned, and fed their children. Sometimes I accompanied them around their local neighbourhood. I spent time with younger and older women when they sat around chatting about various dramas occurring in their lives, and in the slum. I realised early on how unstable their lives were, as events unfolded, be it a fight with one's spouse, mother, family member, a job loss, a cheating husband, harassment by police, local leaders and landlords, illness, death and so on. I also spent a considerable amount of time in the tiny health clinic, observing young women who came for services and the providers, who provided ample information on many of the young women and men in the slum, including slum history and some of the local level leadership struggles. I also managed to locate some young women to speak to at the local clinic. The sudden eviction of residents in Phulbari led to differing outcomes for the young women I followed, with their lives and health adversely affected. For this book, I chose three detailed case studies – Monsura, Roshonara and Sayeeda and their families, who differed in age, family support and social status in Phulbari. The three case studies are distinctive but broadly representative of the experiences of insecurity and powerlessness, as reflected in the total number of case studies collected.

Monsura was extremely poor, a tenant, and dependent on her landlady. Whereas Roshonara's mother was a landlady, and Roshanara and her family lived with her thus relieving her from paying monthly rent. Both Monsura and Roshanara did not work outside the slum. Sayeeda was a health worker inside Phulbari and lived with her elder sister and brother-in-law. Her brother-in-law was a powerful local leader in Phulbari. All of them were vulnerable. Despite their varied status and economic situations, eviction was the equalizer. As they lost materially, economically and socially – income sources, social connections and networks – their anxieties deepened. As cash scarcity deepened, rifts, angry outbursts, and violence increased among young women and their spouses and with other family members.

Fieldwork During and Post Covid-19: 2020–2022

In April 2020, I was able to access a different group of 23 young women and their families, and 11 men and their families (in total 34), who lived in diverse slums in different parts of Dhaka City. I knew these young people since 2006, because of my personal interactions and relationships,[6] and I reached out to a few of them inquiring if they would like to speak to me about their struggles and experiences during this period. Most expressed an interest, while a few that agreed remained unresponsive to calls and scheduling interviews. For those we spoke to, they had the time to share their experiences at length as they were stuck at home during the lockdown. As the country began to partially reopen in June 2020, and subsequently post lockdown, meeting timings and places were adjusted to accommodate their availability, be it at their own homes or their places of work (e.g., selling on the streets). The time allocated for repeat interviews could vary from 20 minutes to several hours, with occasional last-minute cancellations due to income opportunities, arrests, or unforeseen calamities.

I selected three case studies from the total number – Meena, Shuli, and Fatema, along with their families. These case studies document in detail their lives and health experiences over a two-year period, from the sudden lockdown in 2020 through the post-pandemic period until August 2022. While the first round of interviews was done on phones, trust and familiarity already existed and I've maintained contact with many of these young women and their families. All three women work in the informal economy. Meena works as a maid and was the worst off. Her husband did not work, and her mother, while very loving and supportive, was extremely poor herself. Shuli sells towels on the streets and has a volatile relationship with her mother and children. She was married for the second time with a loving spouse. Fatema also sells towels on the streets, and is close to her parents, older brother, and in-laws.

In contrast to the young women in Phulbari from 20 years ago, all the young women in 2022 worked in the city. This is not surprising as increasingly female employment has become key to survival, demonstrating a significant change in practices that challenge traditional patriarchal ideologies. Many women work in factories and in the informal sector, sometimes as the primary earner, making critical contributions to household income. Nevertheless, their incomes are seldom sufficient or stable (Banks, 2013). For the young women in the case studies, their ability to survive shocks, abuse, and harassment from law enforcement officials, was shaped not only by their access to cash, but by the presence or absence of spousal and/ or family support, relationships cultivated within the slums, and external networks in the city, including employers and others.

Both research projects received IRB clearance. The urban research in 2002, (Project A 15054) was supported financially by the Special Programme of Research, Development and Research Training in Human Reproduction, World Health Organization, Geneva, and the second project in 2020, supported by ARISE, IRB reference no. 2019–034-IR.

Experiences of Fieldwork during 2002 and in 2020

When I first entered Phulbari, I was surprised by the large sprawling nature of the slum, tightly squeezed into a bustling city. I was also taken aback by the diversity and heterogeneity of the slum with its four distinct sections. As I walked around from section to section, I was struck by the absence of trees, and the dust and acrid smell of burning tires and wood. In many corners, visible waste lay around, including children's faeces in drains, which were filled with blackish coloured water. Having previously worked in rural areas, the stark contrast in Phulbari's environment was shocking. Even though I had been living in Dhaka City on and off since 1993, I was unaware of the extent of deprivation in living conditions that hundreds of families resided in. My research assistant and I visited Phulbari daily, which initially posed some difficulties with certain local leaders. However, with the support of health workers who vouched for our genuine intent to learn about young women's lives and health, we gained access. Even though we had received permission from a few *mastaans* (local leaders), there were residents and other young leaders who remained sceptical. They did not believe I was 'simply' a research student and wondered if I was working on behalf of the government to plan an eviction, or a journalist snooping around due to the thriving drug trade and other illicit activities in the area. I was harassed in section 3 of Phulbari, and in the corner of section 4, where drug selling was rampant, and I was warned to never return to those areas. Despite this, the considerable amount of time I spent in Phulbari with some of the families and post-eviction with a select few, allowed me to build trust and friendships with young women and maintain cordial relations with some of their spouses, extended families, and other residents. Over time, some of the *mastaans* and well-established residents began to offer me tea, smiled, and waved as I walked around, sometimes accompanied by a health worker or one of the adolescent women I was spending time with. As they became more comfortable with me, many of the residents and young women shared that when they visited other parts of the city, they did not divulge that they lived in Phulbari. They feared stigma and discrimination as they were '*bastee*' (slum) people. Many of them were aware that slums were often seen as sites of disease, disorder, and crime, so they would provide made-up names of more affluent housing settlements to strangers when asked about their place of residence.

Twenty years later, slums have increased exponentially, and, as before, most of them still lack access to basic services, such as poor sanitation, housing and even basic drainage. Congestion and overcrowding persist, and the harassment and control by *mastaans* and powerful brokers continue, with regular police raids, a thriving drug trade, and evictions. The young women rent one-room homes in slums, constructed of bricks and tin, with little to no ventilation and lighting. They also have to share kitchen and latrine facilities with other tenants in the compound. The roads and narrow lanes with broken pavements leading up to their homes are littered with waste. Meena, Shuli and Fatema moved around the city easily, taking buses and local transport when required. Despite this set of data being collected 20 years later, these young women, like their predecessors, married early and, in some cases, more than once. They all began selling goods on the streets at an early age, and during their early adolescence, had love marriages, bore children, cooked, cleaned and cared for their families, all while working outside the home. They also received very little education. Unlike their counterparts in Phulbari, some of these young women and their families did not refer to their locations as slums (*basti*), but called the place by its actual street name or locality. I also found young women and men actively using their phones, watching TikTok, Facebook, Instagram, and online videos. There were shops selling SIM cards, and young men engaged in 'gaming', which was popular in the slums. Some young women covered their hair and wore saris, but many others preferred shalwar kameez (traditional kurta and pajamas). Social media had infiltrated the slums, and I found young men walking around with buzz cuts, and haircuts mimicking famous footballers from Brazil and elsewhere. Young women wore shalwar with leggings, a fashionable choice commonly worn by middle and upper-class women in the city.

During both periods of fieldwork, the young women scrutinised my uneven shaped eyebrows, my hair, weight gain (and loss), and offered beauty advice. Both adult and younger women seemed shocked by my lack of cooking skills, and with affection explained how to skin and clean fish, cook chicken feet, rice, beef curries and lentil dishes. They often asked about my husband and how he tolerated me given my lack of basic household skills.

Poverty is Fluid

Except for three of the young women who were exceptionally vulnerable, two of them and their families came from 'breakeven' households.[7] This means that, while they weren't necessarily extremely vulnerable pre-eviction or pre-Covid-19, they could easily fall into the poverty trap at any point, due to sudden shocks, unforeseen events, and larger crises, leading to a domino effect of instability. Their varying status could also be discerned through their clothing, sandals worn, type of dwelling (single room or larger rooms indicating higher or lower rent) and location, household items such as bedding, clocks, utensils, current employment and income levels. While two households had televisions in 2020, and one had a fridge, this did not necessarily indicate that they could sustain this lifestyle, as such 'improvements' were often temporary. A household may be forced to sell the television or a fan or bed, when in dire straits. For the majority of households, life remained in a constant state of change, subject to the influence of external factors beyond their control. It is, therefore, difficult to box these young women and their families into any one single category, as the spectre of extreme poverty is always looming around the corner for them.

Ethical Dilemmas

Twenty years later, I wonder what happened to the young women and their families that I had continued to follow post-eviction. Were they still alive? Did any of them climb out of their dire circumstances? Given the levels of exclusion and discrimination faced by many of these poorer families in slums and in the city, I am doubtful that any improvement would be difficult to maintain, given the overwhelming odds stacked up against them. Some of the more recent young women I spoke during the pandemic period also continue to struggle.

During fieldwork, spending time with both groups of women (in 2002 and 2020) and seeing how many of them lived, in their tiny dark rooms; in overcrowded areas, listening to their stories and witnessing firsthand some of the shocks and tragedies that befell them, left me with many conflicting emotions: feelings of despair, anger at the injustice of it all and enormous guilt. Sometimes I found it difficult to focus on my own life after particularly difficult day of fieldwork or a deeply painful narrative shared in an interview. For instance, when the eviction took place or when I received news of the sudden death of a young woman's spouse because of a road accident post-Covid, I became anxious, at times depressed for the young women and their families who I had become close to. It was difficult to switch off. How does one regain some balance of mind and soul after hearing so many disturbing events, day after day, week after week? I wondered how they coped and managed, given I was not even experiencing any of their struggles.

We noted down story after story; tiny incidents that remain imprinted on my mind, such as finding a little bit of cash to buy an egg, or the excitement around extra money made from decent towel sales, to finally be able to buy some meat for their children, or when someone told me that they ate one piece of dry chappati (flat round bread) all day, as they could not afford a meal for that day. It made me sad. The stark contrast between their lives and mine could not be more brutal. After hearing endless stories of humiliation and abuse faced by many of these young women and their husbands and family members at the hands of powerful actors inside the slums and the city, I found myself thinking of how I could live in the same city and as a fellow citizen, experience a completely different world. None of their daily concerns affected me. I was living and sleeping in comfortable place, and I had no fear of losing my home. I had access to nutritious food, clean water and electricity and much more abundance and material and social wealth, than they could ever imagine. I did not fear law enforcement officials. My life trajectory was completely different to these young women who had their childhoods stolen and entered adult lives at an early age; either by getting married early and or working to support their families. I had privilege, power and countless options and opportunities, unlike them. While they aspired to have much better lives, stable jobs, it was not clear whether they would ever be able to achieve them; whereas I have had support to achieve many of my own dreams.

Maintaining complete objectivity proved to be an unattainable goal. As time passed, I discovered that I couldn't simply stand by, especially in critical moments of their lives. I felt a strong urge to provide assistance in various small ways, whether it meant taking them to a clinic, offering financial support when they were in dire straits, or covering the medical expenses of a young woman's husband. I also extended help to another woman who had been battling illness for some time. Even during and after my fieldwork, which encompassed events such as eviction and the pandemic, I continued to offer financial support to these young women. I wrestled with the ethical dilemma of whether my involvement might compromise my objectivity or the quality of the data I collected, as well as my relationships with them. Ultimately, I couldn't remain detached; it felt morally right to intervene. I believed that any potential loss of objectivity or disruptions to the research would be outweighed by the ethical imperative to assist those in need. As Cassell (2002) aptly observes, when a researcher is present as a 'living, responsive fellow human being' rather than a detached observer, the individuals being studied will naturally incorporate the researcher into their lives. In the end, I felt it was necessary to compensate these individuals for the considerable time and insight they provided, as I benefitted from our interactions. Although it would never be adequate. This research would have little impact on their lives, and I couldn't simply watch, gather data, and do nothing. I am indebted to them and hold deep respect and admiration for their remarkable strength and resilience in the face of ongoing exploitation and relentless challenges. All the young women and their families displayed patience, kindness, and hospitality.

In their work titled *Unfinished*, Biehl and Locke (2017) underscore the complex nature of individuals' existence and stress that interpretations and theories drawn from data are an ongoing process, capturing only a single aspect of the truth (Biehl & Locke, 2017). My writing primarily delves into the instability of their lives and how it profoundly affects their lived experiences, health and well-being. While there are moments of happiness, shared laughter, celebrations and joy, my ethnographic research unveils that their lives more frequently revolve around scarceness, unpredictability, and trauma.

I am aware that long after my fieldwork concluded, the lives of these young women and their families continued, marked by a blend of both predictability and unpredictability, characterised by a continual series of twists and turns, with the ultimate outcome remaining uncertain. I cannot predict whether this book will alter or reinforce your perspectives on the most vulnerable, but I hope it at least encourages you to reflect on what needs to change in our society, within us, and around us, so that justice can be served to those living on the fringes.

Notes

1 The court interpreted Articles 31 and 32 broadly in light of Article 15 of the Constitution, which makes the right to livelihood and shelter part of the fundamental principles of state policy. The court laid down guidelines for the rehabilitation of *Bostee* residents to be carried out in phases and evictions only to be made when alternate arrangements were in place for shelter. The guideline also requires the government to provide written notice and arrange for the rehabilitation or resettlement of evictees prior to eviction. The Court gave specific directions to undertake rehabilitation arrangement for the Slum residents and to undertake eviction of the slum residents only 'according to the capacity of their available abode and with option to the dwellers either to go to their village home or to stay back leading an urban life' cited in Farid (2013).
2 Professor Muhammad Yunus established the Grameen Bank in Bangladesh in 1983. See www.nobelprize.org/prizes/peace/2006/yunus/biographical/
3 Late Dr Zafrullah Chowdhury was a public health activist in Bangladesh, who has advanced rural people's access to medical care through Gonoshasthaya Kendra (GK, The People's Health Centre) in 1972. https://rightlivelihood.org/the-cha nge-makers/find-a-laureate/zafrullah-chowdhury- gonoshasthaya-kendra/
4 Power, Participation and Resource Center, a leading Think tank Center in Bangladesh.
5 BIGD – BRAC Institute of Governance and Development, BRAC University, Dhaka, Bangladesh
6 Volunteering and working with an intervention that reached out to street kids, many dropped out and I continued to stay in touch at a personal level, from when they were young children to becoming young adults.
7 The term is coined from research done by Jack 1916/1917 (cited in Sen et al., 2004, pp. 25).

References

Adams, V., Craig, S. R., & Samen, A. (2016). Alternative accounting in maternal and infant global health. *Glob Public Health*, 11(3), 276–294. https://doi.org/10.1080/17441692.2015.1021364

Ahmad, A. (2007). *Provision of Primary Healthcare Services in Urban areas of Bangladesh: The Case of Urban Primary Health Care Project*. Working Papers 2007:9, Lund University, Department of Economics.

Ahmed, K., & Islam, R. (2021). The making of a megacity: How Dhaka transformed in 50 years of Bangladesh. *The Guardian*.

Ahmed, M. (2022). Learning loss from Covid-19: Can a generational threat be averted. *The Daily Star*, 13.

Ahmed, S. (2013). Civic environmentalism and the politics of marginalized people: A case study from megacity Dhaka, Bangladesh. *Environmental Justice*, 6(2), 56–61.

Ahsan, A. (2019, 21 November). Dhaka-centric growth: At what cost. *Policy Insights*. Policy Research Institute, Dhaka. https://policyinsightsonline.com/2019/11/dhaka-centric-growth-at-what-cost/

Amis, P. (1995). Making sense of urban poverty. *Environment and Urbanization*, 7(1), 145–158.

Baker, J. L. (2005). Dhaka: Improving living conditions for the urban poor. https://documents.worldbank.org/en/publication/documents-reports/documentdetail/938981468013830990/dhaka-improving-living-conditions-for-the-urban-poor

Bangladesh Bureau of Statistics (BBS). (2015). *Census of slum areas and floating population programe 2014*. Bangladesh Bureau of Statistics; Ministry of Planning. http:// 203. 112. 218.65:8008/WebTestApplication/userfiles/Image/Slum/FloatingPopulation2014.pdf

Bangladesh Bureau of Statistics (2015). *Census of Slum Areas and Floating Population Programe 2014*.

Bangladesh Bureau of Statistics (BBS). (2020). *Statistical Yearbook Bangladesh 2019* (39th ed.). Bangladesh Bureau of Statistics;Statistics and Informatics Division (SID); Ministry of Planning, Government of Bangladesh

Bangladesh Bureau of Statistics (2020). *Statistical Yearbook Bangladesh 2019*.

Banks, N. (2013). Female employment in Dhaka, Bangladesh: participation, perceptions and pressures. *Environment and Urbanization*, 25(1), 95–109.

Banks, N. (2016). Livelihoods limitations: The political economy of urban poverty in Dhaka, Bangladesh. *Development and Change*, 47(2), 266–292.

Bashar, T. (2022). Residential stability of the urban poor in Bangladesh: The roles of social capital. *Cities*, 126, 103695.

Biehl, J., & Locke, P. (2017). *Unfinished: The Anthropology of Becoming*. Duke University Press.

Cassell, J. (2002). Perturbing the system: "Hard science," "soft science," and social science, the anxiety and madness of method. *Human Organization*, 61(2), 177–185.

Chattopadhyay, S. (2021). Much more to do to tackle inequality. https://thewire.in/south-asia/bangladesh-much-more-to-do-to-tackle-inequality

Chowdhury, A. M. R., Bhuiya, A., Chowdhury, M. E., Rasheed, S., Hussain, Z., & Chen, L. C. (2013). The Bangladesh paradox: Exceptional health achievement despite economic poverty. *The Lancet*, 382(9906), 1734–1745.

International Development Committee (2022). Extreme poverty and the sustainable development goals: Fifth report of session 2022–23. House of Commons. https://publications.parliament.uk/pa/cm5803/cmselect/cmintdev/147/summary.html

Center for Policy Dialogue (2023). Reducing out-of-pocket expenditure to improve the quality and affordability of national health care system (Draft Policy Brief 2023).

Etzold, B., Hossain, M. A., & Rahman, S. (2013). Street food vending in Dhaka: Livelihoods of the urban poor and the encroachment of public space. *Dhaka Metropolitan Development Area and Its Planning: Problems, Issues and Policies. Bangladesh Institute of Planners (BIP) Dhaka*. www.bip.org.bd/SharingFiles/journal_book/20140427160

Financial Express (2021, August 3). Growing income inequality in Bangladesh causes concern. https://thefinancialexpress.com.bd/views/reviews/growing-income-inequa lity-in-bangladesh-causes-concern-1627918086

Farid, C. (2013). New paths to justice: A tale of social justice lawyering in Bangladesh. *Wis. Int'l LJ*, 31, 421.

For their outstanding record of promotion of health and human development (2023). *Right Livelihood.* https://rightlivelihood.org/the-change-makers/find-a-laureate/za frullah-chowdhury-gonoshasthaya-kendra/

Giménez, L., Jolliffe, D., & Sharif, I. (2014). Bangladesh, a middle income country by 2021: What will it take in terms of poverty reduction? *The Bangladesh Development Studies*, 37(1 & 2), 1–19.

Haque, S. S., Yanez-Pagans, M., Arias-Granada, Y., & Joseph, G. (2020). Water and sanitation in Dhaka slums: Access, quality, and informality in service provision. *Water International*, 45(7–8), 791–811.

Heinrich Boll Stifthung (2020). Double repression: Lockdown measures in Bangladesh and its impact on informal sector workers. https://th.boell.org/en/2020/05/13/dou ble-repression-lockdown-measures-bangladesh-and-its-impact-informal-sector-workers

Hossain, M., Khan, M., Haque, M. A., Roy, S., & Hasan, M. (2015). *Changing Patterns of Urbanization in Bangladesh: An Analysis of Census Data.* Bangladesh Bureau of Statistics.

Hossain, M. J., Soma, M. A., Bari, M. S., Emran, T. B., & Islam, M. R. (2021). COVID-19 and child marriage in Bangladesh: Emergency call to action. *BMJ Paediatrics Open*, 5(1).

Hossain, M. S. (2006). *Urban Poverty and Adaptations of the Poor to Urban Life in Dhaka City, Bangladesh.* PhD thesis. UNSW Sydney.

Islam, N., Mahbub, A., Nazem, N., Angeles, G. L., & Lance, P. (2006). Slums of urban Bangladesh: Mapping and census, 2005. www.measureevaluation.org/resour ces/publications/tr-06-35.html

Khan, M. (2010). *Impact of Climate Change on the Livelihood of the Urban Poor: A Case of Dhaka City.* Master of Public Policy and Governance Program thesis, North South University, Dhaka, Bangladesh.

Koonings, K., & Kruijt, D. E. (2007). *Fractured Cities: Social Exclusion, Urban Violence and Contested Spaces in Latin America.* Zed Books. https://doi.org/http://dx. doi.org/10.5040/9781350220225

MacMillan, S. (2022). *Hope Over Fate, Fazle Hasan Abed and the Science of Ending Global Poverty.* Rowman & Littlefield Publishers. https://bracusa.org/hope-over-fate/

Misha, F., Imtiaz, S. H., McConnell, M., Cash, R., & Rashid, S. F. (2023). Using mobile financial services to improve community health workers' efficiency during the COVID-19 pandemic in Dhaka, Bangladesh. In *Inoculating Cities* (pp. 167–185). Elsevier.

Muggah, R. (2012*). Researching the Urban Dilemma: Urbanization, Poverty and Violence.* IDRC; CRDI; UKaid.

Perlman, J. E. (2016). Rio's Favelas and the Myth of Marginality. Politics & Society, 5 (2), 131–160. HYPERLINK "https://doi.org/10.1177/003232927500500201"https:// doi.org/10.1177/003232927500500201 (reprinted from 1975)

Preetha, S. S., & Islam, Z. (2020). 1931 brands have delayed & cancelled $3.7bn worth of orders from garment factories during COVID-19. *Business & Human Rights Resource Centre.* www.business-humanrights.org/en/latest-news/bangladesh-1931-brands-ha ve-delayed-cancelled-37bn-worth-of-orders-from-garment-factories-during-covid-19/

Rahman, H. Z., Rahman, A., Faruk, M. S., Avinno, I., Matin, I., Wazed, M. A., & Zillur, U. (2022). *Recovery with Distress: Unpacking COVID-19 Impact on Livelihoods and Poverty in Bangladesh*. https://doi.org/10.35188/UNU- WIDER/2022/144-0

Rashid, S. F. (2004). *Worried Lives: Poverty, Gender and Reproductive Health of Married Adolescent Women Living in an Urban Slum in Bangladesh*. PhD thesis. Australian National University.

Rashid, S. F., Theobald, S., & Ozano, K. (2020). Towards a socially just model: balancing hunger and response to the COVID-19 pandemic in Bangladesh. *BMJ Global Health*, 5(6), e002715.

Roy, S., Sowgat, T., Ahmed, M. U., Islam, S. M. T., Anjum, N., Mondal, J., & Rahman, M. M. (2018). *National Urban Policies and City Profiles for Dhaka and Khulna*. Bangladesh: GCRF Centre for Sustainable, Healthy and Learning Cities and Neighbourhoods.

Satterthwaite, D. (1997). Urban poverty: Reconsidering its scale and nature. *IDS bulletin*, 28(2), 9–23.

Scoones, I. (2013). Livelihoods perspectives and rural development. In *Critical Perspectives in Rural Development Studies* (pp. 159–184). Routledge.

Sen, B., Hulme, D., Ahmad, I., Kabeer, N., Ali, Z., Khan, I., Begum, S., Matin, I., Haider, O., Sen, C., & Shahabuddin, Q. (2004). *Chronic Poverty in Bangladesh: Tales of Ascent, Descent, Marginality and Persistence: The State of the Poorest 2004/2005*. Bangladesh: Bangladesh Institute of Development Studies Dhaka.

Shibli, A. (2023, February 4). What is holding Bangladesh's GDP growth rate down? *The Daily Star*. www.thedailystar.net/opinion/views/open-dialogue/news/what-holding-bangladeshs-gdp-growth-rate-down-3238926

Sowgat, T., & Roy, S. (2013). Pro-poor development: An assessment of the national level policies and programs in Bangladesh. *Plan Plus*, 6, 43–61.

Streatfield, P. K., & Karar, Z. A. (2008). Population challenges for Bangladesh in the coming decades. *J Health Popul Nutr*, 26(3), 261–272.

Wahlberg, A., Burke, N., & Manderson, L. (2021). Introduction. In *Stratified Livability and Pandemic Effects* (pp. 1–24). https://doi.org/10.2307/j.ctv1j13zb3.7

William, S. K. (2022). We need to recognise the diversity of the urban poor. *The Daily Star*. www.thedailystar.net/opinion/views/news/we-need-recognise-the-diversity-the-urban-poor-3121506

Wood, G. D. (2005). Poverty, capabilities and perverse social capital: The antidote to Sen and Putnam. In *Making a Living: The Livelihoods of the Rural Poor in Bangladesh*. UPL.

World Bank (2015). World Bank leveraging urbanization in Bangladesh. www.worldbank.org/en/country/bangladesh/brief/leveraging-urbanization-bangladesh

World Bank (2019). *Bangladesh Poverty Assessment: Facing Old and New Frontiers in Poverty Reduction*. World Bank.

World Bank (2020). COVID-19 to add as many as 150 million extreme poor by 2021. www.worldbank.org/en/news/press-release/2020/10/07/covid-19-to-add-as-many-as-150-million-extreme-poor-by-2021

World Bank (2022). Out-of-pocket expenditure in Bangladesh. https://data.worldbank.org/indicator/SH.XPD.OOPC.CH.ZS?locations5BD

World Food Programme (2020). WFP Bangladesh Country Brief. www.wfp.org/countries/bangladesh

Yunus, M. (2023). The Nobel Peace Prize 2006. *NobelPrize.Org*. www.nobelprize.org/prizes/peace/2006/yunus/biographical/

3   Life on the Margins

Phulbari, 2002

The Phulbari slum was established in the 1980s on empty government land, right in the middle of the bustling suburb of Mirpur. From the outside, it looked like any other slum settlement – a large area divided artificially into four sections. One was comparatively cleaner than others, with a paved road, but all sections were severely congested. Rooms no bigger than 45ft^2 were set out in rows, leaning into each other, with little room for privacy or space. These were the homes of those with whom I worked.

Compounds within the slum might include five to six little rooms, in which women crouched, elbowing each other, maintaining their guard as they waited to access the shared stoves to cook meals for their households. Only a few of the richer households and landlords had their own private areas, delineated for cooking, sometimes with a built-in latrine. In some of the poorer sections, gas was not available, and women cooked on stoves set up right outside homes, buying wood, which was expensive. Smoke fumes filled the space, where I saw young women crouched on their haunches, carefully stirring their pots.

Section 4 was the most neglected part, with no paved road and long queues of men and women waiting to use the one of the two latrines in one corner or to collect water where compounds did not have their own water tap. A putrid stench filled the air on rainy days, as raw sewage, household waste and dirt flooded the narrow lanes and dirt paths. Skin infections were rampant among the children and other family members, who waded through the sludge to get around during the monsoon season. In the hot summer months, cockroaches, rats, and mosquitoes infested the compounds, and people were constantly swatting, watchful as they walked from one section to the next, from one household to next, or simply in their own room.

Phulbari was reported to have 3,500 households, before it was evicted in the middle of my fieldwork, end of July 2002. A sense of being in a community varied throughout Phulbari, with some sections more fragmented than others. Small shops were lined up in rows in different corners, as men and especially women set up stalls in the narrow lanes, selling fruit or snacks.

DOI: 10.4324/9781003467472-3

Children would play wherever they could, close to overflowing garbage or in the corners of the dirt lanes, with bats and balls made from scraps of cloth and plastic. Men would sit around in locally owned tea shops and play cards in the evenings, or drink, smoke, and gamble. Women would sit and gossip in the afternoons, after lunch was eaten, and they had bathed and completed their household chores. Some of them would gather in a neighbour's home to watch television; others would have their hair oiled, or have another woman take lice out as they skilfully weaved their fingers through the long hair. This was particularly so in sections 1 and 2; in contrast, in larger sections, residents didn't always know their neighbours. Until the demolition, Phulbari had three small NGO schools, and a neglected, empty semi-government school. Two of the NGO schools were in section 4 and the third one in section 1. There was only one small health clinic, set up several years ago by an international health organization, in section 4, an area notorious for gang violence and crime. It had four staff, three health workers from Phulbari, and a paramedic, who trekked in from another better off neighbourhood, to sit in the clinic for a few hours every day.

Monsura and Ratna

I met Monsura (17), her husband Sayyied (30), and her landlady Ratna (32) through health workers employed at the clinic, one of several linked to the supporting NGO which focused on women's health. Monsura and her family had rooms in a compound diagonally opposite the clinic, adjacent to other houses and near numerous narrow mud lanes heading in multiple directions. Monsura had large mischievous eyes and a ready smile on her face, and she was usually in good spirits, bursting into fits of giggles and taking great pleasure making fun of and gossiping about Ratna. Monsura detested but was also dependent on her landlady Ratna. For TK450 a month (c. approximately US$8.00 at the time), she and Sayyied rented a small room made of tin, perhaps 40ft^2, dark and dingy with a tiny window, affording very little ventilation. The room was in a small compound owned by Ratna, which included a few more rooms: one was a kitchen; another was occupied by Ratna and her family. One room was empty when I began fieldwork.

Monsura usually wore a long maxi (kaftan with petticoat underneath), one of three: a creased stained brown one, a dark blue floral one, or a faded green and yellow one. She always looked slightly dishevelled, her hair pulled back and no jewellery but for a small gold nose ring. On a few occasions, when I walked along the main road of a T junction leading into section 4, I would find Monsura standing outside the rusty tin gate of the compound, her baby son, Joy (2), on her hips. She'd look slightly amused and bored as she watched the activities along the dusty mud road. On other occasions, I would walk into her room and surprise her. I would find her lying on the bed, gazing at the tin roof, Joy sleeping next to her or playing in the dirt on the floor, naked but for a prayer protection string around his waist, snot running down his lips and chin, his fingers covered in mud and grime. The fan was always on, and a lightbulb would hang from the ceiling, flickering dimly in the room.

Monsura was born in rural Barishal, and she claims she moved to Dhaka city with her mother and older brother when she was around 12 years old, after her father had abandoned the family. Monsura's brother was married, but I never met him. He worked as rickshaw puller, a low paid strenous job and Monsura's mother lived with him and his wife. On a few occasions, I often found Monsura's mother at her place, perched in the corner of the room, holding Joy and playing with him. Sometimes she would listen in and interject when we were speaking and at other times she would leave because Monsura would pointedly kick her out, "ma (mother) go now I have impor- tant things to talk about.' I never fully understood the dynamic of their rela- tionship. Monsura often complained that her mother came to her to sponge off her, expecting meals and wanting to borrow money, not considering her difficult circumstances. Whereas Monsura's mother was also there for her when she had difficult times with her husband, Sayyied, lending Monsura small amounts of cash, and taking her to the village when Sayyied dis- appeared for days and then returned drunk and abusive. Monsura's mother claimed to be a spiritual traditional healer with special powers and healed people with all kinds of ailments.

Monsura married Sayyied 3 or 4 years ago and had been living in Phulbari for the past 2 years. "I fell in love with him (Sayyied) … he is tall, handsome, and fair," Monsura boasted, "(he) told me he fell under my spell. He said to me, 'oh Monsura, you have stolen my heart'." They had met when Monsura was working in a garment factory; Sayyied would watch her as she walked to work daily. They had eloped when she was 15 and he was 28; she stopped working when she had Joy. Her dates were vague, as it was for many people: there is a law against child marriage, and their lives, the date of their birth and present age, had little relevance to everyday life. Usually, a young woman who is menstruating is considered ready for marriage. This persists even now; a report in 2022 states that Bangladesh has the highest prevalence of child mar- riage in South Asia and ranks among the top ten countries in the world. The practice of child marriage is rooted in tradition, socio-cultural beliefs, gender inequality and poverty. This worsened with Covid-19 (Hossain et al., 2021).

In the early days when we used to spend time together, Monsura provided a blissful story about her married life, sharing her fantasies of a loving husband Sayyied, who was attentive and caring, who worked in a good job in the transport sector and earned a lot of money. "He earns over TK10,000 a month (approximately US$176 in 2002), we temporarily living here but will move into our own place soon." The reality was that Monsura was ashamed that she barely had one sheet covering their bed and the two utensils she had were on the floor. Her vivid imagination and tales did not match what I observed in her tiny dingy small room over the period of my visits, which was over a year. Sayyied looked much older than her, with his sunken cheekbones, moustache, and dark circles under his eyes. He was polite whenever I visited but he didn't speak much. In the early days when we chatted, Monsura gave the impression of a blissful married life, of Sayyied attentive and caring, working in a well-paid job in the transport sector. Over time I witnessed a volatile, unhappy marital life. The few times I found Monsura extremely happy, and all dressed up, in her one and only green and gold nylon sari, was when Sayyied took her for an outing, to make up for his violence or bad behaviour. She would put on lipstick, eye liner, pull back her freshly oiled hair and pat her face with Johnson's baby powder. Joy would also be dressed up, with a large black dot reapplied on his forehead, as the family set out for the day. These outings were rare.

A year after marriage Monsura had moved to Phulbari, where she barely knew anyone. Most of her interaction was with Ratna. Shortly after I met Monsura, on my third visit, I was speaking to Monsura when Ratna walked in and said, disdainfully, "Look at your son ... he will fall sick, sitting on the floor putting all kind of rubbish in his mouth." She shook her head in disgust, "Is this the way to take of care of one's child?" I asked her if she had any children. She beamed, "Yes, I have two girls." Suddenly we heard laughter outside the room from one daughter; another was howling in pain. Ratna hurried away towards her room, screaming "You whores, useless whores, why don't you go and help me cut some vegetables ... not a moment of peace with you two devils!" There was screaming and yelling.

Ratna was heavily built and known for her violent temper. Neighbours spoke disparagingly about her because she was always arguing and "going after her tenants." Ratna saw herself as economically and socially superior to the tenants. She would regularly share stories with me about her allegedly "rich family members who spoke English and were educated." Fifteen years ago, Ratna had invested her own savings to buy the plot of land for her compound from the local leaders (*mastaans*). Many residents reported paying different leaders at the time, money for building their homes in the space allocated. As discussed earlier, these local leaders operate in the absence of governance due to the lack of formal legal recognition of slums and tend to control and manage residents living in these slums. They also operate the illegal drug trade in alliance with police and other powerful stakeholders and politicians. In a hierarchy of power relationships, *mastaans* affiliate with government political party leaders, even the police, to hang on to their power.

Ratna had spent a substantial amount of money to build the rooms with tin, brick, and cement, and to instal a latrine and a water tap. Owner-occupiers have no formal rights to the land, lacking the land holding numbers (a formal registration certificate) that prove ownership, but 'owned' the homes that they paid or bought from a local leader (Banks, 2016). Ratna shared that water was available mid- morning for a few hours daily and she regularly paid local leaders (*mastaans*) for continued access to water, gas, and electricity. She shared her one room with her two daughters, Shapna (12) and Jharna (9), and her husband Abdul (36). Abdul worked in a spectacle shop and drew a monthly salary, supplementing Ratna's rental income. Ratna did not work outside and took care of the home and was often found chatting with a few neighbouring women of a local collective, who provided loans on a system set up by the women themselves.

Roshonara and Chachi

Roshonara (21), her two sisters, Razia (17) and Rabeya (14), and their mother, Chachi[1] (50) lived in a largish compound owned by Chachi. The walls were made of a mix of brick, bamboo and tin, and the floor was made of mud. Chachi's daughters were all born in Dhaka and had grown up in Phulbari. Their compound included three adjacent rooms, a narrow entrance area, a small space out the back for bathing, and a latrine. In the front, a small area was used for cooking, with a shelf for utensils, pots, and pans. The large main room was occupied by Chachi, Razia and Rabeya, and had a bed with blankets, strewn with dirty clothes. A cabinet was filled with clothes; there was dusty and partly broken chair. Four jute sacks rested against the cabinet, filled with onions, potatoes, and dry rice.

Chentoo Mia (65) was Chachi's husband, and he visited every few weeks, spending the rest of his time with his second wife in a low-income housing area. Roshonara, their eldest daughter, was married to Mintoo (30) and they had a three-year-old daughter, Lucky. Roshonara had struggled with fertility, and she fell pregnant with Lucky, her pride and joy, after seven years of marriage. Their room in the compound was tiny, with a bed, fan, television, and a cassette player miraculously squeezed into the congested space. A piece of cloth hung to cover the window; cardboard was placed strategically over holes in the tin wall, also for privacy. The third room was rented by an unrelated couple and their daughter, Mamoni (16).

The first time I walked in, the smell of stale lentils and fish being cooked wafted through the air. Razia and Mamoni, good friends, were chatting away, and they greeted me. Razia challenged me: "So we hear, you are working on young women's health? What do you like for yourself, a peeled banana, or an unpeeled banana?" They laughed. I was embarrassed. Razia was a confident, slim, tall young woman, dark skinned, with her hair tied back and wearing a fitted shalwar kameez, red slippers and bright red lipstick. Six months ago, she had married Shahed (25) for love, but they had recently separated, and Razia was struggling emotionally. Shahed had refused to introduce her or take her to his parent's home until her family paid the dowry price. Throughout my fieldwork, I often found Razia pining for him. Although illegal, dowry (gifts and cash given to groom) is widely practiced.

Mamoni, unmarried, was close to Razia and was boisterous. She was giggling at Razia's comment, as they waited for me to react. Roshonara glanced at them, annoyed, and invited me to her room. She was also dark and of medium build, with her hair tightly pulled back in a round bun. She wore a loose brown cotton shalwar kameez and had Lucky on her right hip. She was sweating profusely and there was a faint smell of dampness in the room. She had a very calm, no-nonsense air about her. As I sat down, Chachi came into the room, peeking curiously at me. She gave me a wide toothless grin. Her tongue, lips and remaining teeth were stained red from the betel leaf she was chewing. A tall and heavy-set woman with a pockmarked face, she was wearing a faded and thread bare sari with no blouse. Whenever I visited over the next several months, I always found this compound bustling with activities as visitors came and went, and both mother and daughter rushed around, cooking, and cleaning and taking care of the household members. Roshanara was very close to her mother, who listened to her for advice on major family matters. Roshonara and her family were established residents, familiar in the area, close to some of the leaders, and friendly with the neighbours, health providers, and other residents in section 4.

Sayeeda: The Health Provider

I met Sayeeda who said she was either 25 or 26 years old, at the beginning of my fieldwork when I was walking around Phulbari to familiarise myself with the place. I came across the clinic in section 4 and visited it. Over time, I became very close to Sayeeda and to her colleague Sufia (45). They introduced me to many of the residents, including local leaders, married women, and single adolescent women in Phulbari. They often filled in missing information I needed on Phulbari and its residents. Sayeeda was skinny and plain, with gaunt face, boundless energy, and a razor-sharp tongue. She would talk a mile a minute and knew all the gossip in the area. Sayeeda had had three failed marriages and had been left to bring up her three children, two daughters, Shahana (13) and Nasreen (10), and a son, Shaon (4). People feared Sayeeda because she was well connected. She lived with her elder sister, Mukta (40), who was married to Malek Master (45), a powerful leader in section 1, where they all lived. After several visits to the clinic around end of January, I was invited by Sayeeda to visit their home. As we walked from the clinic in section 4 towards section 1, Sayeeda proudly pointed out the cleanliness of their section, compared to other sections of Phulbari. We walked into a large rectangle shaped room, where Malek Master was sitting cross-legged on a high, four poster bed, reading a document; Mukta stood nearby, chatting to him. Mukta was the opposite of Sayeeda, bordering on obese and very reserved. She rarely spoke and her speech was always measured. Sayeeda introduced me as the "foreigner student who was studying women's health." There was an awkward silence, then Malek Master nodded at me, got off the bed and left the room, saying softly to his wife, "I will be back in the evening." She followed him outside.

Throughout my fieldwork, Sayeeda and her sister's relationship seemed very strained. Sayeeda seemed to be freer and closer to her brother-in-law, Malek Master, than her own sister. Malek Master was a schoolteacher and owned ten homes. Malek Master could be referred to as a *slum elite*, well off, compared to the other 'owners' and tenants, as one could draw a considerable income, from rental payments, allowing for some level of stability and security compared to other residents. The room in which they lived was large, dark and windowless. But there were two lights and a fan above the bed, and they had their own water tap set up in a corner, and a large floor-length cupboard and side cabinet. The floor was cemented and smooth. There was another room adjacent to this, and next to that, the latrine and bathing area. The kitchen was in this main room. Sayeeda explained that nine family members lived in this one room, with space allocated according to hierarchy, position, and age. Malek Master, Mukta and their young daughter, Moina (7), slept on the large bed. Sayeeda's young son, Shaon, also slept with them. Sayeeda sleep on a jute mat in the left-hand corner of the room, sectioned off at night with a cloth to afford her and her two daughters some privacy. Malek Master's son Maher (17) also slept on a jute mat on the floor, opposite to his aunt and cousins. Malek Master's eldest daughter, Polly (18) had embarked on a bachelor's degree and despite failing to complete it, she was admired and respected by her parents and residents. She was given her own room in an adjacent space, with a bed, chair, table, and a desktop computer. Other than Polly, no one was allowed in that space.

Sayeeda walked around with me and took me to different sections in 1, 2, 3 and 4 of Phulbari. Some residents recognised her and were friendly; others, newer residents or women living in alleyways rarely visited by health workers, looked blankly at her. Sayeeda wore a white coat and carried a bag, lending an air of authority and status. Both Sayeeda and Sufia religiously took me on their rounds, introducing me to established families and newly married adolescents.

Twenty Years Later: Young Women from 2020 to 2022

Baniganj slum[11] is one of the single largest slum areas in Dhaka city, roughly between 180 to 220 acres. It is in a prime location, located besides Gulshan and Banani, two posh residential suburbs. In this area, land price is very high, and therefore has considerable potential for urban development. Residents live and work as maids, in garments factories, as street vendors and as helpers in small retail stores. Baniganj is very old, with reportedly more than 100,100 residents. Three parties are alleged stakeholders of the slum: Baniganj – T&T (Department of Telegraph and Telephone Board of Bangladesh), PWD (Public Works Division), and the former private landowners, in a complicated messy relationship over ownership (Mridha et al., 2009). In the 1990s, unoccupied pieces of land in the area were gradually occupied or sold to various lower-level government T&T workers as well as gang leaders and local leaders (*mastaans*), and city government appointed ward commissioners. They began to rent out land and housing to poorer incoming migrants at low rates. As a result of the growing demand for inexpensive housing, the area expanded (Sinthia, 2020), to create Baniganj as it is today.

In 2007, the monthly income level of residents living in Baniganj was reportedly low, with almost 42.67% households having income around TK3,001–4,500 (US$45–65) and 28% with an income of only TK2,001–3,000, others as high as TK4,500–6,000 (US$65–87). At the time, very few households had an income of more than TK6000. The remaining households' incomes are below TK1,000 (Institute for Development Policy Analysis and Advocacy, 2007). In general, income sources are erratic, and people tend to under report their wages and earning. However, for those who were informal workers, salaries tend to remain low or erratic, with daily wages fluctuating.

It was reported that most of the powerful local leaders belong to the current ruling party. There are three political clubs run by young males, who are closely affiliated with local leaders and different levels of politicians. There was an attempt to evict people from Baniganj in 2014, but several legal aid NGOs filed petitions in court challenging the eviction notice on such a massive scale, reflecting the size of the population. The final verdict as of 2023 is still pending, and the future remains uncertain for thousands of residents. As demand for land grows, urban planners and investors begin to push for reclaiming the land. Baniganj has been home to Meena and her family and Fatema and her family for a long time. In mid-2022, due to events in 2021 (discussed in later chapters), Shuli moved into Baniganj.

Meena, Liton and her Mother, Mita

Meena had rented a room in Baniganj since her marriage to Liton, almost nine years ago. Her home was in a busy area near a mosque, with many one room homes, closely lined up next to each other. There were numerous shops on both sides of the street, with four drug shops, four small grocery shops and a few tea shops next to Meena's place in an alleyway. Meena and Liton lived in one of four rooms on the second floor of a two storied place with a cemented floor and a tin roof, and it was boiling hot and stuffy in the summer months. There were five rooms on the ground floor, and a separate kitchen and bathroom on the 2nd floor. Meena and Liton and her children shared a kitchen and latrine and water access with 40 other tenants. The condition of the latrine was filthy, the area stained and stinking of urine. There was cloth hanging for bathing next to the latrine, but each tenant had a separate bucket in the bathing area. Water was in short supply, available once a day for a few hours only, and so tenants stored water in buckets. The road leading up to Meena's place was very narrow, allowing only one person at a time. It was dark and there was a lot of waste lying on the streets, a pungent odour of waste which one could smell in her room. The rent for the room was TK3,000 (approximately US$35 in 2022). They had one large bed, a steel food rack, and some glass jars containing various kinds of cooking masalas. There were also two small table fans in this room, and the clothes they used were hung across a rope which had been strung across the room. In addition, there was a school bag and two shopping sacks where potatoes were kept, a picture of

Meena's mother and father, and a poster with writing in Arabic. In the corner was a tin suitcase with five to six pillows and *nakshi kantha* (embroidered blankets). The bed was clean and tidy. The slippers and shoes were kept outside the door of the room, so the floor wouldn't get dirty.

Meena guessed she was 21 years old, but she also confessed that she did not remember her age. Her husband Liton was either 25 or 26 years old, and they had three children; their eldest daughter was 12 years old when we interviewed Meena in 2020. There were two younger boys, aged 7 and 8 years old. Her daughter was studying in a semi-government school, until Covid-19 when all schools were closed. Meena was worried as her daughter had done little since the school had shut, although she did help with household chores. The younger boys were not enrolled as Meena could not afford it; although tuition was free, she didn't earn enough to cover costs of books, pens, and school materials. Her husband had been sick for a while, diagnosed with tuberculosis several years earlier (there is more discussion on this in later chapters).

Meena covered her hair with a hijab style scarf and wore a worn shalwar kameez. Meena was very dark skinned, thin and frail, with beautiful large brown eyes and a round face. she had slightly protruded upper teeth, with thick upper lip jutting out. Her face was without any make up, except for a gold nose ring, as is common among married adolescent girls. Her young daughter also sat in the corner of the room in a red shalwar kameez, wearing a head scarf. She smiled sweetly and looked like a miniature version of Meena. She listened intently as her mother spoke and occasionally glanced at her brothers who were running around screaming in excitement as they fought over a packet of chips. Meena and Liton kept shushing them. Liton, a tall, gangly looking fellow, sat on the bed in a *lunghi* (sarong) and an old blue checked shirt. In the end, Liton managed to get the two boys to leave the room by offering to buy them some candy.

Meena always looked sad. She rarely smiled and it seemed as if the weight of the world was on her shoulders. Meena had sold goods on the streets since she was about 9 years old, although later, she switched to domestic work. Her mother, Mita, a 40-year-old widow, worried that because Meena sold on the streets, she would meet unsavoury characters, or elope, or even worse fall pregnant so ruining her reputation in the locality. When she was 13 and had begun menstruating, Mita felt it safer for Meena to be married, and married her off to Liton, the neighbouring tenant's son. When Meena met Liton, he was working in a factory and earned an income between TK8,000 to 10,000 (US$85–95). Liton's father passed away when he was in class 4, and he had to drop out of school. His father had two wives, and they lost any land when the second wife and children took possession of the home and the little land the father owned. They relocated to Dhaka city and moved into a slum, and Liton began working, like his mother and sisters, to support the family. Liton was calm and barely spoke; whenever I visited, if he was around, he mainly observed Meena, as she spoke about their life and ongoing struggles since

Covid-19. He only piped up at one point to mention that he was sick and felt guilty that he relied on Meena to run the household.

Meena's mother, Mita lives in a low-income housing area with her 19 years old son, Shahrukh, 20 minutes away from Meena. Mita and Shahrukh lived in a tiny room adjacent to another room, with one door shared between the two tenants, and they had adjusted to the other tenants walking through their room. The room was located near Badda High School Road, with ten grocery shops, electronics shops, mobile flexi-load shops, and a five-storey mosque, and several drug sellers working on the street. Water was available all the time and they shared with several other tenants two latrines, two bathing spaces, and a small kitchen with two gas stoves. Mita's room had only one large bed, glass bottles with spices and a rack for food items and small pots, some rice, pitchers, and buckets. The room was partly made of concrete, and was well lit, with windows on two sides.

When I met her, she was wearing a yellow-brown printed cotton sari. Her hair was in a messy bun, burnt to darkish reddish brown from being in the sun for long hours. She immediately covered her hair with the sari cloth. She explained that she was a devout Muslim and prayers have sustained her mentally as she and her children have struggled since she was widowed, when Meena was very young. Her husband's brother grabbed the land, and Mita and the children were deprived of their inheritance. She moved to the city with her children, to look for work and survive.

Shuli, Shumon and her Mother, and Children

Shuli was 22 years old and had been 'doing street business' as a hawker all her life. She was introduced to this 'business,' by her mother at an early age, and peddling stickers and plastic bags, towels more recently. She was proud of her 'towel' business, pre-Covid, although she struggled to earn enough. Over the years, I often observed as she would weave her way deftly through the traffic and plead at car windows to customers to buy items she carried in her hands. She would always be smiling as sweat poured down her face in the hot midday sun. She was a striking and pretty young girl, tall, slim and fair skinned, with large eyes, her hair was pulled back and tied with a clip. She would sometimes wear eye liner and lipstick. She would burst into giggles every time she tried to sell me items, and I often gave her money without taking anything. Shuli said that she fell in love and ran away with a young man she met on the streets, when, she claimed, she was maybe 16 years old (Fatema said she was not more than 13 years old). The young man earned an income as a police informer, and when he double crossed them, he was arrested and jailed. The marriage ended soon after the birth of two children, and when he came out of jail, after a year, he abandoned her. Shuli moved back with her mother and her two young children, who were very small at the time.

Soon after, she met her second husband, Shumon, 26 years old, who pursued her for six months, courting her with flowers, phone calls and hanging around her, when she sold on the streets. When she married Shumon, she left her children with her mother, Jorina (48 years old), who lived with her son Akash (25) and his wife and Shuli's two children, Shuborna (12) and Jihad (9), near to where Mita lived. Their room stank. It was messy and dirty, dark and hot, with a tiny window in the corner. Insects and cockroaches crawled around the place. Shumon had been previously married too, and it ended when his wife left him to marry another man; he moved to the city to look for work. Shuli found Shumon handsome; he was well built, fair skinned, and dressed in jeans and t-shirts. He had a lot of friends, and he was well liked. She was elated to meet someone 'who was so in love with her,' so soon after the failure of her first marriage, when she felt rejected and abandoned. She was pleased that Shumon took her feelings into consideration when they looked for a place to rent, and that they made joint decisions about their work, their baby and other household matters. Shuli was not close to her mother (see later chapters). She mentioned that her mother had her children begging on the streets to earn money, but she felt she had little control. Jorina was formidable, known to be aggressive and loud on the streets. No one wanted to take on Jorina, especially if there was fight amongst hawkers about selling or if someone was trying to cheat a customer.

Shuli was glad to remarry and move out. She was tired of supporting her mother, and she wanted to get out of her "mother's clutches." When I met them, Shumon and Shuli had been married for over 6 years and had a daughter, Arifa, who was two and half years old when we reconnected in 2022. Shuli was playful and naive. Once when we were talking, she suddenly lifted her kameez (top) and grinned as she showed me the pockets sewn into her top where she kept her cash earned hidden from sales. Shumon smiled indulgently and asked her to pull her top down. She merely chuckled and grabbed Arifa and kissed her on her forehead. Her baby was her pride and joy.

Shuli and Shumon had relocated several times during 2020 to mid-2022, and the rooms ranged from dark and dingy or slightly larger with windows and ventilation, varying in quality and the availability of water, a kitchen, and other services depending on what they could afford. Shuli had collected a few possessions along the way, which moved with them: a small television, a small fan, a bed which could be taken apart and reassembled, some cooking pots, and their clothes. Although they rented in different settlements, each area had the typical characteristics of a slum or a low-income settlement, with rent payments from TK4000 to TK3,500 and usually the shared use of a kitchen, latrines, and water, by rotation – what Shuli called 'serial numbers.' Either paved roads or smaller dirt paths, full of litter and other waste, led to their rooms.

Fatema, Riaz and her Family

Fatema, 19 years old, rented a room with her husband, Riaz (28 years old), and two young daughters, aged three and seven months, in one room in Baniganj. She lived about ten minutes away from Meena, but they rarely met, their lives crowded with earning and household responsibilities. Fatema's room was via several small alleys, crowded with disused and broken water pipes. The alleyways were so narrow that even a rickshaw, used for local transport, could not enter the narrow lanes. Unpaved and without drainage, the alleys easily flooded in the monsoon season. Fatema's room was next to a tin-shed two storied house and a small grocery store; two houses down, her parents, her elder brother Faruk (26 years old), and his wife live together.

The alleyway leading to and beside Fatema's room was filthy, piled high with waste, old broken furniture and other rubbish. All the waste accumulated is, Fatema explained, dumped into the nearby lake; there was no rubbish collection service. There was a pile of dirt at the main gate leading to Fatima's, and then a latrine and bathing area on the left-hand side. There were seven rooms with tenants renting a room. Fatema, Riaz and her two young children lived in the third room on the ground floor and share the kitchen with four gas stoves for tenants to use. The landlord also lived in this place, in a slightly larger room. There were six more rooms the second floor, also rented to tenants and owned by the landlord's sister. Fatema's room was very dark, despite a window. Whenever I visited, she had a fan and two light bulbs on, otherwise it was a very dark space. When the electricity went off, as it did intermittently, the room was unbearably stifling and in complete darkness.

In contrast to the decay, filth, and smells of waste outside the compound, Fatema's room was very tidy, and the floor was immaculately clean. All shoes and sandals were neatly arranged outside. The room was made of cement, bricks, and tin, with the roof entirely of tin. It was well furnished: a bed, a closet, a table, a television, buckets stored in a corner to collect water, a water filter, and a fridge. She also had a long cabinet with glass, to showcase dinner plates, cups and saucers; in the corner there was a clothes rack. Fatema pointed proudly to a calendar picture hanging on the wall and a clock on the table. She also was very proud of the two chairs she had bought with her savings, placed at the end of her bed.

Fatema wore a lovely green and blue shalwar kameez, gold earrings, and a dozen coloured-glass bangles on her arms. Her hair was neatly oiled and tied back in a bun. She recounted how she had met Riaz when she was selling sell towels in Gulshan 1. He would watch her and talk to her. They began to chat often, and he would buy her tea when she took breaks from selling. She was nervous as she was only 13 or 14 and wasn't sure of his intentions and whether he was a "good boy," or trying to "have fun" and was just flirting with her. After several weeks of chatting, he asked for her phone number. She refused, but he got it from Shuli, and he began to call her. She said that she quickly fell in love with him and told her parents that Riaz wanted to marry her. According to her, Riaz was crazy about her. Her older brother Faruk, who is married, initially opposed the marriage, and had grave concerns as Riaz didn't have a job at the time. Riaz begged for Fatema's hand, promising the family that he would get a job. Her parents agreed. Faruk had some additional meetings with Riaz: "She is my little sister, and I didn't want her to marry someone who couldn't hold a job and I wasn't sure about him, but he has turned out to be a good brother-in-law and he is good to my sister." For Fatema, Faruk's approval was critical.

They had been married six years and seem contented. Fatema manages the household but is also the key decision maker on major issues – finance, shopping, education, savings, renting and so on. Riaz's parents and his younger sister do not live in Baniganj, but live close to the Badda High School, where Shuli's mother, Jorina, and her children and Meena's mother Mita and her son live. Riaz's parents provide them support whenever they can. Fatema is close to her in-laws but also wanted to live very close to her parents. Fatema's mother and brother are closely involved in her life, and she is often at her mother's place, eating, catching and chatting with her family members.

During the interview with Fatema, the conversation had to be interrupted several times, because Fatema's 3-year-old daughter woke up and wanted to snack. She opened the fridge door and grabbed a bottle of 7Up (popular soft drink), but Fatema stopped her: "You can't drink it now on an empty stomach in the morning." The girl put the bottle back in the fridge and came to Fatema and demanded food. Fatema told her to go to her mother's home to ask her to buy her some chips from the local shop. The girl walked out, saying, "I will eat iced lollie (ice-cream) from the shop." When Fatema told her she shouldn't eat ice-cream in the morning, the girl ran out, screaming, "I will eat ice-lollie." Fatema smiled at me and replied, "I will beat you." Fatema said it was a relief to have her mother live close by and her children were often there, when she needed to work. As we kept chatting, we heard shouting and abusive language, and a threat to call the police. Fatema informed me that the landlord of the ground floor and his sister (who owns the second floor) had been screaming at each other almost every day because the sister had built a new space upstairs without his permission. Shortly afterwards, Fatema told me she would need to go to the streets to sell towels and I promised to return another day to chat for longer. She picked up her baby girl, locked her room door, walked over to her mother's place, and handed over her baby. She then walked quickly towards Gulshan 1, carrying a bag of towels.

Fatema was tiny, under five feet, and she looked like a 10-year-old girl with a baby face. She was determined young woman, very sharp and adept at managing the household, finances and making decisions on the children and savings. Riaz respected her and listened to her advice, and they rarely quarrelled. She was always inquisitive during our conversations, but also thoughtful when talking about her life, and when talking about Meena, Shuli, Jorina, Shuli's children and others who she knew from the area and from her work.

Young Women Working in the Informal Economy

In Phulbari, in 2002, Monsura didn't work, and Roshonara worked at home, sewing punjabis and earned money for however many pieces she completed. She was part of an informal economy of many women workers in Phulbari, who sewed at home and earned cash, whereas her sister Razia, who was separated from her husband, worked in a garment factory, but still struggled due to her recent separation from her husband Shahed. The exception is Sayeeda who worked as a health provider in a clinic, but she remained vulnerable due to her personal, social and economic circumstances, and dependent on her sister and brother-in-law, who was a local leader. Twenty years later, in 2020, we find three of the young women working outside their homes, two of them – Shuli and Fatema selling towels on the streets and in Shuli's case, begging on the streets to manage their households. Meena worked as a maid, like her mother and prior to that sold toys and other items on the streets. They also belong to an informal economy and are repeating the fate of their mothers – working on the streets or as maids, with low wages and an insecure income.

The informal sector workers range from rickshaw pullers, agriculture workers, construction workers (labourers), street hawkers, rag pickers, transport workers, part time domestic workers (maids), etc. It is reported that 85.5% of males and 92.3% of female workers are engaged in the informal sector. Child workers number around 4.8 million or 12.6% aged from 5 to 14 years of age. Eighty-three percent are employed in rural and 17% in urban areas, and they mostly work in the transport sector, as hawkers, rag pickers, in *biri* and welding factories, etc. (Beaubien, 2016). Workers in the informal sector are left more vulnerable than others, with working conditions unsafe and unhealthy. They work long working hours and earn low wages, (Ali, 2013) often in hazardous working conditions, and have inadequate safety and security (Nastiti et al., 2012). The Labour Law of 2006 is a comprehensive one which was further refined in 2010, 2013 and 2018 providing detailed guidelines for the workers-employers relations and benefits. The informal sector workers are not included. The Bangladesh Worker Welfare Foundation Act 2006 defines informal sector as those

> private bodies where the terms and conditions of employment of workers and other relevant issues are not determined or guided by the provisions of the existing Labour Act, Rules or Policy, promulgated thereunder, and where there is very limited scope for the workers to be unionised.
>
> (Anam, 2020)

Many of them, such as street hawkers, vendors tend to lack recognition as workers, and are disrespected, and many are viewed as nuisances or even as criminals (Abboud, 2022). They also remain in a cycle of dependency and poverty, with income earned never secure or stable enough to substantially improve access, choices and their lives.

Note

1 Chachi is paternal auntie (husband's brother's wife), I never knew her first name as she was always referred to as 'mother of so and so' and I called her Chachi as others did in the locality.

References

Abboud, O. (2022). Recognition and respect could change street vendors' lives. www.wiego.org/blog/recognition-and-respect-could-change-street-vendors.

Ali, A. (2013). Informal labour force. Dhaka, Bangladesh. https://unnayan.org/wp-content/uploads/2021/05/INFORMAL-LABOUR-FORCE.pdf

Anam, S. (2020, March 30). What about workers in the informal sector? *The Daily Star.* https://www.thedailystar.net/opinion/perspective/news/what-about-workers-the-informal-sector-1887409

Anam, S. (2020). What about workers in the informal sector. *The Daily Star.*

Banks, N. (2016). Livelihoods limitations: The political economy of urban poverty in Dhaka, Bangladesh. *Development and Change*, 47(2), 266–292.

Beaubien, J. (2016). Child laborers in Bangladesh are working 64 hours a week. www.npr.org/sections/goatsandsoda/2016/12/07/504681046/study-child-laborers-in-bangladesh-are-working-64-hours-a-week.

Hossain, M. J., Soma, M. A., Bari, M. S., Emran, T. B., & Islam, M. R. (2021). COVID-19 and child marriage in Bangladesh: Emergency call to action. *BMJ Paediatrics Open*, 5(1).

Mridha, M. K., Hossain, A., Alam, B., Sarker, B. K., Wahed, T., Khan, R., & Roy, S. (2009). MANOSHI Working Paper Series No 9.

Nastiti, A., Prabaharyaka, I., Roosmini, D., & Kunaefi, T. D. (2012). Health-associated cost of urban informal industrial sector: An assessment tool. *Procedia-Social and Behavioral Sciences*, 36, 112–122.

Institute for Development Policy Analysis and Advocacy (2007). Accountability arrangements to combat corruption in the delivery of infrastructure services in Bangladesh: A case study. Loughborough University. https://hdl.handle.net/2134/9578.

Sinthia, S. A. (2020). Analysis of urban slum: Case study of Korail Slum, Dhaka. *International Journal of Urban and Civil Engineering*, 14(11), 416–430.

4   Social Position, Relationships and Strategies to Survive in 2002

Survival Networks and Temporary Support

In late March, 2002, Monsura and Sayyied had been living at Ratna's and Abdul's place for the past eight months. Sayyied, 30 years old, was always late paying the monthly rent of TK450 (approximately US$8 in 2002), and Ratna, 32, their landlady was furious. They were now two months behind in payments, and so owed her TK900 (approximately US$16 in 2002). Monsura, 17, and I were discussing this, and Monsura said defensively, "We are not the only ones in the slum to pay our rent late, everyone pays their rent late. Jobs are not secure, and no one can pay on time … she says all kinds of things to me, calling us beggars, and lazy!"

Without personal networks, a migrant from the village and less than two years of living in Phulbari, Monsura spent most of her time inside the compound. One afternoon, on my way out of Monsura's room, Ratna called out to me, "I don't know what that girl (Monsura) was telling you, but Sayyied is a useless husband, and she has an attitude!" She looked over her shoulder to check if Monsura could hear us and whispered, "He is always borrowing money on credit and constantly beating her … and she must plead with him for cash to buy food for herself and for the baby. But when I ask for my money, she misbehaves." Ratna's relationship with Monsura alternated between pity to anger and distrust.

Paying rent is hugely stressful for those whose income was unstable. Sayyied worked odd jobs. Sometimes he drove a rickshaw, other times, he rented a three-wheeler scooter. But often, he was drunk and would disappear for a day or two, leaving Monsura and the baby son to fend for themselves. Sayyied had only studied up to class 3 and his income options were limited. Monsura was barely literate. With regular cash shortages in the household, Monsura was tense about their future. If rent is not paid, a tenant can be evicted. To end up on the streets as a pavement dweller is a tenant's worst nightmare. A study in 2022 reported that there are about 20,000 pavement dwellers living and sleeping on the streets in Dhaka city (Huda, 2014). Regular rental payments to a landlord or landlady ensured security, a roof over one's head, and access to basic services. Having a good relationship with the landlord and their compassion meant that one could negotiate and pay later.

DOI: 10.4324/9781003467472-4

An outward marker of a better-off tenant and landlord was usually a cemented floor, the size of the room and compound, and the number of items and furniture in their rooms – a bed, a television, a cabinet, a fan, and so on, in some homes, although rarely, a fridge and old sofa seats. These items came in handy to sell if one needed quick cash, at times of crisis. But Monsura's room was sparse, with only one *chowki* (wooden) bed with a tattered, stained sheet, covering a thin mattress. There were two pillows and a worn looking stitched *katha* (embroidered cotton blanket). In the corner of the room, she had two cooking pots, three tin plates and two cracked spoons, carefully placed on the floor. The room was tiny, dark, a small window and little ventilation, but there was a small fan stand and a light bulb. As we continued speaking, I realised it was past 1.30pm and she had not cooked. Her pots were overturned and dry. I asked her if she was going to cook later today. I felt guilty that our conversation was keeping her from preparing the afternoon meal. She was quiet for a long time and looking shamefaced, responded: "No, I haven't eaten. Joy's father[1] (Sayyied) has not been home for a couple of days, and I used up the last of my savings. Yesterday I borrowed some rice from Ratna, but it is so humiliating. She reminds me how much rice she gave me and taunted me, 'Where is Joy's father? How come he is not around? Has he left you?' Apa, she is the devil, the way she speaks to me. I maybe poor but I am not a beggar." She covered her face with her hands, holding back her tears. Joy was fast sleep next to her, sucking his thumb, blissfully unaware of her anguish.

No Work and the Need for Cash

I asked her what she would do. She shrugged and said, "Joy's father does not like to work. He likes to drink and gamble. When I ask him for money to buy food, he screams and yells at me. We must pay rent and Joy's father can never pay on time. It is so shameful to live on credit." As we were talking, I could smell lentil curry and fish curry wafting into the room from Ratna's kitchen, next door inside the compound. Monsura hurriedly got up from the bed and banged the door shut. She looked wearily at me and pointing to her baby boy said, "I can still breastfeed my baby, but even my milk will also dry up." Monsura didn't work and was fully dependent on Sayyied. When I asked if Sayyied was perhaps struggling to find a job, she nodded, "Sometimes he rents a tempo (three-wheeler scooter) but now there is a government ban on tempo cars … you know 2 stroke engines were removed from the streets of Dhaka."

Informal workers like Sayyied are completely dependent on macro and micro factors outside their control, from government agendas, donor policies, global regulations, which leads to grappling with corrupt systems, which exclude the poor, and can lead to job losses and other challenges. In 2002, the World Bank had implemented an aggressive policy that required the government to introduce a new carbon-free environmentally friendly three wheelers, and immediate removal of all diesel-run three wheelers off the streets of

Dhaka city. The aim was to reduce extreme pollution levels in Dhaka city (Rashid, 2004; Daily Star, 1998; 2002).[2] While the intentions were to improve air pollution, this policy left a quarter of a million urban poor men and their families suddenly without an income source. Many could not afford the hidden costs of paying for a new license. To get a new license meant paying bribes and they didn't have the cash. Nor could they borrow money: "Who do I know in this place? I hardly leave the room. I don't work. He must take a loan from a friend or his family." She had tried to join the local women's *samity* (organisation), set up by women residents, a group for savings and taking loans.

According to Ratna, Monsura, a fairly new tenant, had barely made enough for deposits and was asking for a loan of TK2,000, and she only had entry because Ratna, a landlady, had introduced her to this women's group. Monsura was kicked out of the collective and had no-one else to ask for financial support. Monsura shared angrily, "Ratna and those women are just trying to make money off me … so I left that samity. Look at my life, and then my mother asks me for cash and my brother behaves like I don't exist!"

On subsequent visits, Sayyied was at home, lying on the bed with Monsura, cradling their baby son Joy. He'd immediately sit up, slightly embarrassed; he'd invite me to enter and usually take off with Joy, leaving us to converse in privacy. I noticed that Monsura was becoming withdrawn, sullen, and less communicative. I asked her what was going on, and she confessed that Sayyied was regularly beating, slapping, and kicking her whenever she demanded he work. He had warned her to not let me know. There was also growing tension with Ratna: she alleged that Monsura and Sayyied borrowed cash again and had not repaid her. Monsura countered that Ratna had pocketed some of the money and was lying about the amount owed. Within a few weeks, the situation had deteriorated: Ratna now began alleging that Monsura was flirting with her husband. Ratna pulled me aside: "Apa (sister), you won't believe it, but I caught her. She is a bad, bad woman. Monsura wants to sleep with my husband … just to get one set of shalwar kameez (outfit)."

I asked her why she believed this to be true, and she explained: "Listen to me. Once I was away for three days because I had to go to Konabari (her parents' home). I know there was a relationship that took place between them. When I am asleep, they meet and laugh … I can hear them outside my door. Sayyied is never around. He is too busy drinking and gambling and disappears for days. My husband works hard, and she is very clever, hoping he will buy her clothes and give her cash."

Ratna was older, heavy set, and she was conscious that Monsura was pretty and slim, and her husband was very friendly with her.

Marriages tend to be unstable. Stealing husbands was a big fear and rumours constantly circulated: of infidelity, hidden affairs, serially unfaithful husbands, and a few unfaithful wives, of single women "being loose and too familiar with married men" and widows having affairs with married men. Whispers and raucous laughter filled the air as groups of women sat together gossiping and sharing explicit details of various alleged relationships. Men's and women's characters were dissected and shred to pieces. I was present when a wife confronted her husband for having an affair with his sister-in-law. Violence erupted, with the wife openly attacking her husband, as a crowd gathered to watch and some of the men intervened to mediate.

Aside from emotional attachment, hurt and betrayal, men are seen as a valuable resource, socially, economically and for protection. Having a husband ensured social acceptance and upheld one's 'good' reputation. A common saying, I heard during fieldwork was, 'that wife cannot eat her husband's rice,' blaming the end of a marriage on the woman, who was viewed as 'difficult' or had 'brought it on herself.' In rural villages, social sanctions took place in tightly knit bounded communities, with threats and sanctions against men who remarried. It was harder to enforce *shalishes* (punishment via an informal judge-jury system) in cities. In slums, men could simply relocate or settle with a second wife in another location. Jesmin and Salway reported that out of the 732 households surveyed in several urban slums, 15% of respondents had experienced divorce or separation at least once (Jesmin & Salway, 2000). In many cases, migrant men start new families elsewhere, creating a new set of obligations and reducing their economic support to their first family. The anonymity of cities also allowed women to remarry, relocate as well.

Ratna's paranoia was not surprising. Monsura, she said, was too talkative, and always found time to chat to her husband; she was dismissive of Ratna, who asked her to refrain from being so friendly with Abdul. Ratna recounted: "You need listen to me, Monsura is not good! Do you know what she did one day? Her husband was not at home, and it was very late at night, and I saw with my own eyes, she brought back a man into her room. When I confronted her later, she claimed that she was offering to massage his head and he gave her some cash for the massage. She shut the door. Who spends time with a strange man and offers to massage his head? My husband was sleeping at the time. Do you know that the man left at 12 midnight, and he came in at 10 pm? So, what were they doing for two hours? She didn't know I was awake and that I saw her. I walked over to her room as soon as I saw the man leave. She is a whore. I confronted her, 'You brought a man to the house, this is not right, your husband is not at home.' Monsura fell to my feet in fear and said, 'Please don't tell my husband and I won't ever do it again'."

Ratna leaned in closer, her face inches away, her hot breath blowing on my face, "If I wasn't here to guard the compound, then who knows how many men would have come and gone from her room?"

A few days later, as I sat in Monsura's room, after lunch, we heard Ratna screaming again at her daughters, "You whores, stop running around and fill the bucket with water." The girls were giggling and one of them ran out of the compound. She yelled, "Prostitute, you don't do any work in the house." Ratna continued loudly, "Wait till I tell your father, he will beat you with a stick tonight. Come back right now and finish your chores." Monsura burst out laughing. She said, "She is very stupid and fat ... even her husband prefers to fuck other women, you should see the way he looks at me all the time. She is so fat, she can't move. She is so jealous because you come and visit me and talk to me ... you see. I am the *fakirni* (beggar) tenant and she is the landlady, how you can possibly want to speak to me over her?" Monsura continued, returning to Sayyied: "He may beat me, but he loves his baby boy. My son is everything to Sayyied. Even Ratna's mother is jealous of me. She has two girls, but I have a boy."

Having a son was Monsura's pride and joy and, although poorer than Ratna, she knew that she was in some ways superior to her, because most women wanted to have a boy child to ensure their status but also their future security. It was believed that a son would look after his parents and not leave the household, whereas a girl child would eventually marry and leave to be with her husband and in-laws. However, the reality with growing urbanization and poverty means that this does not hold true. Parents complained of sons who were not interested in financially supporting their aging parents once married, and I found households, where young women were working to help support their parents and siblings.

Fights between Monsura and Ratna began to occur frequently, over petty things, use of the shared toilet and "taking too much time, keeping it messy," and accusations of "Joy crying and making too much noise." Nasty accusations continued flying back and forth. Monsura began to insinuate to me that Ratna was having an affair behind Abdul's back, with a married man who lived nearby. She also alleged that Ratna was obsessed with her baby boy. Soon afterwards, whenever I visited, Ratna was cold towards me and despite my efforts, it was awkward. She barely acknowledged me and shut her room door, barring me from entering. She may have felt betrayed that I was still visiting Monsura after all that she had shared with me. To complicate matters, as Monsura had pointed out, there was a clear social hierarchy in the slum, and Ratna was the landlady; Monsura was simply a poor tenant. How could I choose to spend time with her tenant?

One evening, after another explosive fight, Monsura and Sayyied were asked to leave. They found another room to rent in Phulbari slum, as Sayyied knew the tea shop owner, whose wife owned a compound across the lane. Sayyied drank tea regularly at his shop, and his friendly relationship with the shop owner ensured the room's quick availability.

A month later, Sayyied and Monsura had returned to Ratna's compound after persuasion from Abdul. Abdul claimed to be close to Sayyied and said, "They are like family, and we should all be able to live together. The wives must stop fighting ... they are like sisters!" Sayyied was not averse to moving back as Abdul occasionally lent him cash. But Monsura was reluctant. In June, another explosive fight took place, and Monsura accused Ratna of trying to "breastfeed her baby" when she was in the toilet. This led to harsh words and counteraccusations, and Sayyied and Monsura moved out again.

I reflected on Monsura's limited life, with few possibilities ahead. She knew Ratna could freely abuse her and her husband, as they were dependent on her for food, rent waivers and for petty cash. Her son she dreamed one day would be a huge support for Monsura, once he was older, but for now, he was an infant and required looking after, and she was struggling. She didn't know how to manage Sayyied and felt lost and overwhelmed with her life and responsibilities. If Monsura was having sexual relationships or offering massages to earn some money, as Ratna alleged, she had little choice. While I would never know the truth of any of the accusations levelled by Ratna or Monsura, the conversations illustrate the instability of marriages, the stressors of poverty which create tense relationships, and the need for emotional intimacy and the desperation for cash. Any of these may force individuals to act in ways that are risky, but provide some personal gain, whether material, physical or emotional.

Weak Social Ties and Relationships

Monsura's and Sayyied's social networks in Phulbari and in the city were weak. Their immediate families gave them little financial or emotional support. Despite the friction, Ratna seemed to be the only person who occasionally assisted them, with free meals and a couple of times with cash. I remember one incident when Ratna handed over TK100 (approximately US$3.47 in 2002) to Monsura when baby Joy was sick, so she could buy some medicines. Sayyied was unwilling to pull a rickshaw, as "it was too hard on his body." Rickshaw pulling required immense strength as one sat on a small triangle shaped plastic seat with little cushioning and pedalling from two to four passengers for each trip. A common sight in Dhaka streets is of younger males as well as elderly males pedalling, looking exhausted carrying a huge weight of passengers/customers as they weave through the busy traffic on the streets. A report in 2019 found that most of these poor men rent a rickshaw as they cannot afford to own one. Usually after peddling a rickshaw for ten to 12 hours straight, one can earn up to only TK500 a day (approximately US$6). From this amount, a rickshaw puller usually pays the owner, and then a smaller amount to police for plying on restricted lanes, and then money is needed to pay for some food to eat during the day. Overall, very little is left for rent and other costs of living required for himself and his family (Jahan, 2019).

Sayyied shared that he could not afford the bribe to get a licence to ride one of the new three wheelers; he seemed to spend his days drowning himself in alcohol. He was seen as a loan risk, and as a new migrant in the slum, was not well known and not considered ideal for an established money lender. He was also reluctant to borrow, leaving Monsura frustrated and anxious about their future.

Family support was almost non-existent. Sayyied had a difficult relationship with his father, who had remarried, and they had little contact. His younger brother had set up a small business in Dhaka city and was viewed as 'successful' and lent him money a few times, but their relationship was strained. While he had reluctantly reached out to his brother twice for a loan, he always forced Monsura to plead on his behalf. According to Monsura, he was scared that his brother would turn him down but would be more sympathetic if Monsura asked. He could not deal with the humiliation. Monsura felt ashamed of the need to ask for money and cringed at a recent memory, when the brother's wife picked up the phone and cut the line on hearing Monsura's voice. But given their desperation, she kept trying until she received some cash from her brother-in-law. On Monsura's side, the situation was also dismal. Her father lived in the village and had remarried. He deserted his first wife (Monsura's mother), who had moved to Dhaka city and survived as a 'traditional healer,' saving whatever little she earned. With unlicensed drug sellers in every corner of the city, her business did poorly. Her mother lived with her brother and his wife and they pooled their meagre resources and lived together. Monsura was seen as burden, and this was amplified because she married a man who didn't work, nor was he supported by his own family. Both Monsura and Sayyied had few networks they could rely on, which led to instability and volatility in their relationship with each other and with others.

Roshonara and Mintoo: Managing Cash Flow

Roshonara, 21 and her family who lived around the corner from Monsura. In contrast to her, had strong networks and relationships, having lived for more than 20 years in Phulbari. Roshonara and her mother also belonged to a local women's *samity* and her mother was also an 'owner' of her home.

In early April, Roshonara told me that Mintoo (her husband), 30, had suddenly lost his job. He used to ride a van-cart and distribute cartons of juices to various shops, but the company had shut down and he now had no income. He had taken a loan and bought the van-cart so he could distribute goods in the city. At the time, this purchase seemed wise, as he had a stable income coming in regularly. This investment now lay idle. Roshonara was in shock, as his job had assured them of steady cash flow. She was extremely anxious and worried that Mintoo may get involved in illicit activities if he was not busy working. She shared, "I am concerned about him sitting around and doing nothing. Many of the men sitting around get into substance abuse or get involved in local gangs." Roshonara and Mintoo had a young baby girl, Lucky, and Roshonara was anxious about how they would run their household. Since Roshonara lived rent-free in her mother's compound, whatever they earned contributed to food and other costs of running their own and her mother's household. Staying with her mother meant she did not have to worry about rent, which can be a huge burden on tenants. With the recent job loss, paying rent can set back a household and place them in a cycle of indebtedness.

When she was at home, other than cooking, cleaning, and keeping an eye on their baby girl, Roshonara embroidered *punjabis* (traditional male attire) to earn cash. I often found her in the late afternoons, sitting in the corner of her room, squinting as she painstakingly embroidered designs on one *punjabi* after another. They were large family, as she and Mintoo lived with her sib- lings, and her father who visited and stayed for weeks at a time. Mintoo was a loving father who spent a considerable amount of time with Lucky, carrying her on his shoulders or his hips, as he took her for treats to the nearby corner shops, often cuddling her in his lap, when he sat around chatting and drinking tea with some of his friends in the local shop.

Strategies to Earn Cash

Roshonara began to strategise ways to earn cash; a few weeks later, she set up a water-melon shop around the corner from where she lived. She lamented that her husband had only studied up to class 6, dropping out to support his family, so his job options were limited. She also complained that since he had lost his job, he had found excuses not to actively look for work and relied on her to figure out how to make ends meet. When she came up with the idea of selling fruit, Mintoo was supportive and they both sat each day with a large basket of watermelons, near a busy intersection of Lane 4, inside Phulbari. Without shade, in the glare of sun, where I stood felt like it was on fire. I thought that my sandals would melt. I bought two watermelons.

Roshanara seemed better than her husband at selling. He sat quietly, while she joked, calling out to passers-by to try some watermelon. Roshonara had cut up pieces of melon and placed them on a tin plate for residents to taste. Several residents stood around tasting; commenting on the taste, flavour and some of them bought half a watermelon. I squatted down next to Roshonara. She laughed and asked me if I wanted to help her sell. I smiled and told her I'd like to keep her company. I observed some boys and girls, aged ten years old running around kicking a ball in the corner lane. Scruffy and in shorts and worn tee shirts, they screamed in glee when one of them managed to get the ball. As I watched them play, Roshonara shared, "You know, Mintoo doesn't like me working outside the home. When I think of working in a factory, my mind, heart, and body starts feeling ill." She continued, "Will you give me a job to clean your home?" I felt Roshanara was taunting Mintoo, who looked visibly irritated and immediately retorted, "No need for you to clean other peoples' homes. I told you I will find a job." He was insulted by her comments, in front of me, and appeared slighted by the implication was he was unable to look after his own household. Men are socially and cultu- rally expected to be the rice-winners of the family, although many women worked, and men did not.

In late April, Roshonara was not in her usual place, selling watermelons. I visited her mother's place and found her there lying down, her eyes were puffy, as if she had been crying. I put my hands on her cheeks and asked her why she was so upset. She tried to give me half a smile and failed. "Our work (selling watermelons) has stopped," she explained. "So many people owe us money, but they have not paid us. We don't make enough money selling the melons. We cannot afford to do this anymore." I had already heard from

Chachi, Roshonara's mother, that Mintoo had a habit of giving away melons, without asking for payment and providing it on credit. He didn't like to haggle or negotiate and wanted to come across as generous, not desperate for money. It was important for his status and his reputation in the local area.

I asked Roshanara what her options were. "I cannot work in a garment (factory)," she replied. "I don't want to leave my daughter at home all by herself. She is so young and (I would) feel very guilty." She was upset as they had little stored food in the house and was frustrated with Mintoo as he didn't want to do hard labour, pulling a rickshaw, for example, to bring in an income. They had sold their television for quick cash, and Roshanara missed this – it was her respite after a long day of work. She also felt that because her mother was landlady, residents assumed they were well off and not struggling:

"No one sees the inside of anyone or of a household. No one knows whether one has eaten or not...all people see is just the outside. I am okay one day and then I am poor, but if I have a lot of items in my home, a television, fan, some utensils, and I am rich. But the truth is ... (she paused) look how quickly one can lose everything. Now we don't have a television anymore, and we may have to sell the cassette player."

From the outside, Roshonara's compound would be considered large compared to the small one roomed home in rows on their lane. It was not surprising that poorer tenants considered them well-off, as the luxury of 'owning' a home with several rooms and having separate facilities in Phulbari was a dream of many, who worked tirelessly to pay rent to landlords and landladies.

In early June, I visited Roshonara again. She had sold the van-cart that Mintoo had bought, and with her mother, had taken a TK5,000 loan (approximately US$88 in 2002) from the local *samity* group. She was an established resident in Phulbari and had been a member for a long time, so it was not that hard to get a loan. To this, she added her savings to put together the amount of TK15,000 (approximately US$265 in 2002) to rent a small tea shop in the slum. She had approached a local leader, who agreed to rent his tea shop, since his brother who usually ran the teashop, was on the run from the police and rival leaders. Running a teashop appealed to Mintoo, as this was more prestigious and not seen as low status as riding a rickshaw in the city or working as a labourer. It was also less laborious in comparison to the other jobs.

A few weeks later Roshonara again seemed beside herself with anxiety. "We have enemies behind our teashop," she explained. "Next door to us, they have taken away a lot of our customers. They also have a teashop, but we were doing so well. I am very worried.... I can't sleep at night." Roshonara said that she was suffering from sleepless nights and a lack of appetite, tense about repaying the TK15,000 loan and meeting other costs of renting the tea shop, along with pending bills for electricity, gas, and water. The competitor was selling tea at much lower prices. This forced Roshonara to rethink her strategy, and she borrowed cash from her mother, and bought a small television to attract customers and reduced the price of their tea. A few weeks later,

Roshonara looking visibly happier shared, "The cable line and television has led to improved sales." She smiled, "Now, I am going to make myself a gold chain with some of the left-over earnings."

No Money, no Meals

Meanwhile, Razia, 17, her younger sister, had separated from her husband, Shahed, 25. They had a love marriage. Dowry disputes and Razia's family refusing to pay any sum of money to Shahed, as they were also financially struggling, was the main reason for the separation. Razia bitterly resented her mother and sister for not caring about her future and complained on numerous occasions to me that her family were unwilling to take a loan to pay the dowry demanded – TK20,000 (approximately US$353 in 2002). Instead, her mother insisted she work and save up money for the dowry demanded by her husband and his family, as she had a love marriage. This was not their problem. Chachi often shared with me and so did Roshonara, that they did not pay any dowry cash to Mintoo and his family when Roshonara was married. Roshonara shared that it was unfair of Razia to expect her parents to pay dowry for her marriage to Shahed, given Mintoo and his family had received nothing. Razia's hope of moving on from the drudgery of her daily existence in Phulbari ended when he unexpectedly left her, after several discussions regarding dowry payments with her family led to little success. This meant that she was now forced to working at a garment factory, but she constantly complained about the "long hours, backaches and eyes hurting," and regularly missed work. She had dreamt of a new life as a bride who would be taken care of by Shahed. Shahed's family seemed to be well off; all of them had jobs and were a close tightknit family. They also had some land in the village, unusual as not many of the poorer residents owned any land in the village. Owning land was a luxury. Roshonara also shared with me in confidence that Razia had gotten carried away and had married "above her economic class," and it was not surprising that Shahed had left her.

Razia felt vulnerable and not supported by her family. As I sat chatting to Roshonara one afternoon, I heard Razia screaming at the top of her lungs, demanding her afternoon meal from her mother: "For the last 30 days I come home, and I don't get food properly. I don't get food in the morning, or the afternoon. I don't get food properly. Why am I always made to wait?" Chacha, her mother, screamed back: "Don't you dare yell at me. All these demands from everyone. What are you, a queen … I barely have any cash left and I can't feed all of you!" Chachi noticing me sitting nearby, winced, and remarked softly, "I hate all these conflicts." Roshonara appeared extremely embarrassed that I was witness to this incident but remained silent.

Razia stormed inside the compound and saw me sitting in Roshonara's room, and continued angrily, "You know why they are doing this? It is because I have not paid my mother for two months, that is why they are doing this to me. If I had paid her my salary, then everything would be fine, and I would get a meal!" Chachi, enraged with this comment, replied, "This girl, she sits at home, and she does not listen to anyone. She goes to work one day and then does not go for another ten days. She prefers to wander about and flirt, talking to men on the streets! But she is always absent from the office (factory)." Rumours had been circulating that since Shahed had left her, she was wandering about with a married man, Khalid (30), who lived in a neighbouring slum. Khalid's first wife lived in the village. Khalid was a popular young man and well connected to local youth clubs and gangs. Her family was upset with Razia's alleged affair and were worried she would create another mess in her life. Razia furious after hearing her mother's response stormed off angrily to another friend – Moni's home. She could not move into Mamoni's room, as Mamoni's father was renting the space inside Chachi's compound. During her stay at her friend's home, Razia confessed to me that since she had been abandoned by her husband and she did not provide cash regularly to her mother, she was being mistreated. She cried, "Who leaves her own daughter to starve?" Hurt by her mother and feeling neglected she was reluctant to move back home again. She stayed at Moni's place for a few days in protest, but after some mediation from local neighbours, including Sayeeda, the health provider at the local clinic, she returned to her mother's home. The relationship between mother and daughter was tense for a while, but Razia also began to go to work regularly and contribute to the household expenses.

These incidents around food, and sharing and withholding meals, were not uncommon. Family members would exclude certain individuals from food and punish them if they were seen as not contributing financially to the household. Some favoured members are served a bigger piece of fish, meat, and others may be left with scraps to eat. Resentment and bitterness would occur when one family member accused another of eating larger portions of a meal, or leaving them with leftovers, or giving them no food. While this not always the case, both subtle and blatant ways of insulting and excluding individuals were used against those seen as a liability or contributing less cash to a household. Scarcity was commonplace, and when cash flow was unstable, it was difficult to be generous. Ultimately however, responses were shaped by family dynamics and the strength of the ties amongst family members in a household.

Sayeeda, the Health Provider

I first met Sayeeda, (around 25 or 26 years old as reported by her), a health provider at the local clinic, in January 2002 when I began to work in Phulbari. She introduced me to Monsura, Ratna, Roshonara and many other young women and their families, as explained in the earlier chapter. Sayeeda was known to provide informal advice and health services to them, and she was liked and trusted by many. As we became closer, she confessed that she earned 'extra cash' by taking clients for abortions. She spoke in a very matter of fact tone. She needed to earn more money to cover all her costs, as her salary as a health worker was approximately TK1,300 per month in 2002 (approximately US$23). She lived with her children at her elder sister, Mukta and brother-in-law, Malek Master's home, which he owned. She didn't pay for rental costs but contributed to other expenses in the household.

We met one afternoon at the clinic, located inside the slum. She had found a patient who was several months pregnant and had taken her to Fair Nursing home for a termination. "She is poor," Sayeeda explained, "and they cannot afford to have any more children." I asked why she didn't bring her to her own clinic, as it provided legal, safe termination services. Sayeeda glancing over to check no one could hear her, and explained: "This is so much easier, and it only takes half an hour to take her." It was located five minutes away from the slum, compared to a half an hour rickshaw ride to the clinic headquarters where abortions were performed. She continued, "The costs for the woman are TK250 (approximately US$4.47 in 2002), and this clinic won't ask too many questions. The main woman (facility owner) pays me TK100 (approximately US$2) for each patient I bring in. We don't get much money from our clinic if I bring a woman for an MR (menstrual regulation)[3] ... less than half of that amount." (See (Crouthamel et al., 2021). The private clinic paid double the amount as commission, a huge incentive for Sayeeda. Sayeeda added defensively: "This is what we must do. It is safe. Otherwise, how will we manage our households?"

Both she and the second health provider, Sufia (45) made additional income as brokers, and took women in Phulbari to this private clinic, where the quality of the staff and procedures remained dubious. They seemed to be unaware of the qualifications and training of the private clinic providers, or their ability to provide safe terminations beyond the legal, safely allowed, 12 weeks period. At times, I found Sufia and Sayeeda bickering as there was fierce competition between them to get clients. One afternoon, Sufia in a very bad mood, grumbling, "Sayeeda took all three patients (MR) patients today, she will earn a lot of money ... she didn't even leave one for me."

Sayeeda also bought saris wholesale from the local markets and sold them to women in the slum when she made door-to-door visits for 'health messaging'. Divorced, she needed to care for her two sons and an adolescent daughter and was vulnerable and dependent on her immediate family for wider social acceptance in the community: "My daughter is 16 years old, and I need to get her married...I must save to cover the costs of her wedding! Who will give me the money?" She was fully aware that she could not rely on her older sister to provide any financial support for her own children's needs. Sometimes on her health rounds to check on women, we would take several detours as she sold saris or collected money owed for saris that had been bought by women in Phulbari. It was interesting to see the interactions between the women and Sayeeda as she was a powerful persuader, enticing women to buy colourful saris, draping them on their shoulders, and at times, she would twirl with the *achol* (a part of the sari draped on the shoulder), as young women nodded and appraised the saris, and pushed each other to buy. She could be charming when she was selling and if the payments were delayed beyond several months, she would become irritated with those women. But she needed to hang on to her clients, so she kept her anger in check.

Sayeeda was pragmatic and her regular income and contributions ensured a cooperative relationship with her elder sister and family. She and her daughter also contributed substantially to household chores in the home, to ensure that they were not seen as a liability. Like most slum residents, for Sayeeda, cash was a priority, as this allowed her independence, security and continued support, and her health worker's salary did not cover the rising prices of food, her children's needs, including clothing and education, and other related costs of living. She had a complicated relationship with her older sister and her children. She couldn't afford to move out and this was the best arrangement for her, given her situation. Malek Master as the leader provided her with status, which would not be available as a divorced woman.

Relationships and Networks

The personal and social networks of these three women – Roshonara, Monsura and Sayeeda – derived from their status (landlord, tenant), economic situation, length of residency in the slum, and family and non-kin support. Although her husband had lost his job, Roshonara's position as a long-term resident and her mother's position as a long-time landlady, gave her options to access her networks. These options didn't exist for relatively new tenants like Monsura and Sayyied, and consequently, they were much more vulnerable. Sayeeda's role as a health provider in an established clinic ensured some level of income stability and gave her legitimacy and status and access to women, who she sold saris to and others who she assisted with pregnancy terminations to earn additional cash. To find a woman living alone without a male guardian in a slum is rare. The young women's narratives demonstrate that life is difficult, unpredictable, and unstable and they worked hard to find ways to manage their day-to-day existence.

There is a heterogeneity of households in Phulbari, like most slums, with poorer tenants less powerful and more vulnerable, than an established resident or a landlord. However, any job loss can catapult families into a cycle of debt and varying degrees of insecurity, but reliable familial and social networks, can keep an individual and a family afloat for periods of time, providing temporary relief from falling deeper into the abyss of poverty.

Notes

1 In Bangladeshi culture, wives do not refer to their husbands by their first name but refer to them as the father of their child (name). For example, Joy's father (her son's name is Joy).

2 A meeting took place on this issue as far back as 1998, called the 'Integrated Approach to Vehicular Pollution Control' which was jointly organised by the World Bank and the Department of Environment. During this period, the Minister of transport took great pains to emphasise that there would be replacement vehicles – 30 Volvo double decker buses, and 100 buses and new Singaporean company of taxi cabs to offset any transport problems the middle class would have with the removal of baby taxis (three-wheeler scooters) off the streets. The Minister did not discuss the thousands of poor families living in urban slums, who were left without any income because of this sudden removal of baby taxis. There was overwhelming support from the middle and upper class to the government's ban on the baby taxis that were seen as a major cause for the pollution in the streets of Dhaka.

3 In Bangladesh, abortion is illegal except to save a woman's life, though menstrual regulation (MR) is permitted. MR involves the use of manual uterine aspiration or Misoprostol (with or without Mifepristone) to induce menstruation up to 10–12 weeks from the last menstrual period. Menstrual regulation (MR) has been available in the country since 1979 and involves the use of either manual vacuum aspiration (MVA) or medications (Misoprostol with or without Mifepristone) without definitive diagnosis of pregnancy to induce menstruation and can be performed up to 12 weeks from the last menstrual period for doctors and 10 weeks for nurses. Menstrual regulation is approved by the government, and safe MR services are offered within government and private health facilities. Brokering continues well into the present in Bangladesh, see (Crouthamel et al 2021).

References

Crouthamel, B., Pearson, E., Tilford, S., Hurst, S., Paul, D., Aqtar, F., Silverman, J., & Averbach, S. (2021). Out-of-clinic and self-managed abortion in Bangladesh: menstrual regulation provider perspectives. *Reproductive Health*, 18(1), 1–12.

Huda, M. N. (2014). Food security among pavement dwellers in Dhaka City. *World Vision*, 8(1), 46–59.

Jahan, N. (2019). Pulling the weight of the world. *The Daily Star*. www.thedailystar.net/star-weekend/labour-rights/news/pulling-the-weight-the-world-1698940

Jesmin, S., & Salway, S. (2000). Marriage among the urban poor of Dhaka: Instability and uncertainty. *Journal of International Development: The Journal of the Development Studies Association*, 12(5), 689–705.

Rashid, S. F. (2004). Worried Lives: Poverty, Gender and Reproductive Health of Married Adolescent Women Living in an Urban Slum in Bangladesh. PhD Thesis, The Australian National University, Canberra, Australia.

Rashid, S. F. (2004). *Worried Lives: Poverty, Gender and Reproductive Health of Married Adolescent Women Living in an Urban Slum in Bangladesh.*

Daily Star (1998, April 28). Two stroke auto-rickshaws should be phased out.

Daily Star (2002, August 3). Two-stroke ban firm on track.

5 Relationships, Networks and Survival during Covid 19, 2020 and After

"It's Who You Know … That Helps You Manage!"

Meena, Shuli and Fatema and their families were desperate to earn cash to manage their households and the costs of day to day living. For all of them, the level of stress and precarity they experienced was directly dependent on the kind of support they had from family, friends, neighbours, tenants, employers, and others. Strong personal relationships with family members, if constant and stable, were a lifeline; so too were relationships with other individuals – landlords, shopkeepers, drug sellers, money lenders and random strangers. All of these young women and their families also benefited from unexpected sources of assistance – money, food, medicines on credit, relief materials and even clothes – when times were perilous (see Bourdieu, 1986; Coleman, 1994; Mpanje et al., 2018; Putnam, 2000).[1]

Liton's illness

Meena explained to me in 2020 that several years ago, Liton was diagnosed with tuberculosis. He suffered from bodily weakness, aches and chest pains, and the entire responsibility of maintaining the household fell on her. He barely worked and spent most of the time at the local teashop or resting at home. Meena was under enormous stress as the primary rice-winner of the family, with four mouths to feed – Liton and her three children who were completely dependent on her. Meena sighed and in a resigned voice, shared that she often turned to her mother, when she struggled with food shortages at home. Her mother Mita, lived nearby, but required her to walk almost 15 or more minutes to visit her mother. She also confessed that she felt bad asking her mother for food, because her mother was a widow. Both Meena and her mother Mita worked as maids in peoples' homes. When Liton worked many years ago, he was earning close to TK7000 per month (in 2017 it was approximately US$86). Life was easier and with her additional income, they could afford food, rent and their daughter's education costs, as well as other wants – buying clothes for the family and children, eating meat quite often and indulging in some gold bangles for herself, and so on.

DOI: 10.4324/9781003467472-5

By 2018, as the single income earner for quite some time, Meena had fallen behind on rent payments and was borrowing money to manage. Suddenly, the opportunity to work in Jordan as a maid arrived unexpectedly from a close relative. "Liton's stepsister lives in the village and informed me and my husband about this opportunity to work abroad as a maid. She said a lot of money can be made if we are interested and she would make all the arrangements. As my husband was reluctant to go with all his health problems, he convinced me to go." Meena shared several stories she had heard of young women earning a lot of money abroad and she was excited with the prospects, but also nervous. Liton and she agreed that she would repay the stepsister for the arrangements of travelling abroad, once she started earning an income in Jordan. She explained, "I thought our struggles would finally end, and we could save, maybe buy land, and build a home in the village." Liton offered to take care of the children and with some apprehension but also hopeful, she left her third child, a nine-month-old baby, with her mother-in- law, and left for Jordan.

Working in Jordan

Meena's time as a maid in Jordan was short lived. With a small bag of her few possessions, and her passport, her hands trembling with fear, she recounted, that she was immediately sent off to a waiting room at the airport by a stern looking man. Much to her shock, she encountered many Bangladeshi women sitting in a room, of varying ages; some were crying. She became scared and unsure: "When I saw so many girls crying, I was thinking to myself what kind of a country have I come to? Why are the girls crying and why was there a foreigner woman yelling at them to be quiet? I had no one to talk to, but there was no turning back. I was here, miles away from my family, from home." Her employers came to pick her up from the airport, and they were not friendly. The car ride to her new employer's place was long and the silence in the car was deafening. A million thoughts whizzed past in her head, but she kept praying. It dawned on her that she was at the mercy of these strangers. Her passport was taken from her, and she was taken to "a tiny room with one mattress, sheets and pillow on it, next to the verandah." She began working the next day, each day late into the night, cleaning a two storied home – the living room, dining area, four bedrooms, four bathrooms and kitchen. She felt isolated and was given little food to eat. She was desperately lonely and didn't know who to turn to for help. Meena spent most of her time working late into the evenings and was confined to her room. She shared that at night, she would cry. She yearned for her family, her children, the neighbours and her home. The lady employer was cold and harsh and only yelled at her, if she didn't clean properly. A month passed by, and the employers sent her husband TK11,000 (approx. US$170 at the time) but Meena was already regretting her decision to come to Jordan. The stories she heard didn't match the reality.

Unable to accept her situation, Meena took a risk and decided to run away. She snuck out of the house early one morning, leaving her few belongings behind. Not knowing where to go and not being able to speak the language, she was eventually found by locals and brought to a deportation centre for workers. The police dropped her back to her employer, who had filed a case. Terrified and hysterical, she begged to be sent home. She was beaten, locked up in a dark room, and given only bread and water for seven days by her enraged employers. Soon after, she was put on a plane and was sent back to Dhaka. She shared that the events leading up to her departure were hazy but she was petrified for her life.

Many poor men and women in Bangladesh go abroad, aspiring for better wages. Reports document that women's migration for labour overseas started in 1980, and since 2009, migration has been an increasing trend, against the backdrop of unemployment and poverty (Sultana & Fatima, 2017). While not everyone has a terrible experience, a survey of 101 returning female migrants, mainly domestic workers, indicates that restricted mobility, withholding of wages, beatings and sexual abuse were common (Naziha, 2013). Bangladesh government policies are either non-existent or do not recognise the gendered nature of migration and its adverse impacts on poor female workers. There appears to be gap in these middle eastern countries where laws and policies tend to discriminate against poor labourers. Ishrat Shamim argues that migration doesn't always equate with empowerment, and women often choose to migrate because of poverty (Shamim, 2006). These women are more exposed to forced labour and sexual exploitation than men and more likely to accept precarious working conditions and poorly paid work.

Finding a Job

Meena's return surprised her family as they had assumed she had been killed, as they had not heard from her for a few weeks. A day of emotional celebrations followed her return as she was greeted by her mother, husband, children, and her neighbours. A meal was cooked for her, and she shared how she cried tears of joy, especially when she was reunited with her baby, who had lost weight. She rested for a few days and then, pragmatic and knowing that her family continued to depend on her, she forced to get herself out bed and began to earnestly search for work. She asked her mother to reach out to her wide network of acquaintances and relationships. "I got my first cleaning job after my return, because of my mother, as she knows many women in her area. She kept asking for a job for me ... one of the *khalas* ('aunt', not related) told my mother about this work option." Meena also asked her neighbours to look out for her: "Many work as maids in apartment complexes, and they often hear if any of the flat owners are looking for people to hire as part time cleaners or cooks." Referral networks and recommendations from these friends and acquaintances were key, as they could vouchsafe to the potential employer the trustworthiness and reliability of the person hired. Eventually,

Meena found part time work in several homes, and earning cash from multiple jobs, she was able to cover rent and basic food costs. Relieved she fell back into her routine, the memory of Jordan remaining a bitter experience for her.

Meena earned just enough to manage each month. When she struggled, she relied on her mother for food contributions. She said, "She lives 15 minutes away from me, so if I am very hungry and we had less to eat at home, she would give me rice or potatoes … sometimes meat, and she also lent me money time to time to pay the landlord, who doesn't want to understand my situation." Life was tough, but manageable.

With Covid and the lockdown in 2020, Meena was let go by her employers abruptly, and Meena was scared. Since her return she had fallen into a predictable routine. The country and Dhaka was shut down and there were police and army on the streets enforcing the nationwide lockdown, with everything shut. Her primary fear was her capacity to feed her children, as she had no job. Liton didn't work so there was little savings available. There wasn't any dry good – rice or lentils stored in the house and the rations given by the government were insufficient. She had only received relief food once, and during this period of a lockdown of two months she counted on her mother for rice, potatoes and small amounts of cash. She and her family basically ate only rice and potatoes, with her children crying and screaming constantly for more food. She felt guilty as her children didn't understand why they couldn't occasionally eat eggs, beef, or fish. She was frustrated because Liton seemed unbothered and continued to spend either all day at the tea shop or slept often, barely speaking with her, even when she taunted him for not finding cash to support her and the children. By the end of April, desperate to earn cash, she defied the lockdown and walked miles daily on foot to Gulshan, a relatively wealthy suburb, to look for work, convincing police to take pity on her when she was caught on the streets. She would carry her baby in her arms and cover her hair and face with a scarf, pleading with them to let her go, explaining she would starve if they sent her back to her slum. The police pitying her, let her go.

She persisted and walked in the searing heat, door to door, visiting her old employer's large two storied spacious home, other houses, and apartment complexes, asking security guards for news of any jobs available. Residents in Gulshan were reluctant to hire anyone, fearing getting infected from slum residents. One security guard, Bari bhai, informed her, "They are not hiring any one during this situation (Covid-19), and they will not permit anyone inside the house from outside, even drivers of many houses have been asked to leave." Desperate for work, Meena gave guards, who she referred to as 'uncles,' her phone number in the hope someone would change their mind, telling them she was willing to work for even less than TK3,000 monthly (approximately US $35), just to earn some cash. She walked for hours on end, her feet blistered and eventually her sandals tore, as she looked anxiously for work. Her mother bought her a new pair, stating, "My poor daughter walks in the heat daily looking for work, so I managed to find a pair of cheap sandals for her. Is she going to go barefoot?" She didn't comment on Liton not working.

Taking Loans

Meena's debts were piling up, and in early May, with the lockdown continuing, she drew on her personal relationship with the local shopkeeper to buy food on credit. She pleaded with him: "I became emotional and explained to Chacha (unrelated, called uncle) the neighbourhood shop keeper, that I will get a job soon, so please let me take some items on credit. I need to feed by children." She asked her mother for some cash and bought some more rice and potatoes, and few vegetables. The cash was insufficient to cover all the costs, but because she knew the shopkeepers, she was given some of the items on credit.

Chacha was known to Meena and many of the tenants in the area and he did the same with long term tenants in the area. He kept a slip of paper and noted down items, but Meena became anxious, as the lockdown continued, and she still didn't have a job. She was tense that the support from the reliable and kind shopkeeper would eventually stop: "How long will he give me on credit? He also needs to eat and feed his family. I feel embarrassed to continue to ask him for credit." He continued to be supportive well into 2021, a year later. Although for Meena, it was important for her own dignity, social standing, and reputation in the area to repay him as soon as possible. Such social relationships were critical in times of crisis, as she continued to struggle to find stable work.

Although the lockdown had been removed end of May 2020, and the country was opening slowly, jobs as part-time maids were scarce, and this continued into the first half of 2021. Employers were initially reluctant to hire maids, as they were seen as 'germ carriers,' but over time, this fear eased. The few stable longer term job openings available were with employers wanting a live-in maid. Meena found some part time work, which was low paid. As Meena had three children, and her husband 'was sick a lot,' she could not agree to be a live in, full-time maid. Her jobs during this period ranged from being a cleaner for a few months, a maid for six months, then as a cook, with jobs erratic, with periods of unemployment.

Meena was filled with remorse as she knew that her mother shared whatever she could, despite her own financial constraints. She began to reach out to other personal and social networks to get cash to partly cover rent and food costs, asking for time from the landlord. Initially she borrowed TK4,000 (approximately US$47 in 2020) from a woman known to lend money, but she had to pay interest of TK500 (approximately US$6), upon repayment. After several months the relationship turned bitter, as the woman began abusing Meena and demanded her money back. Meena with a downcast expression, said, "Despite knowing how difficult it was for me with Liton being sick, she screamed and created a scene." It was humiliating and uncomfortable as nosy neighbours from other homes, gathered nearby and could hear the scathing comments being heaped on Meena. She shared, "I finally gave her some cash and asked for a few more weeks to repay the rest." She also borrowed another small sum from another money lender, "An 'uncle' who ran a local teashop, who knew her well and trusted her to repay him, with a small interest." Meena was tense as she knew she needed to repay each person, as well as ensure rent and food costs were covered. At some point, she phoned an old employer, who she referred to as *nani* (grandmother), who lent her TK2,000 (approximately US$23.50). Borrowing money was seen as the last and worst option. According to Meena, it was always nerve-wracking: "They come and land up in your home and eat your head up with their insults. Who wants to live in anxiety and fear of being abused?" Meena knew that it was critical she repaid everyone, to maintain good relationships as well as ensure future loans and support, when there were emergencies.

Liton could not borrow from anyone, as he barely worked and residents in the area knew this; he was seen as unreliable and incapable of repaying. Weighing up the risks and the ability of individuals even if they were long-term tenants was important for any money lender for his or her business to thrive. This was also important for neighbours and friends, who were not interested in constantly following up repayments, who may default, leave. They wanted reliable candidates. The burden of taking loans fell entirely on Meena. She was concerned about borrowing too much cash, as she knew that the interest was piling up. She also sold her phone for a couple of thousand taka, when she was desperate, which she had purchased for double that amount pre-Covid, but sold it at a loss. She didn't have a choice. Losing her phone was a huge gamble for her, because the phone allowed her to remain connected to the job market and to call her various contacts and potential employers.

Throughout 2020, she turned to her neighbouring tenants, who she knew well. The tenants in her compound were familiar to each other, and comfortable asking each other for small amounts of cash, food items, if a family was struggling. Meena mentioned, "I borrowed TK300 (approximately US$3.50) from an aunt (unrelated, tenant) and she did not charge any interest. There was also no pressure to pay the money back immediately. Suppose if you don't have rice in your house, then we share with each other … but now everyone is suffering from scarcity." However, a year and half into the pandemic, by mid-2021, even tenants were reluctant to loan money to each other, as everyone was struggling with cash flow and rising debts. While the country had opened, the economic losses, meant jobs were harder to find, with reduced work hours and salaries. Meena was pragmatic and was sympathetic to the plight of her neighbouring tenants when they couldn't lend any support. She said, "I wanted to borrow some cash from aunt (unrelated tenant) again, but she was unable to lend me any more money. She is also struggling. She has given me food in the past. These are difficult times for everyone." Meena shared that although she could get an advance on her salary, which was TK4,000 (approximately US$47), she couldn't ask the current employer for a loan, as she had given her a phone to use to stay connected and she received many benefits from this female employer. Meena explained how the job as a maid in this home, allowed her to access a clean toilet, shower daily, and she received hair oil, soap monthly and she was also given leftover food often, which she took home for her children and husband. She also ate a huge lunch of rice, fish, and other items. She shared how she no longer suffered from hunger pangs, when she was unemployed, and because of the food rationing she had to do during the lockdown.

Only when she was at breaking point, did Meena turn to her mother, who also worked as a maid in two households. Her mother also had a compassionate employer who occasionally gave her food to take home. Meena's mother, Mita shared: "The madam I work with gave me 2kgs of rice and a few months later, she again gave me 5kgs of rice, lentils, potatoes, oil, salt. She helped me twice and gave me cash as well. I also went to the house where I used to work a long time ago, and that madam gave me some cash. I gave that money and some of the food to Meena for her household."

Crisis after Crisis

The situation changed for the worse in October 2021, when Meena's mother, Mita, was badly injured while walking to her employer's home. She walked her usual route, when she was hit by a motorcyclist, who went up the sidewalk and didn't see her. She fell to the ground, badly hurt. Left with a slight limp, by December 2021, she found it difficult to work as maid as she suffered from aches and could not bend to lift, cook or clean. She could not stand for long hours. She had to leave her job as a maid. Her employer gave her sum of cash and hired a new maid. Frantic, she turned to begging to earn cash: "I go to another area, walking slowly with my hurt leg and sit in a corner with a bowl. In this area, no one knows me. I cover my hair and partially my face." She was ashamed but had little choice. Mita earned 400 or sometimes up to 600TK or more in a week (approximately US$5 to 7) by begging, but her son and Meena were embarrassed. At the same time, Meena sympathised with her mother's predicament, and realised that she could no longer ask her mother for cash. A series of further mishaps in late 2021 and early 2022 greatly affected Meena's stability. Her relationship with the landlord and his wife deteriorated because of delayed rental payments, and the landlord's wife was openly gossiping with other tenants about this. Meena confronted the landlord's wife for slandering her, and a bitter argument ensued. A few days later, the landlord's wife accused Meena's youngest son of stealing food items from the shared communal kitchen. She was extremely abusive, calling them "dirty thieves who did not pay their rent" before a crowd of residents. The neighbouring tenants stood by quietly. Outraged, Meena and Liton felt they could no longer live in this compound. Meena paid her the rent a few days later, by selling her most prized and only set of gold earrings and borrowing money from a moneylender, with interest.

A week later, Meena, Liton and the children hurriedly vacated the room. The environment was tense and tenants sympathised but avoided her, as they didn't want to face the wrath of the landlady. Meena's situation as a tenant was common; delays in payments could lead to bitter fights and evictions. Meena and Liton wanted to stay in Baniganj (a slum) because they were familiar with the community and had some trusted relationships with the drug shop sellers, shop keepers and others in this area. Liton went to see his mother, who lived around the corner from them, and she convinced her landlady to rent a room to them. However, Meena and her mother-in-law were not close. Meena was upset and frustrated with Liton, because of his failure to support her when his mother abused or criticised her. But she confessed, that she also had *maya* (affection) for him and worried about his health. Meena was in limbo, with few alternatives available. They moved closer to his mother's compound.

Near midnight, on December 2021, Meena was mugged. She was returning after cooking for a party of ten guests at her employer's home. She was taking a rickshaw home and holding her bag, with some of her salary and the phone given to her by her employer. The bag was snatched, and she almost fell off the rickshaw. When she was informed the next day, her employer accused Meena of lying and selling the phone and fired her. Meena left the house in distress and was not paid the remainder of her salary. A few days later, extremely depressed with the persistent 'bad luck' or 'bad fate' as she referred to her life; she forced herself to get out of bed, and began the painstaking search for jobs again, relying on networks of her mother's and her own, and asking the guards of houses in Gulshan to assist her in finding a job.

Shuli and Fatema: Street Hawkers in Gulshan Avenue 1

Both Shuli, 20, and Fatema, 19, are street hawkers and have been selling wares on the streets for around ten years. They knew Meena well, as she had also been a hawker as a child, and they had sold various toys, pens, notebooks, flowers together on the streets of Gulshan Avenue, 1. Shuli and Fatema barely saw Meena now that she worked as a maid, but they saw each other daily, as they spent time on the streets selling towels. Both were extremely familiar and comfortable working on the streets, as they had grown up in this area. They were proud that they knew the hawkers, beggars and the local shopkeepers, pharmacists, guards, security personnel, and other workers. They referred to them as 'grandparents, uncles and aunts, brothers and sisters,' who were protective of them and were 'family.' For Shuli and Fatema, Gulshan Avenue 1 was their 'home away from home.'

Shuli and Fatema struggled during lockdown, post-lockdown and well into 2022. Shuli, Shumon, 26, with their baby daughter, Arifa, relocated five times between the second half of 2020 and early 2022, moving from slum to slum. This was for multiple reasons: moving closer to Shumon's work site to take advantage of sudden short term job opportunities; their ability to afford the rent; and their relationship with certain landlords. They left two places soon after moving in, finding one place infested with bed bugs and cockroaches and another place was without water, sometimes for days. Shuli had a difficult and at times hostile relationship with her mother, and Shumon's mother lived in the village. They had few close relationships in the slums they lived in, and instead relied on ties with friends and other non-kin individuals they knew from work, from whom they sought information on job opportunities, loans, and handouts. Fatema and her husband Riaz, 28, in contrast, had the support of their immediate families and in-laws and lived close to them.

Networks of Support: Stable and Temporary

In May 2020, during lockdown, there were barely any cars on the streets. Shuli took a desperate decision. She used to make a decent amount of money selling towels to richer clients on the busy roads of Gulshan 1. Her husband had a stable income working in the Gulshan markets pre-Covid-19. But towel sales had reduced since Covid, and she began to beg to earn TK60 to 100TK every day (approximately US$0.70 cents to 1.17). She seemed deeply ashamed when talking about it. She fidgeted as we spoke and refused to look at me. She shared how proud she had been of her 'towel business,' how she was quick at selling and had many clients. She shared that begging was humiliating, but Shumon was not always able to find work either, having lost his job since Covid lockdown, and they were desperate for cash to buy food. They had reduced their meals eating only two meals a day, sometimes surviving on lentils, rice, and potatoes, with no fish, meat, and other vegetables. They were both living in fear of the wrath of the landlord, who expected rent to be paid, and was not sympathetic. They didn't know him well, as they had not lived in any area long enough to build strong ties with the locals in that slum.

Shuli met many people when begging outside Tamanna Pharmacy, a well-known small drug shop whose owner she knew well. Being allowed to beg outside his shop was a huge advantage, enabling Shuli to earn a limited amount of cash: "He has seen me sell toys since I was a child … he knows my mother and some of the other street hawkers, so he allows me to sit here with Arifa and beg. Anyone else would have removed me!" Most beggars are shooed away by local guards, their presence seen as detrimental to the image of the shop or a restaurant. For Shuli, another concern was that it was also getting competitive, as other 'newer beggars' began to work the streets to earn an income, especially post-lockdown from June 2020.

Compassion for beggars varied, depending on age, sex, and physical appearance. According to Shuli, children earned the most, then people with disabilities, elderly, and mothers with little babies. She explained that begging was not an option for Shumon, as he was an abled bodied male. She said that if he were to beg he would face derogatory comments: "Why can't you get a proper job? Why are you begging?" She explained, "I have a little child on my lap, that's why people give me money as they see me, a young woman with a child. But people do not give money to young men." She continued, almost defensively, lest I judge her: "We must eat and survive; I do not beg for pleasure." Her usual schedule was mid-morning until evening, in May and post lockdown, as cars were infrequent on the streets and customers were reluctant to purchase goods. Moreover, the money generated from begging was higher than selling towels. Shuki was earning up to TK200 per day (approximately US$2.35). Carrying her baby girl was difficult, as she couldn't rush over to cars as quickly as the other sellers. She looked after her baby girl, carrying cooked semolina in a little plastic container. She was often in a jovial mood, and all of the other younger and older street sellers, were found sitting together, laughing, making jokes, whispering about how much they earned. They hid their earnings inside their blouses or pockets were sewn into the shalwar (pyjamas)to reduce the chances of being robbed when heading home later in the evening.

For almost two years prior to lockdown, Shumon had a stable job in the Gulshan markets as a junior assistant to a shop owner. With lockdown, the owner let him go. Post lockdown, from June 2020 onwards, Shumon began calling his former employee, beseeching him for a job. After several missed calls and a short conversation, he landed up at his old shop, but was gently informed by his boss, that as sales were down, there was no work. Since then, Shumon has taken on any jobs available. His opportunities for work were erratic but he continued to try, even selling towels for a few weeks in Gulshan 1, with Shuli. He was slow and admitted he wasn't as skilful as Fatema or his wife as he was not used this trade. A few times he rode a rickshaw, which he rented from a local owner in the slum, but it was difficult to continue, with police occupying certain roads and the risk of arrest because rickshaws were prohibited from travelling on three major expressways.

Nearly 1.5 million licensed rickshaw pullers and one million unlicensed rickshaws operating in Dhaka city (Shupto, 2019). Rickshaw pullers and their family members are dependent on this occupation, and prohibition of use of certain roads severely impacted their earnings. Shumon also looked for temporary labouring in construction, carrying heavy bags of cement from one site to another. He complained of backaches and chest pains due to acidity and the hard labour, but he persisted working while regularly calling his friends to ask about alternate work opportunities. Shuli shared, "My husband started working before Qurbani Eid (2021), and he got this job in the construction site, through his networks. Shumon called all his friends, former co-workers, and acquaintances for any leads." Shuli lamented that as a woman, jobs and mobility were limited to her, while Shumon "could go anywhere to look for work." For a period of two months, around December 2021, almost one and half years after lockdown, with Shuli, selling towels occasionally, but mainly begging, and with Shumon's cash earning contributions, their combined earnings were TK12,000 (approximately US $138). Elated to have so much cash after a long time, they went shopping for clothes for the baby and themselves. Shuli, was pleased and seemed more relaxed, shared, "we haven't bought anything in so long … my few outfits are torn and Shumon also needs some pants for when he goes to work. We have earned well this month."

Loans

Most months their income was insufficient and the momentary earnings which they had celebrated was not repeated. Both relied on their personal and social relationships to ask for loans, but Shumon was averse to borrowing from money lenders. Neither wanted to accrue interest. Shuli shared, "Many hawkers tell me to borrow money with interest from people. But I am not willing to take because if these people give you 1000TK (approximately US $11.60), they want TK200 (approximately US$2.36) as interest, and then I can't pay. It will be embarrassing...why should I pay so much interest?" Her concern was mounting debts and interest. They had very a small network of individuals to whom they could turn to, and were unsure if loans would be given, but they kept trying. Shuli borrowed small amounts of cash from TK1,000 to 2,000 (approximately US$11.60 to 23.60) from people she knew and trusted her. She relied on the pharmacy owner. In the early days of the lockdown, she also earned some quick cash by renting her phone for a week for a small amount of cash and as Shumon did not like her to borrow money, so she didn't inform him.

As money became increasingly tight, in 2021, Shumon ended up borrowing money from friends and a co-worker to manage their household. Shuli was annoyed with the local shopkeeper in the slum in which they were living, because he would not let them buy food on credit. She said, "No one gives us goods without cash. We had to pay cash up front for our food purchases as this shop keeper will give us anything on credit. The shopkeeper in this area does not know us properly and if they don't know you, they won't give you money." She snorted. "Who has the time to get to know all these people? We don't stay at home all day ... we go out in the morning and enter the house at night, after working all day." Unlike Meena and Fatema, Shuli was not a long-term resident in the slum she was living in. Her networks were primarily with individuals she knew from Gulshan 1, and instead she turned to a few shopkeepers and customers who used to regularly buy towels from her. On February 2021, she asked for help from another *mama* (unrelated, 'uncle') for a loan of 1,000TK (approximately US$11.60). He operated a small digital cash transfer shop via phones in Gulshan 1. She knew him well and often chatted to him, in between selling towels and begging. He did not have the money; his business too was not faring well. As Shuli noted with empathy, "everyone's income is suffering." Worried how she would feed her baby, help came from an unexpected source when a rich man came into the pharmacy and saw her in the corner begging, with her baby on her hips. She caught his glance and pleaded for money to buy milk for her baby. He bought her tin of milk powder for TK600 (US$7), which was the equivalent of a few days of earnings for Shuli. In addition, during the two Eid festivities in 2021, an old customer, who used to buy towels from both her and Fatema, gave them each clothes and extra cash of TK2000 (approximately US$23.60).

In mid-2021, Shuli began to pressure her husband to take more loans as towel sales were low and begging was not bringing in sufficient income. She had had a few fights with Fatema, who she accused to trying to steal her customers. Fatema accused Shuli of being unreasonable and trying to steal her customers, after Fatema was the first one to show up at the car window. Shuli later blamed her 'hotheadedness' for the tension with Fatema, for whom she cared for deeply. She admitted that she was scared as Shumon had not found steady work. When their situation worsened, he reluctantly reached out again to his personal contacts. His friends couldn't help. Shumon decided to ask his temporary employer, a contractor at the construction site. He shared, "I borrowed 1000TK (approximately US$11.60) from him. I met him as I was working for some time as a labourer in one site. I didn't know him for long, but I pleaded that I need to pay the landlord rent money and needed a loan." Shumon assured him he would repay him by the end of the month and was relieved when the man agreed to lend him the cash. Shumon expressed feelings of inadequacy and shame. Left with no choice, he asked two of his former co-workers from the markets for another sum of cash – TK2,000 (approximately US$23.60). He was relieved they did not insist on immediate repayment and did not humiliate him. Shumon, slightly apologetic shared, "I tell Shuli to eat less … whatever we earn, we need to manage. Honestly, I feel very bad saying this to her. I am a man, and I should be taking care of my wife and child! But this past year, I have been earning a lot less." He despised asking for a loan; he felt belittled and was also paranoid about the fights and breakdown of relationships he had seen amongst family and friends when money was not repaid.

In the second half of 2021, Shuli became increasingly worried for her baby girl, who she felt was under nourished. She had been feeding Arifa semolina as a substitute for milk, for many months, but she wanted to buy milk powder. Arifa was losing weight. She reached out to 'grandfather' – the owner of the pharmacy and said, "I don't have TK600 (approximately US$7) to pay for the big tin of milk powder. I called grandfather and explained that Arifa was losing weight. He gave me a large packet of milk the next day when I went to Gulshan 1. But that packet had holes in it from a mouse. How can I feed that milk to my baby?" Shuli instead bought ten small sachets of milk powder for TK10 each, spending TK100 (US$1.18) and kept a lookout for the rich man who had helped her earlier and bought milk powder for her baby. She was also worried about the large sum of cash – TK7,000 (approximately US$82.74) they owed the landlord for house rent. They had relocated and preferred this place, but the rent was higher, but it was closer to Gulshan and Shuli no longer had to take a bus daily to work which was costly. This location was a less than ten-minute walk from Gulshan 1. The landlord's wife had begun asking them almost daily for rent money: "If she sees me, she asks me and if she sees Shumon, she asks him." Shuli shared how her husband and her dreaded going back to their home and facing the landlady, who constantly observed them and harangued them for repayments every few days.

With despair in her voice, she said, "Times are hard, and we have not been cooking. My husband buys some snacks in the construction site, and it is not a stable income. I buy bread roll, and banana and eat that for lunch on the streets." Shuli refused to sell her television, her prized possession, despite their dire situation. She explained that this was the only relief she and Shumon had, watching movies after a long and tiring day of hard work. Shuli was also frightened that the landlord and his wife would find out that Shuli begged on the streets. The fear of being stigmatised by others in this slum, created internal stress. It was important, for Shuli and Shumon to maintain some semblance of stability to maintain their 'face and status.'

Strained Relationships

Shuli had a difficult and tense relationship with her mother, Jorina, 48, who she resented for making her work on the streets at a very young age. Shuli's mother also spent time on the streets of Gulshan 1, monitoring Shuli's two children who also work on the streets. Shuli's daughter Shuborna, 12, sells towels and stationery, and her son, Jihad, 9, begs. When Shuli married Shumon many years ago, her children continued to live with Jorina, and Jorina received all the income they earned. Shuli's children each earn around TK400 to 600 daily (approximately US$5 to 7). Jorina had lost her job working as a cook in a hostel several years earlier. Shuli's children sometimes gave Shuli TK100 (US$1.18), but did not inform their grandmother, Jorina, as she would be furious. Shuli claimed she wanted them to go to school, an opportunity she was never given. According to Jorina, Shuli was greedy and angry because her children's income was not being shared with her. She said, "I brought these grandchildren up in my home. She abandoned them as soon as she got married to Shumon and proceeded to have another child." Between 2020 and 2021, there were several verbal and physical fights, accusations and counter accusations, with Shuli alleging her mother hit her grandchildren if they didn't earn enough daily and Jorina claiming that Shuli slapped her children, if they did not share some cash with her from their daily earnings.

Sometimes, Shuli asked her mother to help her look after Arifa while she was working on the streets, but Jorina demanded payment for keeping an eye on her youngest granddaughter. Despite their difficult relationship, she claimed that she did care for her mother: "I often quarrel with my mother as she is a greedy woman. She has also turned my children against me and sometimes they talk badly about me. But we meet daily in Gulshan 1, and we sit and chat on the side road. In fact, if it is your own mother, no matter how badly she behaves, she is your mother."

In the second half of 2021, Shuli got into another physical altercation with her mother on the streets. Shuli alleged it was because she wanted her daughter and son to stay with her for a few days and her mother wouldn't allow it: "My mother treats me very badly. My eldest daughter wanted to come to visit my place and stay with me for 10 days. But my mother did not agree. We began to argue, and I told her, "Look even if she stays with me, I will give you the money she earns every day.' Then my mother began to yell at me and started calling me names, 'whore, sleeping with my legs open with any man, abandoned my children for sex...' I told her she was very greedy and bad person who used her own grandkids and forced them to beg so she can eat rice and she can feed her useless son."

Shuli's brother, Akash, 24, who she didn't talk to, was a drug addict and lived off the income of Shuli's children. His wife was pregnant and didn't work. According to Shuli, he terrorised the entire family for food and cash. This altercation led Jorina to punch Shuli, who in turn slapped and pushed her, and her mother fell on the sidewalk. They both continued to slap and punch each other. As Shuli recalled, "Luckily the roads were empty, or we could have been hit by a speeding car." Fatema intervened and separated Jorina and her grandchildren from Shuli. Fatema was upset by what she had witnessed: "What kind of life is this for Jihad and Shuborna? I think aunt (Jorina) as a mother, should be kinder to Shuli ... but she favours her son and really made Shuli work hard on the streets as a child." Fatema compared how her own mother and brother support her; but Shuli received little love and affection from her own mother.

Fatema: Pregnancy, Income Sources and Strong Ties

It was late September 2019, six months before Covid and the lockdown. Fatema, 19, was resting at home in Baniganj slum, having just given birth to a baby girl. There was much excitement in their home, because of the baby and because her husband Riaz, 28, had recently landed a stable job in a noodle company, after long periods of unemployment and working odd jobs, with low pay. Prior to him getting this job, Fatema had continued working on the streets, selling towels, well into the eighth month of her pregnancy. "I worked ...walking around in this condition, doing business ... so my physical condition got worse. I needed rest, but I couldn't take rest. Every day in Gulshan, as I walked between cars, looking for customers I was running after customers for hours, in the heat. That's why the baby came earlier, it was all the pressure of working on the streets all day. But I didn't have a choice."

Riaz got this work opportunity in late 2019, because of an 'elder brother' (unrelated), who knew his mother well and recommended him. The new job was stable. The salary was TK7,000 takas (approximately US$83), which covered rent, and basic food items: rice and lentils. There was much festivity in the home when he was hired, and sweets were distributed in the local area, with neighbours and fellow tenants. A delicious meal was cooked and the religious leader from the local mosque was fed. His blessings were sought for the impending birth, and Riaz's new job. It was his family and close network of her parents, in laws and 'uncles, brothers' in the locality, which made it possible for him to get this job. Stable jobs in a company with regular pay-checks were rare for individuals like Riaz. Prior to this, Riaz had found odd part time or erratic work opportunities by staying connected by phone to other labourers at construction sites; they called each other up to pass on information of possible work opportunities.

Managing Landlady and Shopkeeper: Work, Support from Family and Others

With lockdown on March 26, 2020, Riaz lost his 'dream' job. Fatema was rudely jolted into finding ways to earn cash to keep the household running. Her aspirations of being a stay-at-home mother, looking after the household, were shattered. When Riaz began working in the noodle company, he had encouraged her to give up selling on the streets and she was at home, breast-feeding and resting post-delivery. She was enjoying cooking, cleaning, and looking after her baby. Her days were also spent chatting with tenants, watching television, and resting. This was welcomed by Fatema who had lived her whole life selling on the streets. However, six months later, everything changed with Covid-19. In May 2020, during the lockdown, desperate for cash, her husband began to work, surreptitiously, riding a three-wheeler scooter and a rickshaw, risking fines and harassment from the police who were on the streets to enforce the lockdown. Since May and post-lockdown, Fatema went back to selling towels on the streets when her mother's work was finished at around 12 noon or 1pm. "Then I leave my baby with my mother," Fatema explained. "Or sometimes my mother comes to Gulshan and takes care of my child, after she has finished her office job … my mother sits with the baby so then I can sell towels quickly when the cars come. Sometimes we get 20 minutes or less to go from car to car to sell.'

Fatema's father was at home, and I asked her why she didn't leave the young baby with him. She sighed and explained that he smoked a lot of marijuana and "Doesn't do anything." Fatema's mother was the one who kept the family together. Fatema had dropped out from school early on, to sell on the streets to support the household. Her parents' landlord usually came to their rescue when other residents made comments about her father; her parents had been living in the area for 20 years and were long time tenants.

During the initial period of the lockdown, Fatema was supported by her brother and mother, who were very protective of her, and she could rely on them at any time. During a particularly bad period, for two weeks daily, she and her family ate in her parents' home as they couldn't afford to buy food, and they also lent her cash. Her in-laws also sent food and cash. She said, "I feel so blessed. Our family is very close." Fatema had stopped taking credit from the local shopkeeper, once she discovered that he was cheating her and others. She said, "I don't buy on credit anymore as I don't trust the two shops nearby." She was also that the food bill was adding up and that the amount owed had been inflated by the shopkeepers. Fatema began to reduce their food intake and eat at her parents, rather than owe any money at the shop.

Despite sales being low for most of 2020, Fatema persisted in selling towels. In November and December 2020, sales were very low, but she was still able to earn something each day. She didn't want to beg like Shuli and although she made no comments, it was clear she didn't approve. She was frustrated that the government still banned rickshaws and (unfit) three-wheeler scooters from using certain roads, as this created enormous difficulties for her husband. Almost all CNG-run three-wheeler scooters in Dhaka have been scrapped and replaced with new ones. However, some 500 of them had not been replaced, and many were still carrying passengers and driving on main roads, desperate for customers, and risking fines and arrests (Beaubien, 2016).

Riaz found temporary work on a construction site, but Fatema and he calculated that the costs of the bus fare to come and go to the distant site meant he was left with barely any daily earnings. He explored other possibilities. He couldn't ride the scooter on main roads, as it was not allowed by government policy, which meant finding fewer customers and less income earned. He tried to ride a rickshaw but there was little profit in it as most people preferred to walk or paid very little. She explained that one could not earn much from riding a rickshaw. Riaz also shared that this work was very hard on his back, legs and extremely stressful, as customers were abusive, and in late 2021, he was underpaid for a long rickshaw ride an hour away. He shared, "When I objected, the customer began to call me names and threatened to beat me up … I told him, I am a poor man, why can't you pay me what is my due?" According to Riaz, the passenger threatened to call the police, making Riaz nervous, and he left in despair. Riaz claimed he didn't mind working but most of the jobs available were labour intensive and low paid. Faruk didn't agree and shared that although his brother-in-law, Riaz was a 'good man,' he needed to be pushed to work sometimes, and was concerned that he spent too much time with the local boys, who he saw as a bad influence.

As a long-term resident in this compound and slum, Fatema had good relationships with other tenants and neighbours and they supported each other. Like Meena, Fatema and her neighbours helped each other with rice, oil, onions for cooking; they filled up each other's water buckets if one of them was outside working when the water came in the taps for a few hours each day; and lent small amounts of money, when one was in a crisis. Fatema and other tenants decided to approach their landlady collectively, asking her for more time to pay rent. She agreed because as Fatema shared, "She is worried, if we all leave then she won't have any tenants left and then where will she get her income from?" To avoid racking up further debts, news reported that thousands of residents had left the slums and returned to the villages to avoid accruing rent debt.

Meena, Shuli, and Fatema, in contrast to the young women who were residents in Phulbari in 2002, were less sheltered; all worked outside the home and actively moved around the city to earn an income. Their lives are enmeshed in networks that included many others, not only family and neighbours and other residents inside the slum, but others in their area, in the workspace and the city. Their networks proved critical for jobs but also for survival; these networks extended to include employers, well-off individuals, shop owners and friends, who occasionally contributed resources. Every opportunity for the three young women and their families was something to grab as life was so unpredictable, be it getting a job, convincing an employer to hire them, negotiating with landlords, getting food on credit from shopkeepers, taking loans, relocating to save money on transport fares, but they actively strategised to manage. The narratives also illustrate the continual ever-present crisis: from threats of eviction from the landlord, wage loss, loans and debts and food insecurity and at times difficult family relationships. For the young women and their spouses, the smallest of networks mattered; in fact, all networks and relationships were critical. These personal and social relationships were the tight threads holding individuals and families from having a complete breakdown, as they dealt with one relentless struggle after another. All of them kept stumbling along, but their experiences reveal how little power or choice, they have at all levels of everyday life (Das & Randeria, 2015).

Note

1 Scholars such as Bourdieu, Coleman, and Putnam emphasised social capital as a collective asset – Bourdieu's (1986) contribution was on "the size and strength of networks," while Coleman (1990) considered social capital as a resource that can be used by individuals, which can be changed into other capital, including human capital, and Putnam (2000), was interested in social organizations, and looked at "norms, trust, and networks" (see also Mpanje et al., 2018).

References

Ahamad, R. (2021). Slum dwellers pay more rent per sq ft than posh areas. *The Business Post*.

Beaubien, J. (2016). Child laborers in Bangladesh are working 64 hours a week. www.npr.org/sections/goatsandsoda/2016/12/07/504681046/study-child-laborers-in-bangladesh-are-working-64-hours-a-week

Bourdieu, P. (1986). Forms of capital. In *Handbook of Theory for the Sociology of Education*Greenwood Press.

Coleman, J. S. (1994). *Foundations of Social Theory*. Harvard University Press.

Das, V., & Randeria, S. (2015). Politics of the urban poor: aesthetics, ethics, volatility, precarity: an introduction to supplement 11. *Current Anthropology*, 56(S11), S3–S14.

Mpanje, D., Gibbons, P., & McDermott, R. (2018). Social capital in vulnerable urban settings: An analytical framework. *Journal of International Humanitarian Action*, 3(1), 1–14.

Naziha, S. (2013, June 25). Female Bangladeshi migrant workers face abuse: IOM study. *News Global*. www.iom.int/news/female-bangladeshi-migrant-workers-face-abuse-iom-study

Putnam, R. D. (2000). *Bowling Alone: The Collapse and Revival of American Community*. Simon and Schuster.

Shamim, I. (2006). The feminisation of migration: Gender, the state and migrant strategies in Bangladesh. In *Mobility, Labour Migration and Border Controls in Asia* (pp. 155–171). Springer.

Shupto, N. A. (2019, July 21). Rickshaw restrictions: Is it justified?. *New Age*. www. newagebd.net/article/79103/rickshaw-restrictions-is-it-justified.

Sultana, H., & Fatima, A. (2017). Factors influencing migration of female workers: a case of Bangladesh. *IZA Journal of Development and Migration*, 7, 1–17.

6 Police, Gang Fights and Insecurity in 2002

One Needs to Understand the Local Situation to Survive!

It was hot afternoon in late April, 2002 in Phulbari slum. I had come to visit Roshonara and I was greeted by huge smiles from both Razia and Roshonara. Razia asked, "You come and go so often from our slum and your husband doesn't mind you wandering around like this?" Roshonara laughed and quickly responded, almost protectively, "Why would he mind? He knows she visits many residents all the time. She walks around a lot in this slum and she is learning about women's health problems!" The tenant's daughter, Mamoni standing at the doorway of Roshonara's room, laughed and said, "We have so many problems … (she winked at Razia) don't we Razia? Don't your legs hurt from all this walking around?" Roshonara became very annoyed, and gave them both a warning glance, and grabbed me by the arm and brought me into her room. Razia suddenly got up from the bed, went outside, and I noticed she had brought my sandals inside the room and placed it in the corner. This morning, I had left it outside their compound door, as they were very dusty and dirty as I had stepped on a puddle of water.

I asked her why she suddenly brought my sandals inside, which were now dirtying their rather spotless, smooth mud floor. Razia was worried that my sandals would be stolen if left outside. The conversation quickly turned to the spate of thefts by heroin addicts and local boys, that were taking place in the area. A recent incident of a young woman who was violently mugged by local boys was shared. Razia explained, eyes widening, she shared rather breathlessly, "She was found unconscious, near the alleyway. The *wrong baj* (bad boys) pulled her gold-earrings from her ears and grabbed her purse." Gold is valuable and could be sold for quick cash. She went onto inform me that her entire salary for the month was forcibly taken from her. She was left traumatised, with tears and bleeding from her ears. She was a migrant and a relatively new tenant who had moved into the area. Razia shared that many young working women hid their phones under their *urnah* (long scarf to cover the chest), out of fear of being targeted. The muggings took place usually in the evenings, but with heroin addicts, the timing was unpredictable.

DOI: 10.4324/9781003467472-6

Heroin addicts could be spotted occasionally around Phulbari, but this problem of drug use was not openly discussed. I found out that an elderly woman, simply known as Rohel's mother, who had been abandoned by her husband a long time ago, was an addict. She managed her habit by renting out her one room home to young lovers in Phulbari and in the area. I had been speaking to her pregnant daughter-in-law, Rehana, who managed with handouts and support from neighbours and Sayeeda apa. It was alleged that she earned cash by begging, but further away from Phulbari. Her husband, Rohel was also an addict like his mother and didn't work. One afternoon, before entering the clinic, I observed two men standing near to Ratna's house. There was a huge commotion and I noticed that one of them was Rohel, skinny, looking very bedraggled and the other was a slightly older man, with a limp. I was informed that the older male with Rohel was also a heroin addict. Rohel was holding up a *lunghi* (sarong worn by men) and asking if anyone wanted to buy it for TK100 (approximately US$2 in 2002). Suddenly, an older male, shouted and questioned whether it was a stolen item. A furious argument broke out between him and a very agitated Rohel. A loose crowd of ten to fifteen men and women had gathered and were watching the scene unfold. Sayeeda, the health provider from the clinic and I also stood, slightly apart but also observing. I was informed that Rohel and his companion were known to steal and sell items – desperate to buy their next fix. During the heated discussions, feeling my gaze on him, the man with the limp looked over at me, and said to Rohel, "Why don't you get the money from her?" Rohel glanced my way and then shook his head. He had seen me talking to his wife several times and perhaps felt embarrassed. The other likely explanation could be that he knew I was an outsider and from a different socio-economic class.

Rumours about my visits to Phulbari had spread and some of the residents were unsure whether I could be truly trusted and wondered if I was a journalist or a representative from government and powerful. After a few heated words, Rohel and the older male scurried away.

Murders and revenge attack amongst rival gangs was not uncommon. Roshonara and Razia shared about a recent murder of a local boy from Phulbari slum, Awal, 19 years old, who was allegedly responsible for the murder of a rival gang member, Munir from Dho Block, neighbouring area. Four months later, Awal was tracked down living in another slum, with his pregnant wife and his aunt. He was shot dead in front of his pregnant wife, who was kicked in the stomach and had a miscarriage. Roshonara recalled, "He came back after four months to visit Shilpi, his wife, because she was pregnant." Razia nodded, while Mamoni continued, "All the boys left this area, but Awal is a *gadha* (donkey) and returned to Phulbari. He was missing his wife, but fearing for his life, he met her outside the slum. The rival gang tracked him down to the new location." Mamoni, sitting cross legged, near Roshonara, recounted the events in a casual manner, accustomed to hearing about murders and crime in their locality. The rival gang were informed that he had returned after hiding for several months. They had been waiting to exact their revenge. Mamoni shared, "It was late at night and one of the Dho block boys walked in with a gun and dragged him outside. The boys surrounded him, beat him, kicked him, and punched him. They kept violently beating him." His pregnant wife came running out to save him, but one of the boys kicked her in the stomach. She fell on the concrete pavement, doubled in pain. She lost the baby and Awal died. The police did not investigate. This was considered an internal matter amongst the gangs in this area. Internal laws and mechanisms prevailed.

Roshonara, Razia and Mamoni believed that Awal was foolish to have returned as revenge murders were common. It was reported that many young men in Phulbari and the neighbouring locality were members of clubs, gangs and involved in the drug trade. Razia's (ex)husband, Shahed, had a permanent limp because of being violently attacked in a gang fight several years ago. He continued to remain well connected and supported by local leaders in the area. Hence, Roshonara's continual worry that if Mintoo remained unemployed for too long, he too could be lured to join these groups. One could argue the attraction to belong in these clubs and gangs is that most young men remain unemployed, and or are tired of being in a cycle of laborious jobs, earning low wages, with little opportunity for upward mobility. Cash was scarce in general, and membership led to earning large amounts of money, respect, power, and status. As young men view their future as limited and powerless, suddenly they have access to support from powerful godfathers, *mastaans* and other local leaders, and even the police, who become like 'family' for some, even replacing the role and importance of their own family members.

It was well known that Mamun was the most powerful in Phubari and Dho Block area. Dho block was located right next to Phulbari and was notorious for the large numbers of gangs as well. In contrast to Phulbari which was a slum, it was a low-income housing with legal services, slightly better housing, but had similar challenges of congestion and poor living conditions. Although Mamun was currently in jail, he continued to control the trade with his powerful alliances in the area. Mamun previously drove a three-wheeled scooter but was now wealthy and extremely well connected. He had many of the police and others under his payroll and was the most powerful leader in the local area. For younger men, Mamun was a role model, someone to be emulated. Seeing their fathers, uncles and other poor householders stuck in a never-ending cycle of desperation, the desire to get out of this abyss of marginality is normal. Despite being aware of the risks of this path, it was still preferred to monotony of laborious jobs, mostly temporary and unstable. This was the fate of many slum residents, particularly those who worked in the informal sector. The opportunities in the drug trade in the informal economy is available and quickly taken up. The decisions by many of these young men make sense as structural, social, economic, and political barriers are stacked up against them. Belonging to such groups creates an alternate micro-world of solidarity and support who tend to otherwise remain on the fringes.

Social connections to powerful individuals come to use, as most individuals in a slum, do not have access to any formal power or voice. This was the case when more recently Razia, Roshonara's sister had not been paid her salary from the factory for two months. She was in despair and didn't know what to do about the situation. It was common and some of the young women working in the factories in Phulbari complained of facing similar challenges. Razia had also approached a garments union, but they were unable to assist her. Frustrated with her plight, Razia turned to her friend Moni for advice. Moni and her family were well connected in Phulbari. Moni's father was a less-powerful leader and her older brother, Kabir belonged to one of the leader's alliances, which meant he had a lot of 'muscle support,' knew Mamun, and he could rely on a strong network of male friends, during times of need. Moni immediately shared Razia's challenge with her own mother, who asked her son – Kabir (Moni's brother) to intervene and help Razia. Kabir had seen Razia grow up in Phulbari and as she was close to his sister Moni, he felt protective of her. He went with a few of his male friends and threatened the manager at the factory. A few days later Razia was paid her salary shortly afterwards. During this incident, Moni took great pains to explain to me that her brother was not involved in any gangs, and he was a 'decent brother,' who was simply well connected.

It was clear that there was territorial warfare over the drug trade, including control over basic services and many of the leaders ran their own competing gangs, with police and local politicians also involved. As I spent time in Phulbari, I found out over time about several police raids, that took place 'to lock up dealers and criminals', who residents claimed were 'innocent,' as well as reported incidences of several murders, burglaries, and injuries caused by gang-fights, a rape, as well as a death threat to one of the neighbours who lived near Sayeeda. Many of the residents, including Roshonara and her family, and Sayeeda, were loyal to some of young men in Phulbari and blamed the crime on the Dho block boys – the rival gang who were considered the main troublemakers in the area. Sayeeda's nephew was close to and allegedly belonged to one of the gangs, and Roshonara's family knew many of the young leaders quite well in Phulbari. They didn't trust the police and claimed many were in cahoots with the Dho Block rival group. Irrespective of which group they belonged to, for many young men, their position on the lower levels of this leadership can be unstable, particularly if they lose the grace of the 'godfathers' and other powerful individuals in the area and the city.

In 2019, a newspaper reported that according to Police and Rapid Action Battalion sources, there were at least 50–60 adolescent and youth gangs active in various areas of Dhaka city, living in low-income housing and in slums (Mamun, 2019).[1] A study documented organised crime in the city flourishes, via a hierarchy consisting of three different levels. The first are *mastaans* (local leaders of slums) and are the country's organised crime bosses who are affiliated with powerful politicians and the police. The second level are gangs (local boys who may be loyal to different leaders) who exist on the streets and live in the locality and in the slums; the third group are street children, the illicit workers of these groups, who are involved in some of the worst forms of labour. These active *mastaan* groups operate drug businesses, with each group having clearly defined roles, responsibilities, and a system to earn and divide profits. Groups of local youth are headed by a *mastaan* who is supported by an assistant of offsider, who controls the lower echelons of these gangs. The *mastaans* operate in every slum in Dhaka, and they control these settlements by extorting money, in return providing slum residents with access to basic services and other forms of support and at times, protection from the police and rival gangs (Jackman, 2019).[2]

Local *mastaans* (leaders) conduct their activities in collusion with locally based powerful actors, who provide them with immunity. They give them and law enforcement officials a share of the extortion money and provide 'political muscle,' threats, violence and intimidation, and secure votes during elections. They also negotiate areas of influence but remain vulnerable to changing politics and vested interests. Slum residents rarely have direct access to political leaders. Instead, resident slum leaders, tend to be conduits to power who serve as guardians for internal slum welfare, dispute resolution and law and order (Farid, 2013). It is a messy space of survival, money and power. In her ethnography of the *mastaan* culture, Sally Atkinson-Sheppard argued that these *mastaan* groups are mainly under the direct control of lower-level factions associated with the ruling political parties of the time (Atkinson-Sheppard, 2016). Due to endemic poverty, there is even a more vulnerable group of now younger street children who work for *mastaans* and local young men; and carry weapons, sell drugs, collect extortion money, commit political violence, even carrying out contract killings. Some become the foot soldiers and serve as collateral damage, expendable for those who are the most powerful. These young children, like most marginalised residents in these communities, are in reality labourers, doing what is available to survive.

Similar scenarios exist in Latin America, where in poor settlements in urban areas, a world of parallel powers and rule of law exists, due to the absence of formal governance mechanisms in these *favelas* (urban slums). The new warlords, much like local *mastaans* in Bangladesh, become the 'monopoly holders' of local illegal violence, and become the new enforcers of customary justice in the communities. Against the backdrop of exclusion and limited options, this has emerged as a parallel vehicle for social order, integration, and power (Koonings & Kruijt, 2007). As Das and Randeria argue, poverty and vulnerability are differently entwined in various social, economic and political contexts, which "opens possibilities, but also sets limits to the kind of politics that the urban poor might engage in" (Das and Randeria, 2015:S6).

Sayeeda informed me that next to Ratna's home was a teashop in which some of the illicit activities took place, but it was usually late in the evenings. Ratna and Abdul supplied the tea shop owner and the boys and drug-users free tea, and sometimes snacks, so they wouldn't bother them. Ratna also shared how they regularly paid off the 'local boys' so that they could continue to have access to water, gas and electricity in their compound She said, "We keep the leaders (*mastaans*) happy. Then the police will not harm us. My husband gets so terrified." She revealed some names of local leaders in Phulbari who they ingratiated themselves with, for protection. She pointed to the water tap in her compound, and said, "You see the water line ... we bought this. I had to give a few of the leaders some cash for the access, and I pay also for electricity, and I pay them monthly TK350 (a few US dollars a month) so the services don't stop. A person needs to understand the situation on the ground and how to stay protected ... you see, when one lives here, they understand the system."

While the lines were illegal for Ratna and many other residents, this was not seen as a problem, as the leaders had organised a system whereby they could at least have access to basic services. Local boys, who worked for the leaders, extorted a monthly amount from established residents/landlords and if one didn't pay, they could risk being threatened and or having their services shut off. Ratna mocked Abdul in front of me and called him a coward. She mentioned how she managed the local boys, while he stood quietly, ashamed by her taunts. It was critical for landlords to maintain good relationships with the powerful leaders in Phulbari and in the local area, and if possible, with the police as well. For tenants it was critical to have the support of landlords, or other influential persons, who would back them, in times of crisis or conflict. All the landlords in Phulbari slum, including Roshonara's mother paid a customary amount of money regularly to be able to access basic services. Some were given false promises over eventual 'legal' ownership of their homes or had to pay towards fighting cases to claim or hold on to the land, and against any attempts to evict residents from Phulbari. Despite these promises, many seemed to be aware of the temporal nature of their tenure.

Police Raids: We are Innocent, Catch the Real Criminals!

I arrived mid-morning in late April 2002 to find the place unusually quiet. Usually, it was bustling with activity and noise; this time, there were few residents. As I was walking towards the women's health clinic, I noticed that the door was shut, but it was only 11am. The path in front of the clinic had what appeared to be dried blood, red patches scattered on the muddy ground. I was startled to hear a shout and I heard footsteps of someone running behind me. I froze in fear, confused. A few men came running past me and the clinic and turned to the left and disappeared into another alleyway. It dawned on me that I might be in danger. I looked across at Monsura and Ratna's compound and the door was shut. All the homes had their doors shut. The shutters of the tea shops were also shut. Selim bhai, an older man who ran a tea shop near the clinic, asked me what I was doing. He was standing outside his shut tea shop. He immediately advised, "Leave and go home today ... or go inside the clinic, go inside and wait there." Sufia and Sayeeda, health providers at the clinic, hearing voices, immediately opened the clinic door. They saw me, pulled me inside and slammed the clinic door shut. They locked the door from inside. Sufia looked upset and embraced me protectively; Sayeeda grabbed my hand and said, "Today you don't have to work in the *basti* (slum)." We walked over to paramedic Mahmuda's consultation room, which was in another smaller room, next to the larger waiting area.

Sayeeda informed me that there had been a huge fight early in the morning between some local boys from Dho Block and leaders in Phulbari slum, over the drug trade. A prominent leader from Phulbari was viciously attacked and was taken to the hospital; two other leaders were on the run. The hostility had been escalating for some time over stealing of profits and control. We peeked through the window of the clinic to see two policemen arrive. They asked some questions from a few older women standing across the clinic, near an open field. They left within 15 minutes. According to Sufia and Sayeeda, this was "all for show" to justify they are doing their "jobs" to control the drug trade: they knew who the real criminals were and that "innocent men get locked up." There had been a police raid earlier in the year related to another drug related dispute, and a man came running to hide inside the clinic, but was dragged outside the clinic, beaten and taken away. No one knew what happened to that man. Sufia recounted, "These boys broke the table and yelled and screamed but they didn't do or say anything to me or Mahmuda (paramedic) and her daughter. Mahmuda was trembling and holding her daughter tightly as they sat quietly in the corner." Sufia recalled, "I sat next to them. I just closed my eyes and began to pray. We didn't say a word. We were petrified."

Policeman Kicks Ratna's Door Open: Don't Take me to Jail, Please!

Shortly afterwards, I visited Monsura and Ratna's compound to check on them. Ratna's place, located diagonally across the lane from the clinic. I knocked on the tin door. No response. I banged hard on the tin door and spoke softly, reassuring them it was me. After a few minutes, I heard someone unlocking the door. Ratna's face was puffy, and she appeared to have been crying. She grabbed me and held me close and hurriedly pulled me inside, locking the door from inside. She cried, "*Apa* (sister), there was a terrible incident last night. The police came into the slum and took 40 to 50 men away. Only seven men have been released. The rest are still there in jail. They initially grabbed Monsura's husband, but they let him go halfway."

She took me inside her room and sat down. She was distraught and was speaking quickly: "I don't want to live here anymore. I want to leave this horrible place." Her daughter, Shapna, sitting quietly on the bed, interrupted, and said, "They also wanted to take *baba* (father)." Ratna shared, "I begged them (police) and told them, he (Abdul) sells spectacles in a shop. He is not involved in selling any drugs. I begged and pleaded, and, in the end, they didn't take him." She continued, "wh"en they came banging on the door my husband started shaking. He was so scared. They kicked the door, and I asked him to stay inside the room. I told him not to worry, I will sort it out. When I opened the gate, the police shouted, 'why did you take so long?'" Ratna was petrified and lied that she was breastfeeding so she couldn't open the door. By then, Monsura was hysterical and pleading with them to release Sayyied. Ratna suspected that they let Sayyied go because he was not on a 'pre-made-up list' given by gang members to the police. From what I later heard from the residents, it was a common practice for certain police to perform aggressive searches in the homes, kicking doors and destroying possessions and arresting individuals. Money had to be paid to the police for their release.

Abdul walked into the room as we were speaking. He looked terrible. He had dark circles under his eyes, and his face appeared gaunt. He seemed to have aged ten years or more. He was wearing a white, stained sleeveless cotton vest and a crumpled sarong, in contrast to his usual trousers and shirt. Weary and frustrated, he said, "It really scares me to live here. I don't like to be at home. I like to come back late from work. If I don't do anything or come back early, then I must hang out with the slum men. I prefer to avoid this. I finish work at 6pm." Abdul deliberately stayed late at work so he wouldn't have to mingle with the men in Phulbari and feared that "friendly relationships could also lead to enmity" because of the volatile nature of their environment. He shared, "I don't get into fights with anyone here and they don't get into fights with me. If one stays quiet and busy, then they will not do anything to me or my family." He went on to talk about the crime and insecurity that was common, and this impacted on his children, but mainly who were less powerful. Monsura and Sayyied, frightened by the recent incident with the police had taken off for several days. Ratna said, "They have left for his brother's place. They are scared to be here; in case the police return and take him to jail." Ratna herself was planning to visit her family and get out for a few days, as the situation was heated in Phulbari. Ratna shared that she kept the main Phulbari leaders happy and therefore, whatever happened she reassured herself that the police would not harm Abdul or her family.

On my way out of Ratna's compound, I noticed a few men were now gathered outside their homes, huddled together, talking softly to one another. I overheard an elderly male saying, "They always come and take us poor people ... we are the ones who work hard to earn a living and they never get the actual criminals." Another male replied, "We need to pay so much money (TK2,000) to get them out of jail." I walked over to Roshonara's mother's home, but they had locked the doors, and no one seemed to be available. I knocked several times and gave up reluctantly when no one opened the door.

I resumed my fieldwork soon after. For me, the brutality and shock of what happened was still vivid in my memory. Many shops were still shut with the place having a desolate, deserted look. Males seemed less visible and were hiding for fear of random arrests, and there was little socializing among women in the narrow lanes. Children were kept behind closed doors, and the usually noisy, bustling slum was transformed into a graveyard, with an eerie silence pervading the atmosphere. A week later, Phulbari was back to its usual busyness, and except for a few comments now and again, life seemingly had gone back to 'normal' for the residents, predictable and almost tedious in its daily grind. Women were rushing to get water when it was available, tea shops filled with men chatting and drinking tea, women sitting in corners in the afternoon, after their afternoon meal, catching up with each other, while children ran around playing in the dusty alleyways. There were arguments and domestic fights, confrontations amongst husbands and wives and lovers, and furious physical attacks due to money owed, gambling debts and thefts. But it was also not surprising if suddenly an afternoon, morning, or evening could suddenly turn deadly or dangerous, without any warning, with reports of an attempted murder, or a violent altercation occurring in some part of Phulbari. Police raids in Phulbari was not unusual and many of the residents highly distrusted the police.

For many of the residents, they were seen as a bigger threat than the local gangs and leaders.

Notes

1 Newspaper report alleged that there were 56 anti-drug raids undertaken by police in various slums, and at least 91 'criminals' were reportedly killed since law enforcers began an anti-drug campaign, after the Prime Minister had declared a war on drugs. Security forces claim that all those killed were involved in drug trafficking, but human rights organizations have raised concerns, calling these 'extrajudicial killings' (Mamun, 2019).
2 Jackman (2019) argues that extortion, controlling illegal businesses (drug trade) and mediating access to services in slums, are now under an explicitly party-political guise, directly controlled by wings of the ruling political party as well as the police and local level leaders. The police and politicians operate with impunity, given the system is set up to favour the rich and powerful, and the police, as an extension of the system. These more powerful gatekeepers tend to remain above the law.

References

Atkinson-Sheppard, S. (2016). The gangs of Bangladesh: Exploring organized crime, street gangs and 'illicit child labourers' in Dhaka. *Criminology & Criminal Justice*, 16(2), 233–249.

Das, V., & Randeria, S. (2015). Politics of the urban poor: aesthetics, ethics, volatility, precarity: An introduction to supplement 11. *Current Anthropology*, 56(S11), S3–S14.

Farid, C. (2013). New paths to justice: A tale of social justice lawyering in Bangladesh. *Wis. Int'l LJ*, 31, 421.

Jackman, D. (2019). The decline of gangsters and politicization of violence in urban Bangladesh. *Development and Change*, 50(5), 1214–1238.

Koonings, K., & Kruijt, D. E. (2007). *Fractured Cities: Social Exclusion, Urban Violence and Contested Spaces in Latin America*. Zed Books. https://doi.org/http://dx.doi.org/10.5040/9781350220225

Mamun, A. A. (2019, September 7). The menace of teenage gangs. *The Business Post*. www.tbsnews.net/bangladesh/crime/menace-teenage-gangs

7 Arrests and Resistance, 2020 to 2022

For Meena, Shuli and Fatema and their families, and countless others, life is a continual game of evading, strategizing, pleading, and negotiating with the police and other actors/gatekeepers, to be able to continue working and earn some money. How each one copes, at times defiantly continuing to 'break the law,' and when caught or harassed, pleading for mercy and more conciliatory, depends on individual circumstances and the levels of support available to them at the time.

Shuli's Experiences on the Streets of Gulshan 1

Shuli recounts even before Covid hit the country, how she was regularly harassed by police, when selling wares on the streets of Gulshan 2 and she was sent to jail once. She said, "Many hawkers were caught by the police and sentenced, and this was many months before Corona lockdown happened … I was sent to Konabari police station. My mother came running and rescued me with a lot of effort. I was in custody for two weeks and my mother took care of my baby. Then you know we had lockdown … and then after lockdown the police are after us again. One time they grabbed me again. I couldn't run fast enough. I carry a baby in my arms so how fast can I run?" Shuli would be arrested again, in December 2021. As a hawker, she was vulnerable to constant bullying and abuse. Without an official license to sell and unable to pay the costs to set up a shop, street sellers are considered illegal. Like most hawkers Shuli was at perpetual war with the state, and Covid-19 had further increased their fragility and subsequent state policies have weakened the ability of hawkers to climb out of increasing poverty.

How Does One Work on the Streets if the Police Keep Coming After Us?

On June 26, 2020, Shuli described how since lockdown had ended several weeks earlier, she worked very hard to sell towels but had little luck, as there were hardly any cars on the streets and the police were harassing her and others. She was begging and selling towels, trying to earn as much cash as possible. She said, "A few days ago, police came around the corner and I ran

DOI: 10.4324/9781003467472-7

away with my baby in my arm. Sometimes they come and beat us with sticks, yelling at us to get off the streets." It was mainly male policemen and she recounted it was routine to be threatened by the police, who often come at her and other street sellers. She had just begun arranging her towels and was about to go towards the cars waiting at the traffic lights when she spotted two of them walking towards her. Realising she could be fined, or worse jailed, Shuli hurriedly left and waited in an alleyway for an hour, hoping that once the police left, she could go out on the streets again, to try and sell her towels or beg.

One way of trying to manage the police for Fatema, Shuili and other hawkers in Gulshan 2, was to make daily payments to the middleman, Barek Mia who paid the police so they could work without too much harassment. Barek, a 45-year-old man was paid by each hawker and beggar a daily amount of TK20 (US$0.23 cents in 2020). Apparently, the police earned more than TK300 daily (US$3.50 in 2020) from this extortion. Barek, the assigned 'collector' on behalf of the police also paid the police for his use of the Gulshan streets to sell his goods on a *van-gari* (cart). This did not always guarantee that the police would not come after them, but for the most part it provided some mental security for them to sell without constant fear of harassment. As Fatema shared, there were 'good police,' who left them alone, and at times warned them of new police coming on the roads, during a shift change, and there were 'bad police' who despite payments still harangued them, took their towels, and even tried to arrest them. The police had a good relationship with Barek Mia and he served as the broker and buffer between the law enforcement on the streets and the informal workers. Fatema said, matter of factly, "I am very scared of the police. We pay him and he manages them on behalf of us." Personal relationships and agreements, be it daily payments, a middleman, are key and allow street sellers to continue hawking. But there are no guarantees. Fatema shared on a few occasions, when she sat down to eat her afternoon meal on the sidewalk, her bag of towels (to sell) was confiscated, and shared how this took place in September 2021.

She admitted she was a fool and was not paying attention, as she was busy washing her bowl after eating her meal. She was very hungry and tired after all the running around and had left her bag in the middle of the sidewalk. She said, "I saw two policemen put their hands in my towel bag," and immediately pleaded with them to not take her bag and towels, but they rebuked her for leaving her bag on the streets. She lost her income for the day and was left extremely disturbed as she had also lost her towels. Upset and frustrated with nothing left to sell, she walked back home in despair.

State Mandated Covid Guidelines and Penalties

By July 2020, the country was gradually trying to come back to 'normal,' but some customers in cars, waiting at traffic lights, were reluctant to roll down their window and buy anything from street vendors, for fear of catching the virus. The country began to gradually open its shops, factories, restaurants, and other businesses. The role of the police was to monitor mask use on the streets, and fine and arrest individuals who were not following guidelines, as well as arrest and fine those congregating on the streets and seen to violate distance rules. Street vendors and sellers were discouraged from selling to reduce and control transmission. While police are already on their case, these new mandates by the state provided much leverage for abuse of power and no accountability on law enforcement officials. Partial lockdowns were also declared in 2021 and early 2022 for shorter periods; this entailed continued enforcement of mandatory mask use and other rules including restricted movement, at certain times of the day, in the evenings, curfews with harsh penalties, and fines on those seen to violate these rules. While it was very confusing for all residents who lived in Dhaka city, for the poorest, it was traumatizing. It was often unclear what the mandates were and desperate for cash, most were forced to violate these laws, hoping they could still earn some cash and would evade arrests and fines.

A year after the first rigid lockdown in 2020, in April 2021, Shumon, Shuli's husband was looking for income earning opportunities, taking whatever piecemeal jobs were available. One morning he set off with his wife Shuli, to Gulshan 2 circle, and as they were walking, he noticed a parked police car a few metres away. He recounted how his heartbeat went up and he began to silently pray that the police would not notice him and his wife. He said, "A few cops were talking to a man and shouting at him. An older man walked past the police and the man and then walked up near us. Not wanting to draw attention to us, I whispered, "What is the problem? Why are the police trying to arrest him?" Shumon found out that the young man was not wearing his mask properly, it was hanging under his chin. The police threatened to jail him if he didn't pay a fine of a TK1,000 (approximately US$12 in 2021). Pleading with them to lower the fine, as the young man, a labourer, only had TK200 (US$2.35 in 2021) to spare. Shumon shared how he was petrified as he had forgotten to wear his mask and rushed to nearby alleyway to buy one from a small pharmacy shop. He like many of the urban poor residents were deathly scared of the police and he couldn't afford to pay a hefty fine. Rumours in their locality was that some police were fining people TK5,000 (approximately US$59 in 2021). As Shumon shared the details, he seemed visibly shaken by the memory of the incident and from then on, never forget to carry a mask, an old cloth one, whenever he left his home.

Meena's main interaction with law enforcement officials occurred when she left Baniganj looking for work during the rigid and semi-lockdown periods in 2020. She didn't wear a mask and explained that the costs of wearing a mask, and the stifling feeling she had if she did wear it, stopped her. Her strategy was whenever she saw police on the streets, she would immediately cover her face with the cloth of her sari. When interrogated by the police as to why she was outside, she pleaded with the police to let her go. She explained that she had a little baby to feed and was walking to her mother's place to collect rice to feed her child. As she often walked around with her baby on her hip, the police took pity on her, and she was never fined. She said, "I asked them to have compassion for me, a poor young mother with a baby to feed. I told them I was visiting my mother for a meal, as I had no money or food in my home, and I didn't want my child to die of hunger." Despite the fear of facing the police, Meena said that desperation compelled to take such risks. Often after being interrogated and scolded they let her go. Each encounter had Meena tense and anxious, as she could not afford to be fined or be arrested. Her strong faith that she was being protected by a higher divine source, pushed her to take chances, as she walked to her mother's place to collect rice, leave her young child with her, and then walk to Gulshan residential area, going door to door, looking for work.

Poor people must contend with a highly empowered and abusive police force, who were very comfortable and familiar with their pre-Corona routine of extorting money regularly from beggars, street-sellers, road- side vendors, bus drivers, truck drivers, and others. Bicycle-ridden rickshaws and three-wheelers scooters driven by men, if caught on roads where they were prohibited, were often fined, arrested, and beaten. Shuli and her husband, Fatema and her husband, and their families, reliant on the informal economy for cash, were in the past and continue to be the target of the heavy-handed ways of police. Looking for ways to earn an income means also living in daily trauma and continual stress and fears of being caught and harassed. Stories of going to court, finding lawyers who were costly to fight for their release, paying huge fines, borrowing money and jail time for violations, is a routine experience. Shuli had been locked up twice by the time she was 20; her husband Shumon was fined and beaten once and threatened with jail time. While Meena was only questioned, her younger brother Shaon, 19, was fined and beaten for looking for work during lockdown. Fatema, 19, has not been arrested yet, but her husband, Riaz 28 was beaten once, and fined once and arrested twice.

A national newspaper article in July 2021 reported that it was primarily the poor who were being picked up for 'violating health guidelines,' fined for 'occupying roadsides,' and therefore, blamed for spreading Covid in the city. The journalist shared the plight of the vulnerable and reported that at least 5,834 people were arrested in Dhaka in July 2021, on flimsy charges of 'breaching lockdown rules' (i.e., not wearing masks, congregating on the streets, selling items, creating crowds, etc.), with law enforcement agencies continuing their drive to arrest people for flouting regulations. Many people struggled to pay the fines to secure their release. Fines ranged from TK100 to 500 (approximately US$1.17 to $ 6 in 2021). Many had to take loans just to be able to pay the amount (Hossain, 2021).

City Drive Against Hawkers on the Streets: Arrests and Jail time

Between October 2021 and January 2022, according to Shuli, Shumon and Fatema, there were increasingly even more aggressive efforts by the police and even senior law enforcement officers to remove hawkers and all kinds of 'vagrants' off the streets. They had heard from others that there was a city corporation drive declared to clean up the sidewalks and streets, remove crowds, hawkers and street vendors and others deemed to be of public nuisance. There was widespread tension among the hawkers when Barak Mama (the middleman) stopped taking the daily extortion amount for the police. There was pressure from the government to remove all hawkers and beggars from the streets, and therefore the police had stopped taking daily bribes from Barek.

Shuli was arrested in December 2021. She was taken aback when one afternoon a 'senior police officer' grabbed her by the arm and arrested her. Shuli had seen her nearby, but she was not worried, because she (the police officer) was not dressed in the 'usual police uniform.' Police who manage traffic tend to be males and in uniform, but there are senior police officers who are women and men, and sometimes dressed as civilians. Shuli believed she was safe. After her release in January 2022, she shared the details of what happened, "I didn't realise that the police are now dressing in civilian clothes, and many sellers have been taken away. The situation for us hawkers to do our business is very bad. I was taken to the police station a month ago." It was at noon when she was selling towels, when she was grabbed by the arm by the senior policewoman. She was pushed towards a microvan. Shuli, terrified, with one arm holding on to her baby girl, begged her to let her go. Shuli wiping away tears, shared:

> "Madam, please, please, don't take me." She told me that I was forbidden to sell. She shouted at me, "Why are you selling here?" I put my hands together, and bent down, trying to touch her feet asking her for forgiveness, so she would let me go, "Please madam, I won't sell anymore." She pulled me up, didn't listen to me, and said, "I will send you to the police station." I started crying, my little girl started wailing. The madam had no mercy for me, I tried again and pleaded for some compassion, "Madam, my child is small, I have no work. That's why I run this business." She was so cruel, she said, "Give your child to someone in your home because you must go to the police station now."

Shuli called her mother immediately to inform her that she was being arrested and needed to hand over Arifa (her baby girl) to her mother. Initially Jorina could not understand Shuli, as she was sobbing, but she rushed over when she understood the severity of the situation. Shuli shared the trauma and fear that stays with her and other young sellers, as they never know when they might be caught, whether they will be taken to jail, the amount of fines to be paid of fines, when they may be released uncertain, and not knowing the amount of money that might be required to pay off police, and if they had to go to court. Fatema and Shuli as well as Jorina agonised that despite the lockdown in 2020 and subsequent loss of wages and cash shortages, there was little support for them to work or easing of restrictions from the State.

When Jorina rushed over, she was also scolded by the senior policewoman, who threatened to send Shuli to jail as street selling was illegal. Shuli shared, "She told my mother, I will send your daughter to Kashimpur[1] jail for a long time." This was one of the larger jails located far from the city and Jorina began to cry and begged the policewoman, asking for her mercy as there was a little baby girl that would be left behind if Shuli was locked up. The woman was not deterred from her mission of arresting Shuli. Shuli shared, "These people's hearts are made of stone. She told my mother, 'You will contact your daughter there'." Shuli's young daughter, confused and inconsolable, would not let her go, but the policewoman yanked Shuli away and put her in the microvan. Jorina reassured Shuli that she would organise a lawyer and get the money to pay for her release. Inside the van, there were six young and older women sitting inside, all of them arrested for violating the new drive to clean the streets of Dhaka. Shuli also called her husband who reassured her that he would find the money for her release.

Shuli spent lonely days and nights at the jail centre, where many of the young girls slept in rows on the floor, cleaned one section of the garden and toilets, and had to scrub floors and doors. She remembers many of the young women sharing stories of being separated from young or sick children, or aging parents who relied on them financially. Frantic phone calls were made to networks and family, to arrange money for their release. Shuli claims she was released after two weeks. Her mother and husband pooled their earnings and savings to pay TK7,500 (approximately US$88 in 2021) to have her released. She was required to go to court and confess her guilt, "I told the judge I was wrong. I had committed a crime and I would not sell again." The amount paid for her release, is equivalent to covering the costs of rent, food, and other necessities for a month. There were also additional expenses, fees for the lawyer and going to the court, with costs of transport, etc, amounting in total to TK15,000 (US$176 in 2021).

Shuli had lost opportunities to earn money, as she was in jail for two weeks, and then the rest of her selling time was taken up with going to court by bus, meeting the lawyer as the case was pending. She acknowledged that despite her strained relationship with her mother, this recent arrest revealed a softer supportive side of her mother.

Outsmarting the Police: Shuli is Careless, but One

Fatema when recalling the arrest of Shuli, blamed her for own carelessness for getting caught. Sounding slightly irritated, she said "Shuli was taken to the police station twice. She is a little stupid as she doesn't pay attention to her surroundings. We are all very careful and alert each other if see any sign of a police officer around us." It was apparent to Fatema that most of the sellers were on high alert due to the city corporation drive except for Shuli, who was always busy chatting on her phone and in her own world, "Once she starts talking on the phone to her husband, she keeps talking away." Fatema scolded Shuli several times for not paying attention to her surroundings, but Shuli usually became angry and didn't listen, "She yells, don't tell me what to do, I have been selling on the streets for a long time!" Fatema shared how there were many hawkers/sellers including herself who didn't get arrested or caught so easily and accused Shuli of being clueless, often selling at the exact time when the police are on the streets. The police raids took place in the mornings, and other sellers often went to sell towels after noon to avoid being caught, but not Shuli, who had been arrested twice already. Fatema said, "One must know how to manage the situation. I usually come on the streets after 11 am when there are less police around."

Shuli had shared about Riaz's (Fatema's husband) recent arrest, when he was locked up for riding a rickshaw on the main street, where rickshaw pullers are not allowed to play. This was during the post lockdown period in 2021. He had been caught before and usually paid TK100 (approximately US $1.17 in 2021), but this time, the policeman didn't let him go and took him to the Gulshan police station to jail and filed a case. They also seized the rickshaw, which did not belong to Riaz. It was rented. When Fatema got the call from her husband that he was in jail, she panicked and ran to her brother's home and also reached out to her neighbouring tenant to borrow some cash to get his release. She needed TK3,000 (approximately US$35.26 in 2021) and her main fear was the longer he was at the police station, the more likely he would be beaten and transferred elsewhere. She panicked that he may disappear without a trace. Fatema and her husband belonged to the category of those who remain uncounted and invisible, living in slums, with little voice or authority to seek justice. Fatema recounted the incident to me.

She rushed to her older brother's place, Faruk, who hurriedly accompanied her to the police station. To appease the police, Faruk immediately acknowledged that Riaz had 'broken the law' and handed over the cash, as was initially demanded by the policeman. The situation became complicated when the policeman asked for the rickshaw owner to come to the station. They came up with a strategy to manage the police. Fatema was concerned that the policemen would demand even more money, if the owner was forced to show up, and in retaliation the owner would come after her husband; she, with Faruk and Riaz's sister, decided to trick the police. They asked a disabled man, who they knew well, to pretend to be the owner and come to the station. Seeing a disabled man limp his way into the station, the police did not beat him or fine him, but let him go with the rickshaw. They released Riaz because he had paid a fine of TK3,000. Victorious over their duping of the police, there was much triumph and rejoicing as they went back to their home to rest, after a gruelling hour or more, spent at the police station. Fatema's close relationship with her brother, and her sister-in-law, and their mutual networks helped her greatly. Being male, he managed the negotiations with the police, and assisted her with a loan to pay the fine. Faruk's wife, (her sister-in-law) found someone from her network to fake being the 'disabled owner of the rickshaw,' for a small fee.

Between November 2021 to early January 2022, it was particularly terrifying and stressful, as Fatema rushed around, gathering support, money, and made phone calls, visits to the police station and paid off fines. On December 2021, Riaz was accused of being involved in a burglary, and Fatema had to collect TK20,000 (US$235 in 2021) for his release. She borrowed from her sister-in-law, mother, brother, and tenants, as well as a moneylender. She was in enormous debt. She also confessed that the police threatened to take her father to jail, accusing him of selling marijuana in the local area. In both cases, Fatema claims that her husband and father were set up by 'local bad boys' in the area and were innocent. She shared, "I was at his house, and told the policeman, sir, please don't take my father away. Then uncle, my father's landlord came to defend my father. He has known him for many years. He said to the police, 'Sir, he is an old man. He doesn't sell cannabis, he takes it occasionally, and he does not harm anyone'." The landlord who was close to Fatema's parents handed over TK1,500 (approximately US$18 in 2021) to placate the policeman, but he demanded TK5,000 (approximately US$59 in 2021). The landlords cajoled and pleaded and negotiated the amount down to TK3,000 (approximately US$35 in 2021).

Fatema recalled, "Mama (unrelated, uncle/landlord) is very kind. He paid that amount so they my father wouldn't be taken to jail. If they took my father to the police station, just to release him will cost us a lot, maybe even TK15,000 (approximately US$176 in 2021)!" Fatema and Faruk paid their father's landlord back in less than two months. After this incident, there was widespread gossip by neighbours in the community about her father's 'illicit activities,' which had led to the police showing up in their locality. Some of the local women had started gossiping about Riaz being a thief and therefore the arrest by police. Extremely upset, Fatema vehemently defended her father and husband to her local tenants, hoping that the maligning of her family would stop. As the earlier chapters reveal, social relationships are important and maintaining them was critical, to belong and be accepted in the community.

Powerless, these young women and their families are barely tolerated; they 'work the system,' by payment of regular bribes to gatekeepers, mainly the police and other power brokers. The police raids, 'clean up drives,' set out by city corporation have huge, short- and long-term catastrophic domino effects on not only their livelihoods, but on their overall lives (Etzold, 2013). Their low social and legal status is the key driver of their vulnerability, and they face continued exploitation from all levels of power brokers and gatekeepers. Many return to the streets time and time again, to sell their wares, look for work, defy the official rules, and rely on their networks to continue.

Shuli and Fatema: Nasty Comments, Abuse and Harassment

Other than the daily fears of dealing with police, both Shuli and Fatema regularly faced nasty, judgmental, and lewd comments from passersby, and customers in cars and motorbikes. Shuli shared in January 2022, that, in the past year, ever since she began begging with her daughter in tow, she faced numerous pointed remarks by 'well-off women' who were walking on their way to work and back, and sometimes from 'rich women' in cars, who rolled down the window to tell her off, when she approached them for money. She experienced a mixture of emotions, from anger to frustration and sadness, because of the aggression and lack of compassion.

In tears, she said, "I beg around Gulshan 1. A lot of people on the street talk nonsense and say nasty things: A lot of madams who walk to work and back, look down at me." I asked what comments she had to hear. She replied, "They say 'Why do you beg with such a young child in your lap? You can't work.' I used to get upset but I hear it so often that I don't get upset anymore. I can't get upset. Will these madams feed me? One younger woman, she seemed rich, said to me, "You are coming to the streets to beg with such a small child.' I told a madam about 10 or 15 days ago, with a smile, 'Will you give me work in your home? Then I will work.' She did not say anything and kept walking. All big talk, but no one wants to help. Rich people don't give jobs to anyone now."

A woman customer recently accused her of renting Arifa to garner more sympathy and beg on the streets. This remark enraged Shuli who admitted that she was in tears and began yelling at the woman in the car to stop telling lies and making accusations. The wealthy woman in the car taken aback by a young poor street seller shouting at her, screamed, "How dare you speak to me like this? What is the world coming to? You are begging with a little child because it is an easy way to make money. Shame on you!" The woman rolled up her window and the traffic lights changed, and the car drove away. Shuli was left feeling very upset but also humiliated. She shared, "I cannot pay attention to these horrible comments, they won't pay for my survival, will they?"

She couldn't leave Arifa with anyone and needed to bring her to work. Usually, Shuli carried Arifa around on her hip, but she also took breaks as she was tired of always carrying her on her hips. Arifa was two years old and heavy to carry, and Shuli, a slim young woman, would place her on the ground, for some temporary relief, so she could rest her back and body, which hurt from carrying her all day. She let Arifa, a restless child, play on the main island (road divider) of the main road. Her two-year-old daughter would walk up and down the island road divider, from one side to the other. Arifa often played with the young daughter of another hawker, Bahari, 30. The frightening aspect of this was if any one of those two young children suddenly stumbled or pushed each other, they would fall directly on the road, into oncoming traffic of cars, trucks, and buses, as this was a very busy intersection. They would be instantly killed.

Shuli and Bahari would occasionally look over at their daughters, admonish them if they became too rowdy but for the most part, they seemed to be unaware of the dangers of this road, as they chatted to each other or focused on finding customers in cars. Shuli was overwhelmed at times, because she found it difficult to sell, or beg and manage a small baby. She had to carry a bag of towels to sell, as well as a smaller cloth bag which had snacks for Arifa and a change of clothes, if she urinated or defecated. She walked with the bags and Arifa in her arms.

However, what upset Shuli a few weeks later, in early February 2022, was that 'Mama' (unrelated, maternal uncle), the shopkeeper of Flexi-load shop, made a comment about her continuing to beg, despite lockdown being over. She was worried her reputation was at stake and was upset by his criticism: "He has become very disapproving of me begging. He asked me why I was begging. He said to me, 'You have this little girl with you? That is not good for her'." Shuli explained that she didn't have a choice and given towels sales were low, she needed to beg. The shopkeeper unsympathetic of her circumstances warned her that she would face 'bad comments' if she continued to beg from passersby and customers and others in this area. Shuli who had been struggling to make ends meet, replied, "Can any of them feed me and my family? Will they tolerate my landlord's screams for rent payments? Is anyone giving me any work!" However, unmoved by her response, he insisted she try and start some other selling business, as begging was undignified and wrong because she had a little baby girl with her. Disappointed by his attitude, and fretting, she said, "I did not say anything to him, because there is no benefit in arguing, he is an elder and he cares for me and my baby. I feel close to him, and I was hurt when he said all those things to me," but defiantly added, "but people can say what they like, but they are not feeding me or my family. I must do what I must do!"

Shuli mentioned that some sellers sold marijuana and other drugs on the streets, as well as sold towels, and when asked if she faced any sexual comments directed at her, she denied such experiences. However, Fatema was more forthcoming about the lewd comments directed at her, Shuli, and other female hawkers regularly on the streets. She shared, "I had a stomach ache because I was menstruating. Then I sat down on the sidewalk with my hands on my stomach because it was aching. I had cramps. At that time, two well-dressed boys were walking along the road. As I sat with my hands on my stomach, they looked at me and said loudly, 'Look, this girl is sitting with her hands on her stomach. This girl seems to have had sex with someone somewhere'." She didn't react as she knew it would be futile, but she was angry as well as ashamed. They walked off confidently, laughing loudly, knowing that she was unable to do anything.

Fatema said it was common for women hawkers, particularly the younger ones, including Shuli's daughter, Shuborna, who was only 12 years old, to face a barrage of lewd and sexually offensive comments, from drivers in cars, to well-dressed men walking to their office jobs, to young college boys and older men on motorbikes. Comments ranged from "Heh, you want to come with me and have some fun?" or "We know you sell more than goods on the street, why don't you sell yourself?", or "You can earn a quick cash if you come home with me now!" Most of them just ignored the men and went about selling their towels and other goods. Shuli had once threatened to call the police when an older man made some vile comments at her, but he just laughed in her face, knowing that she had no power to call the police. He was after all, a middle-class professional working and living in Dhaka, and it would be the word of a poor female street seller, 'illegally' plying her business, against the word of an educated, well-off man.

Most of the young street sellers brush off these comments, and Fatema explained, "we pretend not to hear these comments, although there was a recent incident, where Fatema, yelled and abused a sexual harasser, a CNG (three-wheeler scooter) driver. The incident took place on February 2022. Fatema shared, "A CNG driver was trying to talk to me as I waited near the traffic signal for cars. I was standing in front of CNG for only 2–3 minutes, when the driver says, 'Hey, why don't come with me. I will give you money. We will have a good time'." Tired of these types of comments regularly being directed at her and other young women, she became furious and began screaming at him, "Sister-fucker, do you think I'm that kind of girl (sex worker)! We work hard and I need to run my household." When the driver simply smiled at her, she threatened to take off her sandals and beat him. She shared, "This horrible man must be over 40 years, with a beard. This guy must have children. Shameless!" Hearing her scream, her street seller friends came closer and the CNG driver, startled and scared seeing a few of the sellers gathering, sped off quickly. She later explained that she was hungry, tired and in a bad mood. Sales were low and she was upset that not only did they have to manage the police, but also a constant stream of men who routinely harassed them with sexual innuendos and offers, while she was simply trying to survive and earn enough cash to manage her household. It was emotionally draining.

Etzold writes on street hawkers (sellers) in Dhaka, and how their livelihood is critical to urban economies, especially in Global Southern contexts (Etzold, 2013). However, all street sellers, be it selling food or goods, are seen as 'disorderly,' and disruptive to any organised urban planning by city authorities and the local elites. Instead of providing adequate legal frameworks, street hawkers are criminalised and 'informalised,' and seen as appropriating public spaces illegally. They are accused of many things: "of being dirty and 'ugly,' of not paying taxes, selling illegal goods, of being unhygienic, of blocking public areas and spaces, being noisy and [...] the underlying complaint by many city administrators, local business, or residents is that they are *there*" (Cross and Karides 2007: 19).

The law is against those who sell on the street, in parks or on a public place, all of which are under the official control of the Dhaka City Corporation. Consequently, it falls on the police to control the streets and prevent these workers, from 'creating a nuisance of themselves' and 'occupying the footpaths.' The law does not acknowledge the steep social and economic structures that they are up against. Continual shortage of cash, makes it next to impossible to set up or rent shops, get a license to operate, in an already exorbitantly expensive city. With little social and economic capital, no connections to Dhaka City Corporation officials, and insufficient cash to bribe them for a license, to set up a small permanent shop near a footpath/ lane, is simply a cruel fantasy. As a result, none are registered, and as Etzold, argues, most informal workers globally are viewed as trespassers of public spaces, but resist and continue to work in these spaces (Etzold, 2013).

Shuli, Fatema's narratives illustrate the gender dimension and risks of their occupations, the judgement faced by Shuli as 'a mother' who is seen as harming her baby, with no recognition of the structures and systems in place, that have pushed her to work on the streets. Both Fatema and even Shuli's daughter Shuborna's experiences of sexual harassment, reveal the persistently male dominated environment, that thrives on harassment, discrimination, and oppression in public spaces. With no power to ask the police to intervene, a few screams, shouting and fighting back when they can, is their only recourse. For the most part, they swallow their rage, feel ashamed, and stay silent and continue to keep working.

A study of two slums in Dhaka city, with 180 respondents (94 males and 86 females), found 57% females who utilise public spaces in everyday life, reported facing harassment from male strangers on the streets, and sometimes by their male peers as well as by stalkers in the neighbourhood locality (Arefin & Rashid, 2021). Etzold argues many of those who live marginal lives have developed resistance to formal rules of governance, and quietly appropriate and use public space, and deny the state its legitimacy (Etzold, 2013). In turn, the criminalization of the poor and excessive use of state violence against them is directly related to the privatization of security and the fragmentation of the city into well-to-do areas for better off and elites, e.g., in gated community, and spaces of the subalterns – slums (Davis, 2006). This results in a cycle of insecure citizenship, fragmentation of rights, discrimination, and vilification, as well as victimization by the police and others (Koonings & Kruijt, 2007).

Note

1 Known as Dhaka Central Jail at Kasimur, Gazipur is one of the biggest jails in Asia. The total land area: inside the jail is 35 acres and outside the jail is 48.5 acres, on which the 4 residential buildings of Kashimpur jail, agricultural land and Gazipur-Tangail highway are located. Present capacity: 2000. Structure: There are six six-storied and three three-storied prisoner buildings inside this jail. There is a hospital with 200 beds. There are four kitchens for prisoners, one gallows, a pond and well decorated flower, fruit and vegetables gardens in the jail. There are one three-storied, one two-storied and four single storey buildings in the production department.

References

Arefin, S., & Rashid, T. (2021). The urban poor in Dhaka: Perspectives on the right to the city. *Journal of Urban & Regional Analysis*, 13(1).

Cross, J. C., & Karides, M. (2007). Capitalism, modernity, and the "appropriate" use of space. In J. Cross & A. Morales (Eds.), *Street Entrepreneurs: People, Place, & Politics in Local and Global Perspective* (1st ed.). Routledge (Taylor & Francis Group). https://doi.org/10.4324/9780203086742

Davis, M. (2006). Planet of slums. *Open House Int*, 8(5).

Etzold, B. (2013). The politics of street food. Contested governance and vulnerabilities. In *Dhaka's Field of Street Vending*. Franz Steiner Verlag.

Hossain, I. (2021, July 26). Breaching lockdown rules: Poor arrestees struggling to pay fines. *Dhaka Tribune*. www.dhakatribune.com/bangladesh/253381/breaching-lock down-rules-poor-arrestees

Koonings, K., & Kruijt, D. E. (2007). *Fractured Cities: Social Exclusion, Urban Violence and Contested Spaces in Latin America*. Zed Books. https://doi.org/http://dx.doi.org/10.5040/9781350220225

8 Battered Bodies, Minds, and Hearts in 2002

Monsura's Tremors

In mid-April, 2002, field work was difficult as it had been raining the past few days. It was after 1 pm and suddenly there was another downpour. It was hard to walk around the tiny, congested lanes. I waded through sewage, as the few drains overflowed; dead rats and cockroaches floated within the water, along with faeces and other sludge. I was carrying an umbrella, but I was not able to protect myself fully from the thrashing rain. I carefully navigated my way to Ratna's place and banged on the tin door several times. The sound of rain against the door made it difficult to be heard, until finally, suddenly, Ratna's mother yanked open the door, holding up an umbrella. She gasped and screamed in shock, "What are you doing here in this rain?" She ushered me into the small compound. I took off my rainboots, washed my feet near their tap and entered Monsura's room. Ratna smiled and yelled, "You will fall sick!" Monsura was half-lying down, propped up on a pillow, playing with Joy. She waved me in. Ratna seemed to be in a good mood and was back to being friendly with me.

Monsura's room smelt rancid, a mixture of urine and dampness, and there was a large puddle of water near the foot of the bed. A bucket with a messy pile of clothes had been placed strategically under the leak of their tin roof. She looked tired. She patted the space across from her. She spoke softly of the terrifying health ordeal the night before. She said, "Yesterday I nearly died. I don't know but I had severe cramps in my hands and feet. The pain was shooting up and down my body. I curled up and my hands and feet became completely cold. I felt numb. I was so frightened." Sayyied became very frightened and rushed to get a cloth to keep her legs from shaking and then he grabbed mustard oil and began rubbing her legs and arms vigorously. When she wouldn't stop shaking, he rushed off in a panic to get Ratna, who came running in, and began to rub mustard oil and praying. Monsura concluded: "My tremors stopped, but it took some time."

She could recall at least four such episodes in the past several months. When probed further, she divulged the condition has been brought on by her incessant worries. She sat up, and with a pained expression, replied, "A doctor

DOI: 10.4324/9781003467472-8

was brought in to administer saline. Sayeeda recommended this pharmacy, and Abdul gave us a loan of TK300 (approximately US$5.25 in 2002), so we could pay for the saline. Some energy did come back into my body, and I felt less weak. But my worries persist, and they will not go away. I have weakness in my body." She pulled at the skin of the bottom half of her upper, tiny skeleton- like arms and stretched them out, then placed her right hand on her heart and rubbed her chest gently. She continued, "Those who worry will fall sick. My body and heart hurts." She looked at me and asked, "Do you even understand what I am saying? I am poor and poor people suffer from worries and we fall sick." When I probed further, she explained, "We suffer from *chinta roge* (worry illness) and a doctor cannot treat this. This illness does not show on an x-ray."

She was silent for a while, then continued, "Everyone has worry illness, those who are poor remain worried." She half smiled, "You won't understand. You are rich. We live our lives sick with worries. This affects our entire body. I can't think and I can't sleep properly because of my worries." She went on to describe her days and nights of insecurity, because Sayyied didn't work reg- ularly, and she was often left eating just "rice and lentils or sometimes rice soaked in water, with chilis." When these sickness episodes occurred, he would take care of her, massaging her body with mustard oil and apologizing profu- sely for mistreating her. Due to her constant worries, she said she experienced restlessness, fever, palpitations, insomnia and at times, body shakes. She picked up a half empty bottle of Cinkara syrup, as Sayyied had been alarmed by these repeated incidences and had purchased a bottle from the local drug shop.[1] Monsura had been taking a teaspoon of this syrup, sparingly every few weeks, to manage her bodily shakes and weakness. The syrup claimed to provide 'energy and vital nutrients,' and cost TK250 (approximately US$4.35 in 2002), sufficient cash to buy some food for a week for the household.

Monsura's mother walked in, wet. She was wearing an old tattered faded green sari, with no blouse, and rubber slippers. Her thinning hair was severely pulled back into a bun. She gave me a toothless smile. Her tongue and lips were heavily stained, dark red, from chewing betel leaf. She plonked herself down on the bed and grabbed Joy and held him tightly to her chest. She was a traditional healer, so I asked her about worry illness. She replied, "Because of poverty everyone worries all the time, this is leading to heart problems, strokes and people have cancer and blood pressure. This era has more poverty and loss of faith. Previously, there weren't any of these illnesses. We (healers) cannot cure cancer and stroke; only doctors can cure these new diseases." Here loss of faith referred to lack of trust in people and the government. She added, "The slum is filled with crime and drugs and bad air and illnesses. We constantly worry about our future and our health, but what does the govern- ment do? Nothing." Monsura and her mother began discussing the absence of sufficient clean latrines, irregular water availability, clogged drains, and the lack of proper gas lines in many homes in the slums, forcing some women to cook on stoves using wood, cloth, pieces of rubber tires, and paper as fuel, causing a myriad of health problems.

Monsura piped up, "Imagine if we don't have money and then we borrow from someone, but if you cannot repay it, then your honour will go away if you cannot repay this loan." Money or the lack of money was constantly mentioned by residents. Daily life was a grind, worrying about the next meal, paying bills, debts, loans and rent and so on. This was a world characterised by uncertainty and powerlessness; cash provided the poor with an important degree of control over their lives. Cash was desperately needed to survive but was extremely scarce, and the shortage of cash was directly linked to worries and ill-health. Monsura's mother described *chinta roge* (worry illness) as a tree and likened the growth of the illness to a tree spreading its roots, over time creating all kinds of diseases inside the body. She went on to explain how persistent tension, from desperately trying to survive, manifested into various illnesses but could also eventually lead to diseases such as cancer and heart failure. Most residents especially married adolescent women and older women, either mentioned in passing or when probed, that their lives were filled with constant *chinta* (worries) and they suffered from all kinds of health problems as a result. Like Monsura, they bought tonics and syrups like Cinkara, saline, and tablets, from the local drug shops, to manage weakness and build strength in the body, improve insomnia and lack of appetite, and to resolve fevers, colds, coughs, bodily shakes, and aches. While these medicines provided some relief, people recognised these measures as temporary (Rashid & Islam, 2019).

Advertisements in newspapers, leaflets, word of mouth, abound for food supplements, nutritious drinks, tonics, and purifiers in Dhaka city, and this resonates in slums, where residents live lives of scarcity and fragility (see also Nichter and Vuckovic, 1994 Nichter & Vuckovic, 1994). The pharmaceutical industry markets medicines to influence treatment options, and many women are advised to purchase tonics and vitamin syrups to treat all kinds of ailments, including loss of nutrients and weakness in the body. Drug shop sellers as unqualified doctors/chemists become basically *de facto* medical practitioners, and serve as health care alternatives (see, Logan, 1983) for most slum residents. This industry has been around since the 80s, since the Drug Ordinance of 1982. This created a market for the local firms for simple generic formulations which were earlier imported or manufactured by the foreign firms. A study in 2017 reported that more than 80% of the population sought care from drug shops (Ahmed & Hossain, 2007). They tend to be largely unregulated and not accountable. Residents living in slums preferred them due to their accessibility and familiarity, their trust with the seller and shorter waiting times. These private drug shops, in every corner of the city and in slums, are open late into the evenings, which is a huge benefit for those who did not want to or cannot take time off during the day and lose a day's wage. Drug shops will sell without a prescription, and in slums will provide medicines on credit, especially those who are loyal customers. This is against the backdrop of very weak public health services, poor quality of care, long waiting hours, high costs, and mistreatment of patients in public facilities, as well as certain private ones. As of 2017, there were reported to be 106,919 licensed and an equal number of unlicensed retail drug shops selling all types of medicines and over the counter medicines (Ahmed et al., 2017).

Poor people are constantly urged by health workers to maintain good health by eating nutritious foods, such as spinach, meat, milk, and eggs, which they can rarely afford, which further desocialises the nature of the problem (Scheper-Hughes, 1992). In some ways, accessing tonics and syrups are an effort to cope with the hunger, anxiety, and other ailments but also the oppression faced; 'the hidden and overt injuries' of class and other forms of social inequalities. The use of such tonics may act as a self-medicating mechanism for the harms caused by oppression. (Baer et al., 1997).

End of April: Beset with Health Problems

A series of health crises from April 2002 created further anxiety and stress for Monsura and Ratna. When I visited Monsura in April, I found Joy as usual, playing on their one room mud floor, soiled and dirty. He was wailing loudly. Monsura's face was flushed with rage. She shrieked, "Shut up, shut up, you asshole!' Monsura seemed completely overwhelmed with the responsibilities of taking care of a baby as well as managing a difficult husband. She didn't work and during the day she was mainly confined to her room, wondering if Sayyied would show up with cash to pay rent or if had done some shopping so she and her baby could eat. When she saw me, she seemed embarrassed. She picked up Joy and placed him to her left breast and whispered that she had been suffering from large boils around her vagina for several weeks. It was painful. I asked her if she had gone to the clinic, but she had not – she said didn't want to be gossiped about and preferred to seek care elsewhere. She was resorting to home treatment, "The boils burn a lot, and it is painful. There is a lot of itching and I feel uncomfortable. The whole area has become very red. I kept scratching myself and it is swollen." I asked if she had told Sayyied. She replied, "I was not comfortable telling him, because it is another cost … to seek treatment. And my younger brother owes Sayyied TK200 (approximately US$3.53 in 2002). He was meant to pay it back, but he has not as yet."

Last night as they were getting ready to sleep, Sayyied saw her furiously scratching herself. He became annoyed with her and asked her to stop, and she angrily retorted, "I can't stop the itching, so what do you want me to do? I need to go to a doctor." She said that he became enraged and abusive, and called her names, demanding she bring back the money owed to him by her brother. He said he had no money, and he could not spend any more on her health problems and called her a 'beggar's daughter who had cheated him out of his dowry.' With a pained expression, she added "It is so hurtful when he talks to me like this. I could not control myself and yelled, 'what kind of a husband are you?'" She quickly left the room, as the argument began to escalate. She knew that by placing herself outside the room, the chances of him hitting her were reduced, as he would be seen by Ratna and Abdul. A few days later, Sayyied finally relented, as her itching persisted, and her brother had repaid the loan. Sayyied took her to a female doctor outside Phulbari for treatment. When I asked her what she believed to be the cause of her boils, she was quiet.

She confessed that she thought that Sayyied may be sleeping with an ex-lover who lived in another slum. Emotionally wounded, she confronted him, and it led to a huge fight, and she was beaten badly: "He may kick me and slap me, but I told him I knew he was sleeping with that whore (his ex-lover) again!" Monsura's life with Sayyied was volatile and she was beaten regularly.

Monsura sat on a broken cart with wheels, parked right next to Ratna's compound tin door, picking at a scab on her arm. She seemed down. She shared that Joy was not her first pregnancy, but her second pregnancy. She was pregnant soon after getting married but when she was three or four months pregnant, she lost her baby. Furious after another fight over cash shortages and no food in the house, Sayyied beat her violently and kicked her in the stomach. This led to her losing her baby. She lamented that she didn't have a well off, older brother who would protect her. Her brother was poor and indifferent, too caught up in managing his own precarious household. She was so ashamed with what had happened she didn't share this incident with anyone. She said, "He is a *harami* (immoral, horrible person). My mother lives so far away and if I want to go to her, i can't, its too difficult." She shared that she could not take out her anger on her husband, but often ended up taking her rage on Joy. She said, "When he beats me, I am so upset, I slap my son." She turned to kiss Joy as he happily giggled in her arms. She felt guilty but did not how to manage her pain.

Poorer, adolescent women, especially those with little support, remained in these marriages, tolerating infidelity, abuse, and partially 'absent and lazy husbands,' rather than be completely alone, because the trade-off was at least continued social acceptance and physical and (to an extent) economic security. Other than affection and attachment, many of the young women were also pragmatic about their reasons for not leaving their husbands. Young women like Monsura, Ratna, Roshonara and others commonly said: "Is it so easy to leave the husband? Can I just leave him? How many times will a girl get married in her life? What if the second husband is worse than this one?"

A fortnight later, when I visited Monsura, she was not at home. Her room door was locked. Ratna immediately informed me that Joy had diarrhoea and Monsura and Sayyied had rushed her off to a hospital some 30 minutes away, in Mohakhali. Ratna lent her some cash to go to the facility, after Monsura became frantic and hysterical about Joy's condition. He had lost a lot of weight and the diarrhoea was uncontrollable. Ratna pointed in disgust to the state of the room, the soiled bedding and rubbish piled up in the corner of the bed. She said that she wasn't surprised that Monsura's baby had fallen sick, "Monsura caused the child to have diarrhoea. The room is so dirty." Abdul walked in and I asked about his health, having heard from Ratna that he had been unwell for some time. He replied, "Some days I feel better but lately I have been very tired and not so well." He went to a doctor in a government facility, as recommended by the local drug shop seller in their slum. At the facility he was asked to do tests to check for dengue, typhoid, and jaundice. He continued, "The doctor is hoping that the test results will be fine. He prescribed some medicines and asked me to rest. I have taken 11 days of leave from my job."

Abdul worked in a spectacle shop, a relatively stable job with a fixed monthly income. Ratna interrupted, to remark "He never takes leave ... and he is lucky his boss gave him leave, it is hard to find decent jobs in this area." Abdul nodded but didn't say anything. He then replied quietly, "I cannot be sick longer than that ... or I will be in trouble!' Ratna explained that she had gone to members of her local *samity* (collective) in the slum and asked them for a loan to cover Abdul visits to the doctor and to buy medicines. She went into her room briefly and came back, with both hands cupping several strips of tablets, that were prescribed for him. They were beside themselves with worry, fearing the worst diagnosis and outcome. When asked what caused this health problem for Abdul, Ratna shared, "He doesn't eat properly, and he works long hours. It is also not easy living here ... with all the violence and insecurity." She pondered on the various causes and said the 'quality of water from the taps was bad,' and there was 'pollution' which may have created imbalances in his body. Ratna added, "He is scared but I am also very fearful. If something happens to my husband, then what will I do with these two girls? They are getting older. If there is no husband, then can I live here?" She began to cry. I put my arms around her to comfort her. Serious illnesses, possibly leading to death, was a nagging, underlying fear in many households. To be left without a male 'protector' in a slum – a close male relative, i.e., a brother, father, husband, or uncle – was an uncomfortable and possibly terrifying prospect. Living as a single woman is only possible, if a young woman had strong support from a local leader or a landlord or has lived in the area for a long time. Despite that, she remains vulnerable to unwanted attention and harassment.

I returned almost a week later to check on both Ratna and Monsura. Ratna was chatting away to her while Monsura sat on the bed, cradling her son on her lap, humming a song to herself. She looked rested and had put on weight, but Joy was looking thin. She shared, "It cost me only TK20 (approximately US$0.35 in 2002) to get Joy admitted. They kept me in an airconditioned room with my baby." She was pleased as she was fed fish, chicken, and rice daily, and Joy was also well taken care of: "Someone came and cleaned the baby's feces ... and I slept a lot." She remained unencumbered by daily chores of looking after a baby and a household. Being able to eat good expensive food items was an experience, beyond her wildest dreams. She smiled and said, "I feel healthier and better, and my son has also recovered."

Monsura confessed that she had been extremely anxious on her way to the hospital because Sayyied was against admitting their child into a hospital. Like most poor people, Sayyied generally distrusted formal providers and expected neglect and poor quality of care. Rumours and stories circulated in the slums, in the communal kitchens, in the queues when women collected water, in teashops where men sat, and among residents sitting around the lanes; they recounted stories of long waits, abuse and mistreatment and even deaths, and the huge costs incurred at these facilities. In general, visiting a government and even private hospital can be extremely daunting for the poor. The fact is that many public doctors have private chambers and patients are forced to or encouraged to seek care from those private facilities, as there is chronic long waiting hours and absenteeism of doctors in the public facilities, which is higher in rural facilities. In addition, quality of care compared to public clinics and hospitals tend to be better.

Usually when they arrive, they are confronted by a maze of floors, elevators and corridors jam packed with patients, long queues, and numerous diagnostic rooms for treating various health conditions, ranging from maternal and child health to other chronic conditions, including those affecting the heart, lungs, and diabetes. Hospitals have signs in English and Bengali, unintelligible to many of the poor who are not literate. They seek advice from unfriendly, overworked staff who usually dismiss their queries. They also need to pay in cash to meet doctors and access any kind of treatment. All in all, the experience is not pleasant. However, if pushed to go, most slum residents preferred to visit a facility and doctor based on someone's previous experience and recommendation. I asked Monsura how she had selected this hospital for her son, Joy. She replied, "Ratna pushed me to go to this hospital. She said it was well known for taking of children suffering from diarrhoea. That is why I decided to go, and it didn't cost me much to pay for Joy's treatment." Ratna added, "Yes, when my daughter was sick many years ago, someone sent me to this hospital and they took good care of my girl." This hospital is unusual as it is well organised and known to provide hugely subsidised care for poor mothers and children in Dhaka.

Sayyied had also been quite unwell recently. Ratna mentioned, "He will need to have an (hernia) operation. It will cost them TK5,000 (approximately US$87 in 2002). I told them that I would lend them TK2,000 (approximately US$35 in 2002), but I told them they would need to get the rest of the money from elsewhere." I had given Monsura cash on different occasions and wanted to wait and see if she could gather cash from others, before relying fully on me. Monsura had also asked her brother-in-law for a loan of TK5,000 (approximately US$87 in 2002) for the operation, but she was not confident he could lend them the full amount. She was debating whether they should have the operation in her home village, as advised by her mother, or stay in Dhaka. She preferred Dhaka, as his brother lived in the city, and she could call them in an emergency. Based on discussions with Ratna and Abdul, and some advice from Sayeeda, they decided that in Dhaka treatment would be better, compared to that which was available in the villages. I asked about Sayyied's symptoms and Monsura shared, "He feels a swelling down there (groin) and he has pain. He cannot lift anything, and he wants to lie in bed all the time." Sayyied had completely stopped working at this time, fearing that any pressure could worsen his health, and he seemed depressed. Monsura was worried, but also frustrated with him. She mentioned that if he had worked regularly in the past, they would have had enough savings to cover the costs of his operation.

Both households were in crisis. Good health was mandatory for survival. For very poor households, health was an asset, in fact their only asset, as their 'body' was the material possession they had and being able to work was survival (see, van der Heijden et al., 2019). Abdul had a stable job. He had studied up to class 8 and was able to get this job, but he feared that if his illness persisted, he may be fired. Such jobs were hard to find. Most slum residents worked in the informal sector, and a smaller percentage had formal employment in factories. Sayyied was still gathering money for his operation, and the thought of undergoing surgery terrified him. Fears of chronic or more serious conditions, including surgery, created panic and dread. To add to their woes, a lot of cash is usually required for treating persistent and long- term health conditions, a luxury they could ill-afford. Ratna and Monsura were concerned that 'if something were to happen' to their husbands, this would have devastating consequences. Ratna's future security depended on Abdul's health, although she had strong family networks and was a landlady in the slum. The same situation applied to Monsura, except she was a tenant, and more vulnerable, with fewer networks to access and had a little baby. They observed how female-headed households tend to be much more financially constrained and vulnerable, and neither woman wanted to suffer the same fate. As others have also noted, in both urban and rural areas, widowed, divorced, and abandoned women constitute 20% to 30% of the population (Afsar, 1996), with women remain part of the very poor (Ahmed & Ahmmed, 2015).

Razia's Unplanned Situation: The Hidden Clinic

The importance of maintaining relationships, even at great cost to one's health, is a consequence of the gender related vulnerabilities for women living in slums. In late April, I visited Roshonara and Razia at their mother's place. Razia was still working in a garments factory, but she had recently fallen pregnant and decided to have an abortion. She told me that she had sex with her husband, Shahed. I knew that Shahed and she were separated due to unpaid dowry money that his family was demanding. I asked her if they had reconciled. She shook her head, and said, "I sometimes go to see him, but he hides it from others (his family)." According to her, he wanted to have sex with her whenever he saw her. She said, "I have affection for him. I didn't want to have sex with him because I am so hurt by his behaviour, but I didn't want him to go elsewhere. He is a man, after all." She was pleased that he still desired her, as rumours were swirling in the slum that he might remarry. I asked her about Khalid, because I last heard she was seeing him, during her separation from Shahed. She laughed and shrugged these off as 'nasty rumours' and claimed that she was still involved with her husband, despite what people said.

Roshonara, her elder sister, reached out to Sayeeda for advice. They did not want to use the NGO clinic in the slum. They asked if Sayeeda could take them to another clinic, a private one, that would allow Razia to maintain her anonymity. I advised both Roshonara and Razia to use the local clinic, which was safe and legal, and she would be referred to headquarters, where there were qualified personnel. But both were adamant about their decision. As noted in an earlier chapter, Sayeeda's income was low, and she earned additional cash by also working as a broker and was paid for each woman she took to this private clinic for terminations. This facility catered to all women, and those who did not qualify for a legal termination because they were more than 12 weeks pregnant, as per the law. Although from what I gathered, Razia was well within the 12 weeks of her pregnancy, but I didn't probe and just asked if I could accompany them when they went. They agreed.

When the time was fixed, we rode on two rickshaws to the clinic, Sayeeda, and me in one rickshaw and Roshonara and Razia in the second. It was a ten-minute ride, and the clinic was tucked away in an obscure street corner with no visible signs outside the door. We climbed a steep flight of narrow stairs, with only a dim light to help us navigate our way. The steps were filthy and littered with papers and the walls, once white, were now stained a darkish brown and grey, with marks and stains. The place had a strong odour of a popular, toilet cleaning detergent, Harpic powder. When we got to the third floor, where the clinic was located, there was no sign. We were met at the narrow entrance by a surly guard, who asked us to remove our slippers and wait. Sayeeda called someone on her phone and then an older woman, in a white coat, opened the door and let us in. We were asked to wait in a small waiting area, while Sayeeda went inside to another room to discuss Razia's case. Razia looked nervous. She looked at Roshonara and said, "I am scared, will it hurt you think?" Roshonara looked annoyed and replied, "Well you should have thought about all this when you had sex with him." Razia looked like she was about to cry. I quickly reached over and grabbed her hands and held them. She smiled gratefully at me. The woman came back into the room and ushered Razia into another room, where the procedure would take place. I asked Roshonara why she was being so hard on Razia, and she just shook her head and said, "You don't know Razia … I know her, she is my sister. She brings trouble on herself." She became quiet. I didn't say anything.

The entire procedure took about 20 minutes. Razia was ushered out and given a prescription to buy some medicines for pain. She had been given no anaesthesia during the vacuum aspiration procedure, as this would have cost too much. Razia was slightly hunched over and had her hands in front of her belly, hugging herself. Roshonara hurriedly got up from the chair and went closer to Razia and put her arms around her. We walked slowly down the stairs with Sayeeda following closely behind us. Razia had tears streaming down her face, and she said, "It feels like my lungs, liver … everything was being torn from inside. It was so painful. I was petrified but the woman didn't even comfort me. She barely spoke to me." The lack of empathy and disrespect shown by health providers to patients from poorer households was quite common in clinics and facilities in the country. It is not surprising that unless one needed a medical intervention, most preferred to visit a local drug shop.

We went back to Roshonara's mother's place so Razia could lie down. I swung by a few days later to check on Razia to find out that she was still persistently bleeding. The bleeding continued into the second week and Roshonara decided to ask Sayeeda to come and check on Razia.

I was with Razia when Sayeeda walked in. Razia explained, "My work is affected now because the bleeding is still happening. It has been 14 days, and the bleeding doesn't stop." Sayeeda seemed to be defensive and responded, "Why don't you wait a few more days ... and then we'll see!' Then Sayeeda asked if Razia could do an ultrasonogram. Roshonara was annoyed and said, "But this will cost money and why would she need to do this? We already spent money on this (termination)." Razia piped up, "I did the WASH[2] (i.e., common term to refer to the termination) and I took medicines, and I am still not better." Sounding irritated, Razia said, "Sayeeda *apa* (sister), we can't keep spending money on this."

Sayeeda sighed and said, "Look, doing a termination is never good for one's body." Razia was upset and replied, "I didn't do it on purpose, I got myself into a situation, where I had to do it. I didn't have a choice. If the man doesn't want to take responsibility for my pregnancy ... then what choice do I have?" She was getting excited and Roshonara told Razia to calm down. Sayeeda and Roshonara stepped outside to chat. Razia, who had dark circles under her eyes, lay back on the pillow, looking defeated and sad. Suddenly she started groaning and whispered that she was feeling faint. I yelled out to Roshonara and Sayeeda to come back inside. They rushed inside, and Roshonara rushed to the water tap to get some cold water, which Sayeeda began to pour on her head. Sayeeda asked Roshonara to get some warm milk for Razia and asked for mustard oil. Sayeeda looked visibly shaken and began to vigorously rub the oil on Razia's legs, hands, and feet. Roshonara was assisting Sayeeda, and I began to also assist them. After a few minutes, Razia opened her eyes and shared that she was feeling slightly better. Roshonara gave her some milk to drink. Sayeeda advised Roshonara to buy some spinach, eggs, and chicken which Razia needed to eat over the next few days, and she rushed over to her INGO clinic and came back with some medicines for Razia to take, including some antibiotics and more pain medication. She didn't take any money for the medicines.

Sayeeda and I left half an hour later, when Razia appeared to have improved. Sayeeda promised to take Razia back to the clinic where she had had the termination for a follow up check-up, in a few days. As we walked towards Sayeeda's home, she shared, "If anything happened to Razia, then I would be in jail. I am always scared, what if a woman dies ... I was so scared ... but now she is okay after getting her body massaged." She was pensive. After a few minutes, she added, "Her body does not have blood and that is why she has become weak." I asked if it would have been better to have just taken Razia to the clinic where she worked, given these complications were occurring. She snorted in derision and said, "Well Razia is claiming this is her husband's baby, but we all know she has been wandering around with Khaled. It must be his baby." Noting my surprised expression, she added, "Didn't you know … this is what everyone is saying. She was hoping Khaled would want to marry her when she fell pregnant." I was taken aback by this news, but I understood why Roshonara and Razia were adamant about going to a private facility, and Roshonara's cutting comments to Razia, right before the procedure.

Although pregnancy terminations are legal in Bangladesh, most women prefer to keep it quiet and avoid judgement when seeking to end their pregnancies. Young working married women who came to the INGO clinic, asking for a procedure, faced open and covert snide comments and gossip and allegations about having affairs on their husbands and trying to 'get rid of an illegitimate baby.' Older women were ridiculed for being sexually active well past the acceptable 'age' as 'grandmothers' and, embarrassed by their situation, they often sought a termination in secrecy. Unmarried girls and their mothers cooked up stories of a shotgun wedding gone wrong and the need to terminate the pregnancy. Either way, Razia was too embarrassed to divulge she was sexually active with Khaled, given that she was already married. However, her relationship was in limbo with her husband, who seemed to have abandoned her. Being separated or unmarried, particularly after a certain age, made one vulnerable to taunts and ridicule in the slums. Razia was 17, well beyond the age of marriage, which in 2002 was on average 13 to 14 years of age. Razia was desperate to start a family and had been pining for her husband to return to her for quite some time, but he had not returned.

Mamoni, a good friend of Razia's and the tenant's daughter, confided to me that Razia was very depressed. She shared, "She just cries in the room all day. Roshonara and Chachi (Razia's mother) are worried about her but they are also getting impatient with her." Mamoni felt that they didn't understand how deeply affected Razia was emotionally and mentally by the rejection by Shahed and now Khaled. She went onto explain how young women drank poison or did 'crazy things' in the name of love and was concerned for Razia and was keeping an eye on her. According to Mamoni, Razia desperately wanted to be married, have a 'husband, baby and finally a *shongshor* (household) of her own,' but those dreams were brutally ripped away. She was let down by her husband, and now felt betrayed again by Khaled, her boyfriend, who she thought would be happy to commit once he heard she was pregnant. Razia was tired of being talked about in the slum. Separated young women were often gossiped about, insulted during quarrels, and referred to as 'bad women,' and those who left their husbands were referred to as 'the wife who could not eat her husband's rice' – a serious insult as it casts aspersions on a woman's character. Razia was also craving affection and love, after being so brutally rejected by her husband.

Mamoni's fears of Razia 'hurting herself' were not unfounded, as I had heard a few stories of young women, and of a young man attempting self-harm, due to a love affair gone wrong or getting rejected. Despite being emotionally distraught, young women didn't seem to receive much sympathy, other than from very close friends, but rarely from family members and relatives. Many of them like Razia were adolescents grappling with 'adult' predicaments and tried to cope the best they could, in a place where there was a lot of judgement on emotional entanglements, outside of marriage, which was viewed as immoral.

Death in the Family

On top of this recent crisis, Roshonara's father, Chentoo Mia, suddenly died of a heart attack in early May. He lived between two households, dividing his time, spending some time every few weeks with his first wife, Chachi, and his daughters, and the rest of his time with his second, younger wife, who lived in another slum. When we met briefly in late March, he was complaining about his heart condition: "I have bad health. I have heart *roge* (heart disease). I feel for Roshonara, she is always looking for ways to earn money and Razia has been abandoned by her husband ... because we can't afford to pay the dowry money." He smiled wearily at me, standing slightly hunched. He was a tall man, but he seemed to look half his size. Their current plight seemed to have diminished him both emotionally and physically. He shared that he had taken some medicines from the local drug shop seller: "The pain comes and goes. When my worries increase, then the pain in my chest increases. This is our fate ... the fate of a poor man!" My last memory was of him sitting on his chair outside their compound door, wearing a sleeveless vest and *lunghi* (sarong), with his battered old radio turned up, blaring out Bengali songs, one after another, as he smiled to himself, nodding at passersby, and smoking a cigarette.

Smoking among males was popular in Phulbari, and it was a common sight to see men smoking as they chatted and drank tea at the local shops, or after work, sitting outside their homes. Chentoo Mia admitted that the habit was expensive, but it was his only vice, since giving up alcohol a few years ago. He was a heavy smoker, often chain smoking when he visited his wife – Chachi and his children. A study of urban slums in 2015 in Bangladesh found that the prevalence of tobacco consumption among adults was significantly higher (64%) than the national average (35.3%). The study also showed that there was a direct link between economic inequality and health inequality caused by cigarette use, with poorer populations bearing a heavier financial burden from tobacco expenses, increased healthcare costs, and lost productivity (Nargis et al., 2015).

It was Friday morning and I had just entered Roshonara's mother's place, and I found Roshonara sobbing uncontrollably. I panicked as I knew something terrible had happened. Chachi walked in, took a deep breath, and shared in an emotionless tone, "He has died, he is no longer alive." I was informed that Chentoo Mia died a few days ago, from a heart attack. Razia had found him collapsed on the floor of the main room. This was where most of the family members slept, on the large bed and on the floor. The rest of the day was a blur, with neighbours coming in and out of their home. Roshonara and Razia were crying but Chachi seemed to have her emotions under control. She was barking orders at Roshonara's husband who was running around planning burial arrangements. The family had to pool any savings left over and take a large loan from a money lender and the *samity*, to pay for the transport to carry his body back for burial in his home village, a few hours outside of Dhaka city. They had to pay a religious leader to organise a *milad* (prayer reading) in the village and feed all those in the community who attended the prayers for Chentoo Mia. These rituals are mandatory and a socio-cultural norm, to ensure 'safe passage of the departed soul to meet their creator, in the afterlife.'

Notes

1 Cinkara is a non-alcoholic vitaminised herbal tonic claiming to provide optimum quantities of essential minerals, trace elements & vitamins required by the body. https://hamdard.com.bd/product-detail/syrup-cinkara/
2 'WASH' was the term used to state that a termination was the 'washing out of the insides of the uterus.'

References

Afsar, R. (1996). *Onus of Poverty on Women in the Poorer Settlements of Dhaka City.* Dhaka: Women for Women Research and Study Group.

Ahmed, N., & Ahmmed, F. (2015). Problems and challenges of deserted women in Bangladesh: An observational study. *Journal of International Social Issues*, 3(1), 1–11.

Ahmed, S. M., & Hossain, M. A. (2007). Knowledge and practice of unqualified and semi-qualified allopathic providers in rural Bangladesh: Implications for the HRH problem. *Health policy*, 84(2–3),332–343.

Ahmed, S. M., Naher, N., Hossain, T., & Rawal, L. B. (2017). Exploring the status of retail private drug shops in Bangladesh and action points for developing an accredited drug shop model: A facility based cross-sectional study. *Journal of pharmaceutical policy and practice*, 10, 1–12.

Baer, H. A., Singer, M., & Susser, I. (1997). *Medical Anthropology and the World System: Critical Perspectives.* Bloomsbury Publishing.

Logan, K. (1983). Part 5: The role of pharmacists and over the counter medications in the health care system of a Mexican city. *Medical Anthropology*, 7(3), 68–89.

Nargis, N., Thompson, M. E., Fong, G. T., Driezen, P., Hussain, A. G., Ruthbah, U. H., Quah, A. C., & Abdullah, A. S. (2015). Prevalence and patterns of tobacco use in Bangladesh from 2009 to 2012: Evidence from International Tobacco Control (ITC) Study. *PloS one*, 10(11), e0141135.

Nichter, M., & Vuckovic, N. (1994). Agenda for an anthropology of pharmaceutical practice. *Social Science & Medicine*, 39(11), 1509–1525.

Rashid, S. F., & Islam, M. I. (2019). The invisible illness of life: Women's health narratives in a Dhaka informal settlement. https://blogs.lse.ac.uk/southasia/2019/05/20/lse-uc-berkeley-bangladesh-summit-2-the-invisible-illness-of-life-womens-health-narratives-in-a-dhaka-inform.

Scheper-Hughes, N. (1992). *Death without Weeping: The Violence of Everyday Life in Brazil*. University of California Press.

van der Heijden, J., Gray, N., Stringer, B., Rahman, A., Akhter, S., Kalon, S., Dada, M., & Biswas, A. (2019). 'Working to stay healthy', health-seeking behaviour in Bangladesh's urban slums: A qualitative study. *BMC Public Health*, 19(1), 1–13.

9　Health is a Battlefield, 2020–2022

Meena's Persistent Illnesses

Meena had reported suffering from bouts of weakness, insomnia, fever, colds, as well as menstrual problems, for the past two and a half years. She had suffered for as long as she could remember, and her health had deteriorated considerably. She worked around this since she had sole responsibility of managing the household. Liton had stopped working six years ago, when he was diagnosed with tuberculosis. Meena was frustrated because she wanted him to work, even if it was occasionally, but he rarely did. Even during severe illness episodes, Meena usually kept working, as she was terrified of losing her job as a maid or having her salary deducted. She did take sick leave a few times but only when she had no choice, and was simply unable to force herself to get out of bed to go to work. Meena usually walked to the homes she worked in, a 30-minute walk daily, each way. She rarely took a rickshaw to save money, and only took one, if she was feeling unwell, but had to go to work.

A major anxiety was she was no longer menstruating. In late 2020, she sought advice from *Mama* (uncle) Alam, who was the local drug shop-seller in their community. His tiny little medicine shop was tucked around the corner, in a muddy alleyway. He was popular with many of the residents. He informed her she was weak and had no blood in her body, and this had affected her menstrual cycle. He advised her to buy bags of blood to replenish her strength. This was not an option for Meena, because each bag of blood cost TK450 (approximately US$5.30 in 2020). She said, "I am barely managing financially, and I already have so many other costs to manage … food, rent."

Mama Alam was a crucial lifeline for Meena, and regularly provided strips of 'napa (for fever, body aches) tablets', and other medicines, syrups, and tonics, allowing her to pay later, in instalments. She was very close to him and didn't hesitate to seek him out, whenever needed: "I am very comfortable with him. I have known him for many years." By the end of 2021, she felt ashamed to ask him for any more medicines, as she owed him more than TK2,000 (approximately US$23.50). She did pay him, bit by bit, but it was many months later, and by gathering some of her monthly salary, and borrowing from her mother. But Meena was forever embedded in a cycle of debt to Alam, as she needed

DOI: 10.4324/9781003467472-9

medicines often, for the constant fevers, coughs, colds, body aches, and other ailments, from which she, her children, and Liton suffered.

Meena blamed her constant ill health on her being the sole primary rice-winner for the family, the long hours and demanding work schedule, the daily walk to work, and not eating enough. "I don't sit still for a minute. I am always on the move, cleaning all the rooms, washing clothes, helping the cook with food preparing meals ... and sometimes massaging my madam's (employer's) shoulders, back and head ... so in a few days, my body can't take it anymore and it reacts." She continued, "I walk in this heat every day. I don't have a day off. My legs ache after a few weeks ... our food quantity is much less, and we barely eat fish." Liton fidgeted uncomfortably while Meena was speaking. He interrupted to explain that his tuberculosis prevented him from working, "I feel so guilty as Meena works so hard. She feeds me and the children. She could have thrown me out, but she still takes care of me. I used to work, earning a lot of money in the past." Meena looked at him, but the expression on her face was unreadable, as he listed his physical symptoms: "bad knees, chest pains, weak legs." He was lamenting a life he previously lived and had, but now felt unable or was unwilling to resume, given his sickness. Despite his complaints, for most of 2021 and 2022, Liton was often idle, with a lot of his time spent at the local tea shop, or he stayed in bed, while Meena worried about the future. Meena mentioned that Liton and her daughter took care of her and did the household chores when she fell sick, "Liton often washes my head with cold water, and when my body hurts, he rubs my hands and feet with oil ... and sometimes he will even cook a meal (she smiled)."

According to Mita, Meena's mother, it was in fact, Meena's daughter Pinky, 13 years old, who was extremely resourceful and took care of the household chores, cooking and cleaning and caring for her mother. She was silent when asked about Liton. She later shared that Meena hung on to the marriage, because they had three children and it would be difficult to get Pinky married without a male guardian in the household, as local communities ask about the father of the household. This was shared by other married adolescent women, whom I spoke to. A divorce was highly stigmatised.

Meena Worries About Tuberculosis

In late 2021, Meena had a persistent cough and became concerned that she too might have tuberculosis. She had not separated Liton's plate at home, despite the advice of a health worker. She claimed it was impractical and difficult to do so. She also didn't want to hurt Liton's feelings who had reacted emotionally when she tried. They had very few plates, ate jointly and lived in one small room, the five of them slept, cramped together, on one bed. The room was dark and poorly lit, with a tiny window, not allowing for much ventilation. No one in their locality, except for Alam *Mama*, knew he had tuberculosis. According to her, the neighbours and other residents knew he was perpetually ill, and assumed it was from various ailments. The stigma of tuberculosis persists, and in 2019, a qualitative research study in Bangladesh found that tuberculosis patients and community members reported feeling depressed and anxious due to isolation of their utensils, and sometimes sleeping arrangements by family members, due to fear of getting the disease (Paul et al., 2019). For men and women, hiding the disease was paramount. They didn't want to be gossiped about and left out of social gatherings and job opportunities, and young unmarried adolescent females feared being considered 'unmarriageable.' Low self-esteem was widespread and discrimination from others was not uncommon.

Meena lay in bed for a few days hoping she would recover. When her cough continued for a week and she felt worse, she rushed to consult Alam: "I was very sick by now. I also had a cold, fever, and headache. I was suffering from chest pain for six days. *Mama* (Alam) told me to get an x-ray done immediately. I told him an x-ray costs a lot of money and where will I find the money? Uncle said he didn't know what medicine to give me, and he needed an x-ray to understand what my disease was." He insisted she borrow money and get it done as soon as possible. Meena, terrified by his insistence, feared the worst outcome: "what if I have a major disease? Will I die? What about my children? How can I manage the treatment cost!" She had sleepless nights, feeling her entire world was collapsing. Liton knew this wife was extremely depressed with her health situation: "Usually when my wife is lying down, I realise that she is not feeling well. She only stays in bed if she very ill. She is a very hardworking person. She has been crying because she is frightened that she may have my sickness, and we don't have money." He added, "We have been married for more than 15 years, so I know she is anxious. She cries quietly, turning her face away from me and she thinks I don't know."

Having no alternative and not being able to rely on Liton, Meena decided to visit her mother, Mita, for advice and solace. She felt guilty as she was aware since her mother's accident and leg injury, her mother was begging to earn an income. Mita was injured in a road accident in October 2021, as she walking to work. After the accident, she could no long work as a maid. She struggled to stand or walk for more than an hour, and now sat at street corners, begging for a living. After chatting to her mother who was very upset to hear about Meena's health condition, Mita reached out to her old employer, asking for a loan of TK2,000 (approximately US$23.50). Her old employer who was very fond of Mita gave her the amount. Meena used TK1,500 to pay for the x-ray at a nearby hospital and some cash for medicines, 'to ease the congestion in her chest.' She didn't have much money left, but she was very relieved she didn't have tuberculosis. During this period, Meena asked for sick leave for several days from her employer. Her current employer was furious. She was hosting a dinner party the next evening and was relying on Meena to clean half a dozen fish and chicken and help the main cook to prepare dishes to be served for 40 invited guests. Meena pleaded with her to allow her a few days of sick leave. Her employer didn't insist Meena come to work but deducted TK350 (approximately US$5) from her monthly salary of TK4,000 (approximately US$69 in 2021). Upset by this, Meena shared, "Does it matter this sum of money? She is rich, but this is a lot of money for us." But she was relieved she was not fired, and believed her boss was overall happy with her as she was punctual and hard working.

Meena is Sick Again

In March 2022, Meena reported she had jaundice and was unable to work for a few weeks, and she lost a month's salary. With her mother's help, Meena visited a local religious healer, buying a coconut and giving him 'a gift donation,' and visited *Mama* Alam for medicines, which she received on credit again. She was emotionally exhausted and in distress in early April 2022, because her employer had begun looking for a full-time live-in maid who would be available all the time, and she didn't want a part-time worker. She had warned Meena earlier in the year that this was a possibility. A maid was found from her employer's home village, and she let Meena go in early April 2002, with a full salary for the month. Meena's employer was also generous and sometimes would give her leftover food to take for her children, vegetable curry and sometimes left-over chicken. Now Meena was once again without a job.

In late April 2022, Meena began suffering from severe body aches and fever. I was on my way to visit her. I was overwhelmed with the smell of burnt rubber and sewage as I navigated my steps on the narrow uneven roads, with litter, bricks, and sand everywhere, to reach her place. This was a familiar experience when walking around slums or low-income settlements. I walked in and noticed the floor of their new place was cemented, with a tin roof. There was a cabinet in the corner with a few rumpled clothes, and two pots and two pans, and a few plates, stacked in the corner of the room. The room smelled musty and of sweat. Meena was lying on her bed. She appeared tiny and frail, covered by a threadbare thin, red cloth. The room was dark. Her two sons ran around the room, squealing and shouting, bare bodied, streaked with dirt and dressed in ragged shorts. Their hair was a blondish brown, the colour of hair when it has been out in the sun for long, unwashed, and uncared for. One of the younger sons had snot running down his nose. Liton pulled him over a few times to wipe his nose and face, with his *lunghi* (sarong).

Liton sat near the corner of the bed, near Meena's feet. She tried to lift herself up when I walked in, but failed to do, and lay down again. She was very depressed. She spoke haltingly and softly, "*Apa* (sister), I don't know what to do? I don't have a job and now I am sick again. How will we survive?" Liton, who was sitting near her feet, retorted, "I tell her to eat more, but she eats less, saves all the food for the children and for me." Sounding annoyed, Meena managed to raise herself up, and replied, "I must make sure I have enough cash to buy food. A fear of mine is if he (Liton) doesn't eat well, he will die." She paused, and then added, the price of vegetables is going down now but fish and meat are still very expensive to buy." She bought fish twice in the last one month, but her children were upset and fed up with eating mainly potatoes, rice, and vegetables most days.

She mentioned that Liton was absent minded and couldn't be trusted to go to the market as he often bought 'rotten fish,' and didn't know how to haggle and lower prices with shop keepers. He remained quiet throughout this exchange, and then abruptly got up and left the room. Meena became quiet and then sighed loudly, "I need to look for work again, but I am so tired of always worrying about the future. This is my fate, *apa* (sister) … the destiny of a poor person. My heart is sad, and I am sick again." I was quiet and I didn't know how to comfort her. Her children continued to giggle and scream, kicking an empty plastic bottle of coke at each other, oblivious to Meena's pain and dread about the future. She looked at them, with a mixture of exasperation and tenderness. She apologised and indicated she needed to sleep. I left shortly afterwards.

Shuli's and Shumon's Chronic Health Conditions

Shumon and Shuli were close. They both worked hard and supported each other. They talked on the phone often, sometimes twice or thrice in a day. With a grin on her face, Shuli shared, "We have sex often." She looked at me questioningly and added, "Why would someone get married and not have sex? He is my husband, and he wants it … and I can't live without it!" Shuli was on the pill, which Shumon bought for her monthly, from a drug shop near his workplace or in the slums they lived in. She was adamant she did not want any more children. She already had two children from her first marriage, who lived with her mother, Jorina and a baby girl, Arifa, two years old, with Shumon, husband from her second marriage. They claimed that they didn't suffer from 'serious life-threatening illnesses,' and dealt with some 'persistent health issues', but 'it was part of life and they needed to keep working.'

Between 2020 and March 2022, Shumon worked in temporary jobs, despite repeated 'chest pains, and aches in his stomach and abdomen.' He was diagnosed with acidity and gastric problems, and he bought medicines from various drug shops. Shumon's gastric problems increased in the second half of 2021, but he continued working, only taking breaks when he couldn't find work. Most of the income earning opportunities available were temporary. One of the drug sellers asked Shumon to have an x-ray done. As cash was tight, Shumon did not do so. He managed his discomfort and uneasiness by taking tablets, and 'prayed and hoped his health condition wouldn't worsen.' He also believed that doing a series of tests would not stop this illness, as his work aggravated his condition. He ate fried foods and street snacks for his afternoon meals. As a labourer, it was difficult for him to carry home-cooked food to the construction sites. Shuli and Shumon usually ate a small breakfast in the mornings and they both headed out to work. Shuli bought one or two bananas and bread from a local tea shop and that was usually her afternoon meal. She carried semolina for her baby. They ate a cooked meal in the evenings, after they returned from work. Shuli remained anxious about Shumon's 'chest pains,' but mentioned they didn't have enough money to do x-rays. She was also worried that if the doctor demanded more tests, this was not possible. They didn't have sufficient cash for an endless cycle of tests, medicines and waiting hours in health facilities to see a doctor.

Shuli was quite dismissive of her urinary tract infection symptoms. In 2021 and in early 2022, she shared that suffered from burning sensations when urinating and felt discomfort. Only when she felt it was unmanageable, she consulted *Nana* (unrelated - grandfather) at the Tamanna drug shop in Gulshan 1 for some medicines. He didn't charge her for medicines, as he had known her for a long time. He advised her to increase her water intake and gave her some tablets. She shared, "I walk around in the hot sun, and I don't drink enough water. I can't keep drinking water then I will need to go to the toilet a lot." She limited her water intake, because she wanted to reduce the number of times she had to use the free public toilets, located in the markets of Gulshan 1. Another obstacle for Shuli was that she couldn't keep leaving Arifa with other hawkers and beggars if she constantly made visits to the toilet. She preferred to keep Arifa close to her. While she admitted that 'they were all like family,' and some of the hawkers would assist, everyone was busy looking out for potential customers on the roads. She had learned to hold in her urine as much as possible and didn't think much of it. It was part of her daily life, because of the nature of her work. Similarly, Fatema, who also sold towels on the streets, mentioned that she avoided drinking water to minimise her toilet use, to only twice a day: "my goal is to sell, make cash and return home as soon as I can to be with my children. I don't drink much water, even if I am thirsty. I can hold it in up to an hour or more, and then I drink more water when I am home." The few free toilets available for them were filthy and stank of stale urine and faeces. There was water available, an old bucket and a small mug, inside the toilet, and the floor was often wet and streaked with dirt. Soap was rarely available. There was another toilet in the markets, which was cleaner, but people had to pay TK5 each time they used it. This was costly for Shuli and Fatema, as each taka earned was critical. On rare occasions, Shuli and Fatema had access to a toilet in the one of the high-end retail shops on the main road, as the manager knew them. For the most part, both managed the best they could, as they had no other alternative.

Health was a worry, but not being able to work meant no cash, and this was needed to buy food, pay rent and to manage daily social relationships. Poorer residents feared being evicted by the landlord or landlady and ending up on the streets. A reputation was critical in these communities, to be able to rent and make payments was important, if one had to leave from place and rent another place in the same slum. Health was only a priority if it meant life or death, as Shuli explained: "We are poor people … we do not have the time to worry about all this, we must keep working."

Death and the Kindness of Strangers

On March 9, 2022, Shumon was tragically killed in a road accident in Moha-khali. He was on his way to work with his friend, who was riding a motorbike. The work opportunity was an hour away in Gazipur. Shuli sat in the corner of her bed, cross-legged, her back up against the wall, holding her baby girl in arms. In between tears and long pauses, she recounted the events leading up to his demise: "I was waiting for him to come home for dinner that evening … I called him, but he was not answering his phone. We talk at least twice a day wherever we are. In my heart, I was feeling uneasy. But I couldn't explain why. I later find out that the accident happened in front of BCPS (Bangladesh College of Physicians and Surgeons), in Mohakhali." Shumon was in a coma for five days and then passed away while his friend was killed immediately. Shuli was informed by her landlady and immediately rushed to the hospital after midnight. She took a rickshaw and with her baby daughter in her arms headed over the hospital which only a few minutes away, as they were living nearby. An older male tenant helped her find a rickshaw.

Shuli was met by a young student at the hospital. His name was Shiva, and he had found the landlady's number on Shumon's phone. He called her and asked her to inform Shuli. He had been drinking tea with his friends when they witnessed the accident in the evening. A few of the students along with Shiva admitted Shumon at the government hospital. Shuli continued: "Shiva is a third-year student at Open University and lives in this area. They heard a loud bang and thinks the driver might have lost control and a bus was involved." Soon after, a crowd of local shopkeepers and some pedestrians rushed over to help the injured men, and some of them gathered around, waiting for the police to come before they could take them to the hospital. Shuli mentioned that Shumon and his friend were not wearing helmets. She said, "The (landlady) gave me the news at night and my head began to spin … I didn't know what to think. I was praying that they had the wrong information, but I came to the hospital, and he was there." She was frightened to see him nonresponsive and hooked up to a ventilator. The doctor informed her that his chances of surviving were less than 10%. She was in shock and consumed with fear and anxiety; the thought of losing him and the daily costs of keeping him alive at the hospital. The five days of treatment came to more than TK20,000 (approximately US$233); the equivalent of five months of rent for Shuli or buying hundreds of towels wholesale, to sell on the streets. Desperate, Shuli turned to Shiva for financial support: "I cried to the young man (Shiva). I was helpless. I told him I was poor, and he was educated. I had no money and I begged him to help me." Shiva mobilised donations from friends, students, and local shopkeepers in the area, and raised TK15,000 (approximately US$175).

Shuli used TK3,000 (approximately US$35) of her own money, pawned Shumon's phone and received some cash. She didn't want to sell his phone now, but planned to do so later, when she needed more cash. Pawning a phone is usually done with known persons, so the phone is returned and payment is assured. She also sold her gold earrings, which Shumon had given her three years ago: "I sold my gold earrings at the gold shop. After three days and my husband was still in hospital, I went to the shopkeeper and told him that my husband had an accident and I needed money. He offered me TK4,000 (approximately US$46.50), but Shumon had bought it for TK7,500 (approximately US$87). She agreed as she was desperate. Two of Shumon's friends came to know about his death and paid TK6,000 (approximately US$70) for an ambulance to take his body back to his village for the burial. As her daughter played with her hair, Shuli appeared listless, her voice void of emotions. She continued talking: "My husband died in the afternoon … around 5 pm on March 13, and at 9 pm that night, we went to the village with my husband's body. My husband's village home is Faridpur." While Shuli was accompanied by her children, her mother didn't accompany her: "She did not come. She (mother) came to the hospital once, and after that I heard she was sick." When asked how she felt about her mother not travelling with her to the village, Shuli admitted she was in shock and hadn't slept for many days: "I was crying all the time and Fatema told my mother that she should support me. My mother told her she couldn't go to the burial with me as she was unwell. My brother also didn't come to see me." Shuli's main support for the past eight years was Shumon, and she had a strained relationship with her mother. Fatema was very critical that Shuli's mother did not provide financial or emotional support, nor did she accompany her daughter with the body back to the village: "She is her mother, she should have been there. This is such a tragedy for Shuli." Shuli did not work for almost two weeks and therefore could not earn any money from begging or selling towels. She had no income, and her savings were gone. She continued to be depressed, and Fatema said that she barely saw Shuli on the streets during most of March.

Road accidents are a serious public health problem in Dhaka city. A study in 2021 reports from 2015 to 2020, a total number of 1746 road accidents were recorded in Dhaka city; with 89.75% victims who were pedestrians. 17% of them were between 36 to 40 years old and 13.4% were between 21 to 25 years old (Jianxin et al., 2021). The vehicles responsible for these accidents, include buses (35.24%), motorbikes (12.31%), and heavy trucks (10.14%). About half of the total pedestrian accidents were found to occur while a person was crossing the road at level crossings, overpasses, and underpasses (Podder et al., 2019). For the poor, this involves injuries, permanent disabilities, or death, and families may incur massive financial costs for treatment and care. This is an enormous set back, as we see for Mita, Fatema and Shuborna: being injured affects one's ability to work and the impact can be devastating. The death of Shumon, which was a typical road accident that occurs often in Dhaka city, left young Shuli a widow, alone to navigate herself in the slum and on the streets, with a baby girl to raise on her own.

Fatema's Accident

Fatema found out she was pregnant again in late February 2021. She was very unhappy. This was unexpected, and with the stress of the past year with Covid-19 lockdown in 2020, job losses, mounting debts and loans, this was unwelcome news. She already had a one and half year-old daughter. She shared, "I knew I was pregnant; I had stopped taking the pill for some time. I forgot with all that has been going on in the household. I began to feel sick a lot, my menstruation had not happened. I was tired … I already have a daughter … so I went to *Mama* (unrelated, referred to as uncle) for some medicines to get rid of this pregnancy." *Mama* was Alam, the same local drug seller who provided medicines regularly to Meena. Fatema was worried about their financial situation, but he admonished her and advised her against ending the pregnancy. She continued: "*Mama* told me you will work and have enough money in a few months to look after a second child. Look, I can make a profit and sell you medicines, but I know you and your family for a long time. I think you need to think about this decision. You only have one child so a second one will be good. A child is a blessing from Allah."

Fatema was apprehensive and recalled her first pregnancy, pre-Covid in 2019 and the huge costs incurred. Fatema was told by the doctor to have a caesarean, which cost her TK26,000 (approximately US$308), for delivery, surgery, and hospital costs. She was confused and felt bullied into the decision by the providers. She used her savings from working until a week before delivery, and cash from her brother to cover the costs. She said, "I worked for a long time and saved TK20,000 (approximately US$237) from selling towels, as I wanted to go to this known hospital. Many in this neighbourhood have given birth there." As this was her first child, she relied on the advice of trusted older woman who took her to the hospital. A caesarean was required. Her mother-in-law and sister-in-law cooked for her and brought food over, post-delivery. Despite being close to her brother and parents, she didn't expect them to financially support her given everyone was managing their own households and had cash constraints. She shared, "How much will my parents give me? And where will my older brother give me so much money? My brother must work, and he supports my parents. Why should I take cash cost from my own family and deprive them?'

However, Fatema was confused and trusted *Mama* implicitly and knew he cared. He was after all 'like family' and not just a drug shop seller. For many residents, trust and relationships were important. The fact that he was referred to as an uncle, meant that his advice was taken very seriously. While in public health we may simply categorise someone like Alam as an untrained drug shop seller, to Fatema and Meena, and many others, he was like family; someone they knew in their community, who they have turned to over the years, during a health crisis. This deep bond is critical to recognise and cannot be overstated. While many qualified trained doctors and the formal health sector view drug shop sellers, religious healers, and traditional healers as 'quacks,' for the residents, they are known, depended upon and respected. One cannot discount the importance of social relationships, trust, and religious and local understandings of an illness, which inform and influence behaviour and health decisions.

Fatema's husband supported her decision, but her mother and sister-in-law were against the termination and believed it was wrong. Fatema felt guilty because her sister-in-law had been struggling to conceive for some time and she was upset to hear that Fatema was looking for ways to end this pregnancy, while she was desperate to conceive. Her sister-in-law had visited several *kabirajis* (traditional healers) and religious healers in her home village and in Dhaka city and had visited a clinic recently. The neighbours were already gossiping about her sister-in-law and often taunted Fatema about when Faruk's wife would have a baby, and 'if she had a problem.' Fatema's brother Faruk had been married for three years. Fatema was very protective of her brother and his wife and became extremely upset when she heard these 'nasty remarks' about her family. Faruk was worried about his wife's mental state: "she agonises about her fertility. She doesn't like to eat much … she avoids talking to people in the community. I know she is anxious. I went to a doctor with her because she insisted, and he said there is no problem. My mother-in- law has taken my wife to many different providers … it will happen when Allah decides. I told her it is in Allah's hands!" Fatema explained that her brother had a love marriage and was deeply religious and had full faith that his wife would conceive in the future. For a young woman, a baby is considered an essential part of a marriage. A child strengthens a woman's standing in the household, and strengthens the relationship between a husband and wife, and with one's in-laws. Usually when a young woman struggles to conceive, the woman is seen as the problem and blamed, never the male, and there is always a fear of one's husband remarrying or desertion (Nahar, 2021).

In the end, Fatema listened to *Mama* (the drug shop seller) and didn't go against her mother's and sister-in-law's wishes. While pregnant, she continued selling towels on the streets, saving money, until a week before she delivered on October 2021. Fatema is less than five feet tall, and as her pregnancy progressed, her stomach was very visible, protruding, as she rushed from car to car, in the hot sun, desperately looking for customers to sell towels to. She mentioned that in the last few months of the pregnancy, she "felt heavy … it was like carrying a large bag on my body." She also increased her food intake, having more than one banana and several bread rolls and her mother would sometimes bring a rice and curry meal for her in the afternoons. After the delivery, Fatema rested for only a few months, breastfeeding the baby, but she was forced to return to hawking on the streets in early 2022. Money was tight in the household, and it was getting difficult: "We need more cash, as I need to buy diapers, baby clothes, oil, and soap for my baby every month. These are extra costs, and it is expensive to run a family. My husband has a job, but the salary is low."

The Rich Drunk Driver

It was in early April 2022, during Ramadan (the month of fasting) and close to evening, when traffic slows down, and all the activities quieten, as people go home, ready to break their fast. Fatema shuddered as she recalled the evening when she was hit by a car. Excited with the daily earnings, she had bought some food to celebrate: "I had a good profit that day, almost TK400 (approximately US$5). I had left my baby girl with my mother and my young daughter with my father. I went to buy some *biryani* (popular meat and rice dish) from the corner stall … I called my mother to tell her I was going to bring some boxes home for her and father and family to eat." After working all day, Fatema and Suborna (Shuli's daughter) walked out from the lane with the packets of food, and they began to cross the main road of Gulshan 1, expecting there to be no traffic. "It was about 6 o'clock and then suddenly out of nowhere, a car came at a very high speed and hit us. I can't remember, I think I blanked out, but I was hit, and I fell backwards. I was in excruciating pain and my body was slammed and thrown to the side. The car went over Shuborna's legs. She screeched in pain. Another hawker, Bahari, was also hit and fell. But Shuborna was really badly injured, compared to me."

The police arrived on the scene and promptly arrested the 'rich drunk, criminal,' as Fatema referred to him. Apparently, according to the hawkers, this was not the first time he had run over pedestrians and hawkers. Fatema was rushed by her mother and brother to a nearby hospital, Cure Medical Centre, a private facility in the area. The costs of an x-ray, medicines, and bandages cost Fatema TK8,000, which her family and husband gathered from their own money and money borrowed from a lender and her father's landlord. The police came to Fatema's place several days later and asked her whether she wanted to sign a piece of paper for 'the criminal's release,' or go to 'court' to challenge the criminal. Frightened, she replied, "I don't want to go to court and do a case … I don't have the money or the time. He is a rich man, and I don't want any trouble." She simply asked the police that the perpetrator pay her back for the costs she incurred from her injury. She signed but she didn't understand what the paper stated, and she didn't want a drawn-out case. She was hopeful that if she agreed to his release, he would pay her the TK8,000 (approximately US$93). She was very upset: "We didn't get one *paisha* (one cent) from the criminal," and was helpless to protest, and the police didn't seem sympathetic to her situation. Only after she signed the paper, the police informed her, "The one who has suffered the most will get money. We let you know but the other girl (Shuborna, Shuli's daughter) was very badly injured, and she will not be able to work for many months."

Helpless yet frustrated and angry with the police's response, Fatema replied, "I lost 15 working days because of this accident, who will give me my time back? I lost a lot of earnings, and we need to repay others for the hospital costs and medicines!" Despite her own predicament, Fatema was sympathetic towards Shuborna's plight – she was a young girl, only 12 years old and she would not be able to work for several months. Both her legs were in plaster. She also didn't know how much cash Shuborna or her grand-mother received from the perpetrator, but she had heard 'rumours' that the cash given didn't cover all the costs. Fatema reflected that "he was arrested initially, and he has three or four cases against him, but the police eventually let him go. He must have given them a lot of money."

Weak enforcement of road safety laws in Bangladesh, poor accountability, and bribes to law enforcement officers, a bureaucratic court system, and money and time to pursue cases, means that those who are poor, have the least capacity to demand justice. Their marginal status weighs heavily against them. When Fatema was unable to sell towels and lay in bed, resting her injured foot, her mother and brother supported her financially and provided her and her family with daily meals. Her husband, Riaz, continued to work in temporary jobs, and brought in some cash to keep their household afloat. She returned to the streets to hawk, a few weeks later.

References

Jianxin, Y., Rabbi, F., Siraj, M. B., & Zhenzhen, L. (2021). Road traffic accident situation in Dhaka City, Bangladesh. *Journal of Transportation Systems*, 6(3), 23–34.

Nahar, P. (2021). Childlessness in Bangladesh: Intersectionality, suffering and resilience. https://doi.org/10.4324/9781003050285.

Paul, S., Afzal Aftab, M. R., Nazneen, S., Azmi, R., & Hossain, S. (2019). Subjective experiences of stigma related to Tuberculosis: A qualitative exploration at Peri-urban, Bangladesh. *Am. J. Prev. Med. Public Health*, 4(2), 27–36.

Podder, V., Morita, T., & Tanimoto, T. (2019). Reducing road traffic accidents in Bangladesh. *The Lancet*, 393(10169), 315.

10 Displaced Lives in 2002

Eviction and Instability

July 24: The Day Before the Demolition of Phulbari

Phulbari was one of the larger, more notorious slums, known for its 'drug trade and criminal gangs.' It had been established in Mirpur, in Dhaka City, in the 1980s. I walked in to find the place abuzz with news that the slum was going to be demolished the next day. Announcements on the loudspeakers stated it was a government order, and all residents would have to leave or would be forcibly removed by armed personnel. Men were going around in three-wheeler rickshaws, reinforcing this, urging residents to leave with all their belongings by 2 pm on July 25.

I had entered Phulbari through section 1. A few women had gathered around, and I could hear murmured conversations, women sharing that they would go back to the village, others saying they would wait and see if all the homes would be demolished. An older woman turned to me and whispered, "I went to the bazaar. You know what the shopkeepers said to me, 'If you leave who will we sell our vegetables to? Here we are serving so many communities ... how will we manage?'" A younger woman, standing nearby, narrowed her eyes and said, "The bazaar people are saying this but what will happen to us!" I sensed bewilderment, confusion, and anxiety.

Roshanara was in tears: "I have been here since I was a child. I came here wearing half-pants ... I would play here. Now they are saying that we must all go!" Roshonara had recently taken a loan and invested in a tea shop. The cash situation was finally stable after a long time. But she lost it all with this demolition. Her father had recently died and they had no other family in the city. The announcement of eviction was sudden; they were unprepared and in shock. She sighed, "My mother will have to go back to the village. We have no options. Everything we owned is gone with this slum!" After trying my best to comfort her; failing to do so, I promised to return and rushed off in frantic search for Monsura.

Monsura, Sayyied, and Joy had moved to a room across from Ratna's place. When I walked in, I found Monsura frantically sorting out her belongings, the few that she had, scattered in the tiny room. Joy lay in the corner of the room, screaming his head off again and sitting in a pool of his

DOI: 10.4324/9781003467472-10

own urine with snot running down his face. Monsura was screaming at him, threatening to beat him; he continued to wail hysterically. She found me standing at the entrance of her tiny room, and gave me a tired, slightly embarrassed, and impatient smile. She had dark circles under her eyes. Her hair looked messy and unbrushed, and her sari was crumpled. She waved her arm around the tiny room, "We need to pack and move out as soon as possible." She squatted on the floor and started putting her meagre belongings into a large polythene bag and another cardboard box. Sayyied had left to find a new place to rent, and he was selling the fan to earn some quick cash. Monsura calmly said, "Let them break this place. Now Ratna's arrogance will be destroyed." I asked Monsura if she was feeling sad about leaving the slum. With anger, she replied, "Why should I feel sad? I want to leave. I don't know anyone here. The landlords in this place, they treat us like dirt. They always demand rent, and they don't have any compassion for the tenants. Look at Ratna and how she treated us!" Monsura was a new tenant without strong ties in the slum and she was not a homeowner; leaving was not as big a loss for her and her family, compared to Roshonara and Sayeeda.

Slums are heterogenous communities, with varying structures, but tenants are usually dependent on landlords and other gatekeepers, including local leaders (*mastaans*). Those who owned homes in the slums lost their security, established networks and income, either because they lived rent free or received rental income from tenants. I left Monsura's place and walked across the lane to check on Ratna. The tin door to her compound was flung wide open. I walked in to find her sitting on the floor. Her head in her hands, she sobbed uncontrollably. This home was her pride and it had provided security for her and her family for 15 years. Oblivious to the chaos unfolding, her two daughters were giggling and chasing each other near the now empty kitchen. She was in no state to talk.

I walked over to the clinic to check on Sayeeda and Sufia. Sayeeda looked visibly distressed and shouted, you must have heard by now ... they are demolishing the slum tomorrow." She continued speaking rapidly: "*Dula bhai* (brother-in-law, Malek Master) is meeting with others ... they will try and stop this from happening." The clinic walls were being dismantled by some men. Sayeeda was peeling posters off the tin walls and Sufia was quietly organising patients' files and placing them into a cardboard box, ready to be taken to the office headquarters in Lalmatia, a suburb, almost an hour away. Forced eviction of residents was taking place the next day and everyone was jittery and worried. The manager of the clinic from the main office had arrived to supervise the shutting down of this clinic. She mentioned since women in the slum would still need health care, the NGO might re-establish this clinic in a new slum. However, no clear decision had been taken by senior management, and Sayeeda and Sufia were anxious about their jobs.

As I waited around, Sayeeda told me how that morning (July 24) the police had violently attacked residents who were conducting a peaceful demonstration on Mirpur streets. Police began spraying tear gas on the crowds and then started indiscriminately beating them with their batons. Several of the landlords and a few of the leaders walked over with one of the slum leaders to a home, pleading for help and support to stop the eviction, but Sayeeda told me, "His son came out and abused us. He said, 'Go away. My father did not win on your votes'." She continued, "How badly they treat us poor people! We rallied and got him his votes. But, in the end he kicked us out like dogs." Defeated, most residents returned to the slum and continued dismantling and packing.

Meanwhile, speculation was rife about possible betrayal from some factions within Phulbari, who had vested interests, with a few leaders, including Malek Master, identified. When Sayeeda walked outside the clinic, Sufia whispered to me, "Her brother-in-law, Malek Master and some of the other leaders took money from us, every month. They told us that this cash was required to fight cases against eviction and from any kind of takeover of the land here. I don't know ... why this is happening, but we have been paying for years!" Reports varied that payments were made as early as the 90s. I came to know that almost all the landlords, in addition to purchasing a one roomed space from various leaders in different sections of the slum, continued to pay a monthly amount, in the hope of becoming 'legal' landowners one day, or at least to avoid eviction. Like Bangladesh, Das and Randeria describe that in India, local leaders (*mastaans*) in slums engage in party politics, running around the courts, seeking legal support from human rights lawyers and any bureaucratic connections to strategise on how to counter evictions (Das & Randeria, 2015). Although looming in their lives is a level of uncertainty over how secure their tenancy is, most are used to the lives of temporality given they lack any legal recognition.

As I walked around, I noticed large crowds of people gathering to discuss the eviction news. There were rickshaws and van carts were being filled with boxes, as people began to sell off or move their belongings to a new slum, or to return to their natal village if they had family support.

July 25: The Demolition of Phulbari Takes Place

> The government ordered the demolition of Phulbari, despite court orders declaring that evictions without providing rehabilitation for residents are illegal. On the morning of July 25, 2002, seven bulldozers demolished all the homes. Thousands of poor men, women and children watched in shock. Many were openly sobbing, while hundreds of armed government policemen stood nearby, ready to confront any resistance. Within three hours, residents' lives had been turned upside down and they had lost everything. Many had lived here for more than twenty years. Not a single home remained, only empty, barren land and rubble. [field notes]

From the beginning of my fieldwork in January 2002 until the day of eviction of residents, there were persistent rumours of getting kicked out of Phulbari. People relied on but also mistrusted the leaders, who were seen to have their own agenda and were allegedly paid off by the government and local politicians. Insecurity and fear were periodically woven into most conversations and people were uneasy about the future. Many had saved up cash and bought one or three roomed homes in the slums from local leaders. Landlords had invested in a bed, a cooking stove, and utensils, radio, television, and electrical connections. Some had taken loans to cement their floors, others had placed tin or cardboard and plastic over the dirt to try and make their rooms less flimsy. Those who could had invested in separate latrines and water taps or tube wells.

On the afternoon of July 25, the slum looked vast, desolate, and empty. Hundreds of people were standing around. As several bulldozers began crushing the few concrete structures; there was pin drop silence. With a pained expression, Roshonara's husband, Mintoo said, "Now the main problem is that during the monsoon season they are evicting us. Why didn't they evict us in the dry season? We are poor people, where are we meant to go? One room that was TK400 (approximately US$7 in 2002) yesterday today costs TK1,500 (approximately US$26)." Landlords in neighbouring slums had hiked up their rent prices, anticipating an influx of tenants from Phulbari. As bulldozers continued to demolish whatever was left, there was a collective loud sigh – the last small brick structure, the tiny local mosque, frequented by the men, was knocked down. Families looked bereft, some walking around in a daze, others crying openly. But most stood, almost numb and in shock, watching the line of policemen, with sticks and hand rifles, ready to combat these defenceless residents. The entire space exuded grief and pain. Many long- term residents would lose their large circle of personal and social ties and networks; the trusted people, friends, and others who they had relied on over the years.

A week later, I went back to where once Phulbari once stood, and found some families sitting at the empty spaces where their homes were once located. They were hopeful that they could return and rebuild. Roshonara had asked me to meet her there, on several occasions, defiantly telling me, "You will see, we will get our home back. We won't let them take our home away from us! I heard some of the leaders are fighting for us to come back." As I sat on the ground, next to her, I was less optimistic of the outcome. Within three weeks, the families gathering at what was once Phulbari had dwindled to only a few. Roshonara and her mother were there almost daily. Within a month, a large official sign had been erected, declaring that the land was private property and that trespassers would be jailed. Rumours were swirling around that the land had been sold to a real estate developer to build several high-rise apartment complexes, and that some of the leaders had done a deal with some of the politicians. A few weeks later, there was a barbed wire around the empty land. Anyone trespassing would be jailed.

The Politics of Evictions

The demolition of Phulbari was not unique. The 1990s saw a sharp rise in demolitions of slums, uprooting hundreds of thousands of people despite persistent social mobilization. Much of this was politically motivated; greed for land ownership and the rhetoric of 'clearing slums' were justified as 'efforts to curb crime and terrorism.' Often, unexplained, mysterious, and 'accidental' fires led to the sudden destruction of slums and the displacement of their residents. These were widely perceived to be ploys to force eviction, in which a network of actors such as political leaders, police and sometimes particular local slum leaders work together to get a place demolished (Farid, 2013).

Slum demolitions and the forced evictions of residents continues, as recently as February 2023. There was a Supreme Court decision in 2000 but the government can evict slum residents, as it chooses, provided there is a rehabilitation plan for them. However, that is rarely the case. While some of these evictions have been challenged successfully through public interest litigation (Pereira, 2004), this is often an exception. Although eviction drives have decreased in frequency, the government has made no long-term efforts towards a housing policy for displaced slum residents (Farid, 2013).

Usually, the ruling party of the day has *de facto* control of the slum area by way of patronage to the various networks of local slum leaders, allowing easy access to potential vote banks (Banks, 2016),[1] and depending on vested interests, evictions take place. The urban land administration in Bangladesh is complex, bureaucratic, with many of the relevant laws outdated. The National Housing Policy (1993) provides guidelines to serve the urban poor, but it is not implemented (National Housing Policy [Draft of 2008], 2008). The Constitution of Bangladesh provides for several fundamental principles of state policies (FPSP) and rights, but access to justice remains a huge obstacle for the poor. Despite an existing legal apparatus, residents of slums remain suspended in a perpetual state of invisibility and in limbo, excluded from urban governance structures and processes (Farid, 2013).

The situation for residents in slums is made worse by the land ownership structures, which are extremely asymmetrical. Seventy percent of urban residents do not own any land at all, while the distribution among the 30% is extremely unequal, with allocation and development skewed towards influential political groups, including wealthy businessmen, bureaucrats, military officers, and members of parliament. Land is acquired or distributed at subsidised rates (Haque, 2012). Land in Dhaka city is extremely expensive and increasingly valuable as the city gets even more densely population, and the lucrative business of buying, selling, and owning land continues to grow. The capital city is also the service sector hub of the country and most of all government agencies are located here. Dhaka therefore is a key site for capitalist accumulation and the resulting dispossession for many urban poor and marginalised residents (Haque, 2012).

Post Eviction, 2002

December 2002: Monsura's Abortion

Monsura lay writhing on the bed, in a narrow dark room in a new slum, Baganbari.[2] It was Monsura's and Sayyied's third relocation since they had left Phulbari.[3] Monsura's mother and an older lady, the landlord, were standing beside her. Monsura flung her arm out and grabbed my hand, and gripping it tightly said, "I should have listened to you ... I took some pills and then I lost the baby." She had been bleeding for several days. When I had received the call from Monsura, I immediately called Sayeeda (health provider from Phulbari) and told her that Monsura was in trouble and may need her help. She had an abortion. Sayeeda agreed to accompany me to visit Monsura. I wasn't convinced that Monsura had only taken pills and I wondered if she had tried to use a cruder method that might be fatal. Once the family members left her side, I scolded Monsura for possibly seeking clandestine means of getting rid of her pregnancy. She explained: "I owe my mother money, about TK300 (approximately US$5.30), and how will I pay for 'the termination' (menstrual regulation)[4] ... she is angry with me because she has been going through difficult times and he (Sayyied) is not working again. What will I do?" She also didn't know how to reach out to Sayeeda or any of the other health providers since the demolition of Phulbari.

Sayeeda immediately recommended some medicines, which I asked Sayyied to buy for Monsura. I handed him some cash. He rushed off to the nearby drug shop, looking extremely scared. Sayeeda suggested Monsura come to the clinic soon, now operating in Dho Block. I handed money to Sayeeda to cover the costs for Monsura's visits and requested her to bring Monsura from this slum to the clinic, otherwise she would get lost. She agreed. Sayyied was unreliable, and I was wary of giving any more money to him. He didn't work regularly and routinely beat Monsura. I informed Monsura that I would be back in a few days to check on her health situation. She nodded and said in a low voice, "I knew you would come for me. You always do. I have no one. I have you. I know you care ... you care for me ... life has been so difficult for many months now." I was depressed to see Monsura in this state. She was always a fighter and in good spirits; now she looked so defeated and scared. I reassured her I would be back. On my way out, I glared at her mother, who had been pressuring Monsura for money. She looked frightened and kept watching Monsura. They had a complicated and difficult relationship shaped by extreme scarcity.

Monsura was already four months pregnant when she decided to end the pregnancy. Sayyied agreed. After their eviction from Phulbari, their situation had worsened; they had moved around numerous times, and by now, they had a list of debtors to repay and dwindling family support. Sayyied's brother no longer accepted their phone calls and avoided them. The new landlady in Baganbari was less accommodating of late rent payments than Ratna and had threatened to evict them. On advice from a friend, Sayyied bought Monsura some pills from a nearby drug shop, but it was not clear to me what she took. I also didn't know if had used some other method before or after ingesting the pills. Sayeeda was convinced that this was the case: "She won't tell us what she and her husband did to get rid of this baby, but I think she might have tried other methods as well ... they are so stupid because they don't realise that she could have died."

December 2002: Sayeeda Moves Out

As we left Monsura's place, I asked Sayeeda about her situation. I knew that the clinic had been set up in Dho block, near to where Phulbari had been, in August 2002, a month after the demolition. She was relieved to still have her job as a health worker. She was also trying very hard to build relationships with women in the new slum and to restart her sari business. She stopped this in October because "business is slow ... the women don't know me so well and they don't want to buy." She didn't want to give the saris on credit, as she barely knew the residents. She was trying to manage on her clinic salary and was still a broker for clandestine abortions at the private clinic, although client numbers were down. She recognised that trust and familiarity were crucial in any community to be accepted as a health provider, to be an effective broker, and to have a successful business; this would take time.

After being evicted from Phulbari, like others, she had faced financial pressures, because she and her family had moved into a low-income area, renting a brick flat with three rooms close to Phulbari. Moving into a concrete structured building nearby, was also strategic but more befitting of Malek Master's status. The rent was TK4,000 per month (approximately US $70); prior to the eviction, they had lived for free. They had lost the income from the other homes Malek Master had owned and the regular rental payments from tenants. He used to also receive a salary as a teacher at the school that used to be in Phulbari.

One consequence of the eviction was that everyday civility, and the fear of previous leaders was crumbling. Built-up resentments and hostilities were now expressed more openly within households and in the wider, but now scattered community. Some residents who had relocated nearby were sharing secrets and stories of various families and households. There was no need to maintain 'face,' or fear retribution. A month after the eviction, Sufia, the health provider who was Sayeeda's colleague mentioned that 'everyone knew' Sayeeda was having an affair with Malek Master and her youngest son, five years old, was reported to be his child. The official narrative was that the child was from Sayeeda's third marriage and her husband had abandoned her after several months of marriage, leaving her pregnant.

Arguments were more frequent in Malek Master's household. Relationships between family members had deteriorated, with accusations flying around and petty disputes over 'who ate the last piece of meat,' to 'missing saris from the cabinet,' 'stolen cash,' and insinuations that 'certain people were not contributing enough to household expenses.' Sayeeda was fed up with living with her sister and her family. Her daughter Shaheen, 13 years old, had been fired from her job at the garments factory because she missed several weeks of work, because of jaundice and persistent weakness. Sayeeda said that her sister, Mukta was unsympathetic and had demanded that Shaheen look for work quickly and contribute to rent payments. Sayeeda was also unhappy that food was being distributed unfairly, and she grumbled that her children were regularly given stale rice, bones, and gravy while her elder sister's son and youngest daughter was given larger, choicer, and meatier portions. Household work fell mainly to Sayeeda and her daughters; Mukta sat around ordering them. On top of that Sayeeda was anxious that since her daughter had lost her job, she seemed depressed and thin, and was spending most of her time away from the flat.

In November, I witnessed an ugly confrontation between Sayeeda and Malek Master. I had walked in unannounced, while Sayeeda screamed at him, "You know what you did to me?' You know what you did ... and I kept quiet." She was shaking as she screamed at him. I stood there in shocked silence. I had never seen Sayeeda challenge Malek Master; the relationship had always been very deferential. Her hair was open and unkempt, and she was wearing an old sari. She was always thin, but now she looked especially gaunt and had aged in the last few months. Malek Master lay quietly on the bed, not saying a word. He looked neither at me nor at Sayeeda. He was staring at the ceiling and appeared depressed.

Mukta walked in, hearing the commotion, and calmly said, "Sayeeda, shut up and go and do the bazaar. We don't have time for your drama!" I couldn't tell what Mukta was thinking. I left the apartment as quickly as I had entered. I wondered what had prompted Sayeeda to confront him so openly. Was it because he was no longer a leader and had fallen on hard times? Malek and Mukta were no longer powerful or in control, and the power dynamics had shifted between them. Sayeeda did not need them anymore, although she had enjoyed the advantages of living in their home in Phulbari, which afforded her respect, status, social benefits, and protection. Was she intimately involved with him because it benefitted her or because she had an emotional connection with him? Or had Malek taken advantage of her sexually and she had kept silent all these years, because she didn't have a choice as he was a leader and her sister's husband? After the eviction, did she feel empowered to speak out because she felt exploited by her brother-in-law and elder sister?

By December, Mukta was pressing Sayeeda to increase her monetary contribution to household expenses. Her sister was abusive, and the rent was exorbitant and not possible given her meagre earnings. Sayeeda informed me that she was no longer comfortable living in this environment and was looking at other options. She hinted that she might move closer to her brother, who lived in another slum, near the railway station. She requested that I didn't mention her plans to Mukta and shared that Mukta was also looking for work: "My sister is now talking about how her life is so hard, that she may need to look for a job ... she has no skills, and she is too old for garments work. She may ask you for a job ... maybe to cook in someone's home." Mukta did not ask me. It would have been too humiliating for her. Once a leader's wife, owner of several homes, mediating conflicts in the community, she was now reduced to looking for 'a low status job.' Her elder son, Maher, was a drug addict, and he didn't work. Her elder daughter Polly had fallen in love and gotten married and moved out, a few weeks before the eviction. Savings were running out. Sayeeda had limited income. Tempers were running high.

By early January 2003, Malek Master had gone into hiding. I did not see him at the flat when I visited. Mukta informed me that he was busy with paperwork and trying to get Phulbari land back. He was allegedly renting a room in a hotel, in an undisclosed location, to be closer to his lawyers. Some of the previous landlords from Phulbari had increased the frequency of their visits, looking for him. Mukta took over the role of 'temporary leader' and held many 'closed-door conversations' with them, possibly trying to placate them and buying time. Allies of Malek Master joined her at these meetings. Although I asked her about this, she was evasive, but she appeared increasingly tense. The residents I ran into during this period were openly accusing Malek Master and some of the other leaders of extortion over the years, and some accused him of being paid off to allow the eviction to take place.

A few others were convinced a deal had been made, and they (Malek Master and his family) would receive plots of land in another part of the city. I would never know the truth of these claims. Sayeeda felt that the situation was becoming risky for her, and she moved out with her children, nearer her brother. He lived in another slum. It was the end of January 2003. The new place was located far from her clinic in Dho Block, and she caught the bus daily to come to work and return home, which was costly, but she didn't have a choice for now. I don't know how long Sayeeda would remain separated from Mukta and the family but for now she was no longer living with them.

Roshonara: Hard Times

After the eviction, Roshonara had separated from her mother's household and was living separately with her husband and daughter, Lucky, renting a room in cleaner, smaller slum located near the Mirpur area. They chose to stay in the same neighbourhood, as it was familiar, rather than move too far from this suburb. Phulbari was once located in Mirpur, before its demolition. She had sold the television since they had relocated to this place, as they needed cash. They were renting a tiny room, which only fitted their bed, and they did not have space for anything else. Roshanara shared the communal kitchen with eight other tenants and needed to time her cooking on certain hours of the day, as there were only three stoves and cooking took place on a rotation basis. Water collection was easier as there was a tap set up near the compound, and water came in for a few hours in the evening, when house-holders queued with their buckets to fill with water. Like the kitchen, the one latrine and bathing area was shared by eight households and their family members. Roshanara complained, "The soap gets stolen, and I try not to use the latrine at night as I don't know how safe it is in this new area." She wrinkled her nose in disgust and continued, "The latrine is so filthy. These people don't know how to be clean." She was so used to her mother's home, where she had access to their own kitchen, latrine, and bathing whenever needed. She was now a tenant. She was trying to develop cordial relationship with the other tenants, to make it easier to negotiate when using the shared facilities. She was struggling as some of the other tenants were difficult and fights would break out, when women did not want to follow the rotation and time allocated for cooking.

Her mother, and her younger sisters Razia and Rabeya, had moved too, half an hour away from Roshonara. She accompanied me to their place; I would have never found it on my own. Most of these less established slums did not have addresses, and this was especially so for those located on the periphery of the city and less built up in terms of structure. The slum was small, with tin rooms, perched precariously on stilts, built on land over a water-body area. This meant that during the monsoon season, the entire place would be deep in water. This would lead to an increase in waterborne diseases such as diarrhoea and typhoid amongst residents. There was an open latrine, made from bamboo, with a cloth covering it for privacy and located at the edge of the water, shared by several tenants and their families. Chachi looked ashamed as she observed my expression when I saw the latrine and the thin, muddy lane leading up to her place. She explained, "The rent was very cheap, and this is all I can afford now. But we will move to a better place soon." I was embarrassed she caught my expression, but I could not control my utter dismay at where she was reduced to living. Chachi and her daughters didn't use at the latrine at night for security reasons: "This is a very bad place," she told me. "It is unsafe and I don't know any of the people here, but we have already heard of many incidents ... I lock Rabeya, 14 years old, inside the room, if I need to go to the market or any place later in the evening." There didn't seem to be any shops in this area. I found Rabeya sitting crossed-legged, on a wooden bed. The floor was dark and there were a few large cockroaches, roaming freely. The room was empty except for the bed and a few utensils, placed on the floor. The room smelled foul, of waste and faeces. The entire slum smelt of waste. There was a stunned silence when Rabeya saw me. She smiled stood up and hugged me tightly, and said, "I can't believe you came to visit us. I wondered what had happened to you?" She had been sewing *Punjabis* (or called *kurtas,* a traditional long shirt worn by males).

By October, Chachi had finally found work as a domestic maid in a land-lord's place in the slum where Roshonara lived. Roshonara had found the job for her mother. Chachi was older and she didn't think she would end up cooking and cleaning someone's home, but she admitted with a weary look that, since the eviction, she had limited options.

Her life had been turned upside down. Rabeya was sewing *punjabis* to earn some cash, and her own job as a maid brought in an income, which covered their rent and food. Razia was working in a garment factory but continued to be unreliable and did not always give her mother money. Roshonara explained when I visited her a few days later, "I cannot support my mother. It is hard enough to manage my own household in this new place. I am cooking, cleaning, and sewing *punjabis* ... I must manage my husband and make sure my daughter eats. I try and do what I can for my mother, but it is hard, we are not in Phulbari anymore. Mother got rent ... any money saved was used for us to support each other ... we had friends in that place ... and we managed our household."

By November, Roshonara was planning to look for work in a garment factory. She was discussing an arrangement with her mother, whereby she would pay cash to her younger sister Rabeya to babysit Lucky, while she was at the factory all day. In December, when I visited Roshonara, I found her very depressed. She informed me that Mintoo had been found smoking heroin with 'some bad boys' in the area. Fed up and emotionally exhausted, she confessed: "I cannot take it anymore. He was high on heroin ... this has been going on for some time. I got in touch with his younger brother, Kashem, and his friend Sobuj." Kashem lived in the village and had come to Dhaka to support Roshonara. He and Sobuj had tied up Mintoo and locked him up in a room in another slum. She said, "They are taking turns to give him food. I have also gone to visit him, but other than me, Kashem or Sobuj, no one can enter the room." I asked how he was responding to this forced intervention, and she replied, "He does not scream or shout. He starts shaking. Sobuj told me water comes out of his nose and eyes. He calls for me and his brother but none of us go inside. Sobuj said that we need to observe and keep him like this for several days so he can stop taking heroin." She shook her head and became silent.

In January 2003, Razia eloped with Khaled, the boyfriend who had rejected her and she had been forced to have an abortion. However, a few weeks later they had reconciled, but this elopement took her family by surprise. Chachi was now living alone with her younger daughter Rabeya and given the situation with Mintoo, they were now thinking of pooling their income and renting two rooms side by side in a new slum, so they could live together again. Roshonara explained: "I think it is best if we move closer to each other. Razia has left and I need help with Lucky. Mintoo ... I don't know how he will be, but I am hoping he will get better. Ma (mother) needs help." They relied on each other for emotional, social, and economic support; and being close to each other was a better strategy, given all the recent challenges and changes that had happened in their lives.

The lives of Monsura, Sayeeda and Roshonara and their families changed irrevocably when they were forced to leave Phulbari. For Monsura, without contact with the NGO clinic and health providers like Sayeeda, who she knew she took some risky decisions surrounding her pregnancy termination. Instability and poverty had resulted in direct adverse reproductive health consequences for Monsura. In addition, relocating several times and facing little support or compassion from family members and the new landlady, left Sayyied and Monsura in a precarious situation. Sayeeda's brother-in-law, once a powerful leader, was now on the run. As formal systems oppress and exclude them, leaders such as Malek Master are driven to improve the conditions of their lives and work to develop strategic alliances to be in power, which also create relationships of support, extortion, and exploitation of residents. Sayeeda's relationship with Malek Master may not simply be one of her being a victim or a willing partner. As we see in Roshonara and Chachi's case, an eviction can also leave well-off families and landlords falling through the cracks, as access to power, networks, and income sources are removed. Chachi was left with no home and was now working as maid. She worried about her youngest daughter, at risk of sexual assault in the 'shady' slum they were living in. Being a widow, and with no male guardian, made her feel doubly vulnerable. The relationships and people you can rely on are key to your survival. Poverty is fluid and any major crisis, can push residents, who already live precarious and insecure lives, deeper into poverty.

Notes

1 Slums are important vote banks for all political parties – capitalizing on the plights of the poor to advance political interests.
2 This slum, Baganbari, was demolished, many years later in 2015.
3 It was five months after the eviction from Phulbari.
4 Abortion in Bangladesh is legally restricted under the Bangladesh Penal Code. However, menstrual regulation (MR), which is defined as a method of ensuring/ confirming non-pregnancy for a woman at risk of being pregnant, is allowed. The World Health Organization (WHO) defines menstrual regulation as 'early uterine evacuation without laboratory or ultrasound confirmation.'

References

Banks, N. (2016). Livelihoods limitations: The political economy of urban poverty in Dhaka, Bangladesh. *Development and Change*, 47(2), 266–292.

Das, V., & Randeria, S. (2015). Politics of the urban poor: Aesthetics, ethics, volatility, precarity: an introduction to supplement 11. *Current Anthropology*, 56(S11), S3–S14.

Farid, C. (2013). New paths to justice: A tale of social justice lawyering in Bangladesh. *Wis. Int'l LJ*, 31, 421.

Haque, K. N. H. (2012). *The Political Economy of Urban Space: Land and Real Estate in Dhaka City*. https://bigd.bracu.ac.bd/publications/the-political-economy-of-urban-space/

National Housing Policy [Draft of 2008] (2008). www.nha.gov.bd/pdf/national_hou sing_policy_(rough).pdf

Pereira, F. (2004) 'When the Will is Far from the Way: Rising Concern over the Non-Implementation of Court Judgements', *Daily Star*; UCA News, 1989

11 What Lies Ahead in 2022?

Sex Work

In May 2022, Meena was still unemployed. She was desperately looking for work, any kind of work, cleaning, cooking, even selling wares on the streets again. But she acknowledged, "I wouldn't know where to begin as it has been so long since I last sold toys and candy as a child … I don't know the business anymore … not the way Fatema and Shuli do." I asked her what she would do now. She became very quiet, and then turned to her two boys, lying on the bed, and asked them to leave the room. They didn't want to get up, but she kept nudging them gently off the bed. Cranky and sleepy, they left. Her eyes teared up and she shared, "I may be poor, but I won't do the kinds of work that I have been offered."

She hesitated, "In early January 2021, I had no job … my employer was going abroad so I knew I wouldn't have work in a few weeks … I walk to Gulshan, Banani and even Badda (three suburbs) … everywhere … and I asked the guards, the doormen, drivers if anyone was hiring maids. Most of them responded that they would let me know and I gave them my number. I also kept asking my mother and her friends to keep a lookout. A month later, one of the drivers outside the gated compound proposed something that was shameful." She dropped her gaze but continued speaking: "His Sir was looking for someone to clean his home … but he preferred a male domestic. I said I was desperate for work. I told him I was strong, and Sir would be very happy with my cooking and cleaning." The next day, she followed up. The driver explained: "If Sir calls you to come at night or you need to stay late, will you agree?" Meena was taken aback and confused and asked the driver to clarify. He said that the job required her to have sex with his employer and she would be paid a generous amount of cash. Meena was deeply humiliated and ashamed, "I told him I can be poor, but why do you think I would be willing? I would rather die than do this!" Meena wiped her eyes as she recalled the experience. The driver laughed in her face and taunted her. "There are younger and more beautiful girls who are happy to be in these arrangements with the sirs in Gulshan. What is wrong with you? Who do you think you are? Don't pretend you haven't done this before!" Meena was dark and skinny, not

DOI: 10.4324/9781003467472-11

an ideal beauty by Bengali standards. He implied she was 'fortunate to get such offers' and accused her of pretending to be naive. Meena left that apartment complex, outraged, helpless, holding back tears. Some male drivers, standing around, smoking, laughed at her as she hurried away.

Meena said it was not the first time she had received these offers. In early 2022, she had an offer from a foreigner, "There is a guard whom I meet often when I go to work and back from my madam's (where she worked) home ... I was worrying about my job, since my madam told me she was looking for a full-time worker. I shared with *Khalu* (uncle – the guard at the complex) my predicament, and asked him to let me know of any opportunities ... A few weeks later, he told me, 'A foreigner who lives here ... well if you have sex with him 2 or 3 times, he will give you TK1,000'." Meena was shocked and asked him how he could even make her such an offer, especially when she treated him like an uncle. Unfazed by her reaction, he justified, "You have shortage of cash, so what is the problem to do this? You must just think about the money and don't think about anything else." Meena began to cry, "I have been poor my whole life and if I wanted to do this, then I could have done this a long time ago ... I could have earned a lot of money, but I cannot do it." She added that many of the residents in her slum were looking for work and she was not alone. But even though their situation was dire, this option was unthinkable.

When asked if she had mentioned these incidences to Liton and her mother, Meena replied that she was not comfortable telling Liton, as he would become suspicious about her going to work in the future. She did inform her mother, who comforted her and said she would find a job soon and to remain patient. To add to her mental anxiety. Meena was outraged when a tenant, with whom she was close, informed her that the landlady at the last place they rented had been gossiping about Meena's late work hours, implying she was a sex worker. Meena did not want to confront because the woman was a landlady and well connected; Meena was a mere tenant. She was upset and shared, "The rich people I work for in Gulshan get up late and eat dinner late. I must stay late, and then I take a rickshaw home. I don't have a choice. Everyone in my family knows what I do. God is my witness. I have not committed any sin. I have all the responsibilities of my family, and who will feed me if I just sit at home getting upset by peoples' hateful remarks? I don't know why she despises me, maybe I'm too poor ... I don't look good, I don't dress well. I work in people's homes." Even within a slum, a hierarchy existed based on money, status, position, and networks. Meena and her husband were one of the households at the bottom of the social hierarchy. Not only was she a tenant, but she was also very poor. She worked as a maid, a low paid informal job, available to those with little to no education. She didn't have any powerful male or female relatives in this slum. If word had gotten around that her mother begged, then there would be further stigma. Her husband didn't work.

With continued financial uncertainty in June, Meena made a difficult decision. She decided that her eldest daughter, Pinky (14) should work in a garments factory. She had been studying at a local NGO school near the slum but had stopped studying as schools closed in 2020 due to Covid-19. Schools were reopening in 2022, and although it was free to re-enrol her, Meena couldn't afford to purchase the books and pens required for her continued studies. The two-year break from the school had also dulled her daughter's interest in school. The plan was that Pinky would accompany Liton's sister to the factory and apply for work there. Her sister-in-law was reluctant as Pinky was young, but Meena begged her to try and get her a job in the factory given she was already employed, she could request the manager. Meena needed cash urgently to pay for rent and food: "I didn't want her to work as I was hoping for a better future for my child. My dream was she would study and not work like me and have better opportunities … at least she is not a maid." Her voice trailed off, and she became very quiet.

There are literacy requirements to work in a factory but given Pinky had studied and despite her youth, most likely would get work. Child labour in factories and other income generating activities is not uncommon. Shuborna, 12 and Jihad, 9, Shuli's children both sold goods and begged on the streets. A report on Bangladesh by Beaubien found that children under the age of 14 who had left school for jobs were toiling an average 64 hours a week (Beaubien, 2016). The survey of nearly 3,000 households in the Dhaka slums found children as young as six employed full-time and others working up to 100 to 110 hours a week; on average children earned less than $2 a day. Most of the girls were employed in the garment industry as of 2016. While boys commonly worked as day laborers on construction sites or making bricks, 13% also worked in garment factories or other parts of the textile industry. Others sold products on the streets or worked in shops. In very poor households, young boys and girls drop out of school to support their families. The dropout rate of Dhaka district is 15.1% where male and female dropout rate is respectively 16.9% and 13.4%, with male dropout rates higher than females (Bangladesh Bureau of Statistics, 2015; 2020).

Shuli and Shuborna: Difficulties and a Foreign Patron

In May 2022, Shuli told me that she was struggling to manage since Shumon had been killed in March. "This morning I ate left-over rice and made *pantha bhat* (rice in fermented water) and then again, I ate the same meal in the afternoon. I don't have any money … I don't have any money to buy one kg of rice or anything else. I also have this persistent headache. When Shumon was here, he would take me to this doctor in Rampura and buy me headache tablets which I'd take daily." With a sad expression, she continued, "He is gone now … but my mother-in-law lives with me. She is an old woman, and I can't just feed her *pantha bhat* only. I will go to Gulshan and beg today, then I can buy rice and some fish with the money earned."

A long-time customer 'madam' who bought towels from Shuli, and gave her occasional cash, took pity on her, and offered her a place temporarily, rent-free, on her private, empty land, in Moghbazaar, an hour from where Shuli worked in Gulshan 1. Newly widowed, feeling vulnerable and low on cash, she agreed. The plot was small, with unkempt grass, and an old decrepit two floor, partially constructed flat, with one latrine, a kitchen room and a tube-well. There were two other families living there, working for the 'madam.' Shuli was given a room to live in with Arifa, but she faced hostility as soon as she moved in.

The families living there began to complain to the 'madam' (owner of the land) that Shuli's baby was always crying, and it was difficult to sleep with all that noise. They also accused Shuli of being defiant and unapologetic when they complained about the noise. Shuli was asked to leave several weeks later. Shuli was worried as she needed to find a place to rent quickly but she also needed cash to do so. She felt overwhelmed and became anxious. This was something that Shumon had always taken care of.

Shuli had no family support. Soon after Shumon died, her mother, Jorina began nagging her to move back in with her. For Shuli it would be the worst arrangement. She didn't trust her: "I know my mother wants me to move in, work on the streets and give her all my income. She is a very greedy woman. I would rather die than be back in that home with her and my useless brother." She continued, "I told her, you don't have to worry about me. She was angry but she didn't say anything." Shuli felt used by her mother, since she was sent to work on the streets as a young child. She had also resigned herself to the fact that her children would never live with her. They were closer to her mother, and they grew up with her, and she had been absent from their lives for a long time, since she had remarried.

Shuli understood that as a young widow, 20 years old, with a baby, it would be difficult to run a household on a single income. How would she find enough cash to pay rent, food and other expenses? Having a young baby would garner sympathy and possibly deter harassment from men and gossip from others, if she rented a room in a slum: "I told the landlady when she asked who I would be moving in with, I explained I was widowed recently with a baby … and that my mother-in-law will live with me." For Shuli, her mother-in-law would provide her with some support, and she wouldn't feel lonely. In addition, she was young and pretty and she could be vulnerable to unwanted male attention. Having an elderly woman live with her provided some security. She had convinced Shumon's mother to relocate to Dhaka city. Her mother-in-law was fond of Shuli; she had known her for almost a decade and had visited and stayed with Shumon and Shuli. As she had moved frequently with Shumon, they had not developed any strong ties or personal networks in any of the slums. Her networks were where she sold her towels and begged. Her mother-in-law shared, "Shuli is a very good girl, and she has always looked out for me. My son and Shuli would send me money … she used to call me and talk to me. You know my son is dead, but my son's wife has asked me to come and be with her. I will stay with her ... Poor Shuli is having a lot of trouble, as she runs the family alone, I feel very bad. I will help her out and I can take care of my granddaughter."

Shuli found a room to rent in Baniganj slum for herself, her baby and her mother-in-law and they moved in. This room was small, costing her TK2,600 (approximately US$28); in the past she used to rent larger sized rooms for TK4,000 (approximately US$43), combining Shumon's income with hers. She had sold a lot of Shumon's items, including his phone, to get some quick cash, but had held on to the television. This is one of the few possessions she would not give up and her only enjoyment left. Her mother-in-law also loved watched television, while Shuli remained busy working in Gulshan 1. The elderly woman cooked, cleaned and took care of Arifa when required. Her mother-in-law sometimes would walk with Shuli to Gulshan 1, carrying Arifa in her arms, making sure she was fed while Shuli sold towels. When Shuli begged, she would grab Arifa from her mother-in-law – a small baby usually garnered more sympathy and cash.

Through March, April and May of 2022, Shuli spoke of how she was struggling without Shumon. There were days when she would lie in bed and cry at night. She missed hearing his voice:

We would talk often. He was always there to comfort me ... we rarely fought ... he took care of me and our baby. I don't know why Allah took him away so soon. A husband is the best friend of a wife ... I miss my husband every day. I think how Shumon would take me by the hand and help me cross the street. He would go to the shops and buy food and manage the landlord. He would call me 3–4 times in a day, to find out how my business was going. Now I go home, and I feel empty inside. I sit and I eat and then the next day begins.

She was depressed and tired. She had to manage the continuing police case and visit the court when she was arrested end of 2021, for selling towels during the city corporation drive 'to clean the streets.' This also required visits to the local clerk/lawyer every few weeks. His office was in old Dhaka city, hours from where she lived. Shumon used to accompany her on these trips. Lonely and often overwhelmed, Shuli strongly felt that the 'increased tensions' in her life had now led to severe headaches, occurring every few days. She was taking 'tablets' to manage the pain. "When my husband was alive," she told me, "I would come home and share my thoughts with him. We would plan and discuss what we would do ... I knew I had him for support. But now I must think and plan everything on my own." Shuli feared the future and what lay ahead for her.

By June, however things had changed. Fatema mentioned that Shuli was preoccupied with a possible new romance. She sounded disapproving: "I hope she doesn't rush off with this man ... she should not get married again. She already has three children." She continued, "I feel bad for her, because we have grown up together, since we were both little. We have been selling towels since childhood. If she still had a husband, her life would have been beautiful. The little girl (Arifa) lost her father and was deprived of his affections (after a pause) if she remarries, that is up to her." When Fatema confronted her, Shuli was evasive, but Fatema was convinced 'something was going on.' She had recently observed Shuli and a young man interacting, and Shuli was on her phone often, 'giggling and chatting away.' Shuli was a very pretty girl, and it was not surprising that she received attention from young men in the area. Poverty and the economic, social, and political environment had accelerated Shuli's journey into adulthood. She had become a mother and wife, was pregnant, bore children, and experienced sexual intimacy at a very young age. This was for the case too for Meena and Fatema, in contrast to middle- and upper-class women in Dhaka city, for whom such transformative life events occurred in their 20s and 30s.

When I asked Shuli if she was interested in anyone, she was quick to emphasise she didn't have time for a relationship. Perhaps she was embarrassed as Shumon had passed away only a few months ago. However, she was only 20 years old, and had very little family support, except for an aging mother-in-law who relied on her financially. She may have been unsure about the relationship, and reluctant to share details, particularly because of the disapproval of young widows to be sexually active, so soon after the loss of one's husband. In Bangladesh, marriage is the only legitimate site of sexual expression. Women marry because it brings social acceptance and the 'legitimate' opportunity to have children, but it is also a site for love, pleasure, affection, and happiness. Women who have or desire relationships that are not socially sanctioned, because they are single or widowed, marry to avoid gossip and stigma (See (Hawkins et al., 2011)). While wanting to fall in love and having someone to love, be loved and cared for, is a human need, this was further fuelled by existing norms and social media, films and television, where romantic dramas are often aired, but also marriage presented as the culturally appropriate option. Young women's sexual lives tend to be regulated by communities. Aside from potential economic support from a suitor, Shuli may have been craving intimacy and companionship. Since Shumon's death, life was even more precarious for her, and she was lonely.

I asked Shuli about her daughter Shuborna since the accident, but Shuli mentioned that she had barely had any time to visit her. She had been busy working. She had heard that 'an older foreign man' had taken responsibility for Shuborna and was paying for her enrolment into a school and providing some cash to the family. She didn't seem to know much about this benefactor. I was curious though, as Shuborna was only 12 years old. She was living in a one room space with her younger brother, Jorina (her grandmother and Shuli's mother), and in the next room, was her drug addicted uncle, Akash and his wife. All of them lived in Badda Link Road, a low-income housing area with relatively secure tenure. Like the slums, low-income housing areas were congested, with poor water, sanitation, and latrine facilities, but with some basic infrastructure and services provided legally.

When I walked into the room, I was confronted by the mixed smells of marijuana, tobacco, and stale urine. The room was filthy, with sand piled in the corner, dirt strewn around the room, and five or six cockroaches of various sizes roaming around the floor and crawling up and climbing on a large, overturned cooking pot. There was a large bed, a jute mat, a small wardrobe in the corner, a steel rack with clothes hanging on it. There was also a small fridge, a television, and a big tin trunk, a chair, a fan, and a light in the room. There was no electricity for about two hours, as was common, and the small window in the corner of the room allowed very little light or ventilation. It was extremely hot and felt suffocating sitting in the room. I was perspiring heavily. Shuborna sat on the chair with two crutches perched on the side. Her hair was covered with an *urnah* (cloth) and she was wearing a kurta and pyjamas. She lifted her pyjamas to reveal the scars on her legs, from the accident.

Shuborna's grandmother, Jorina, refused to leave the room during the conversation, claiming she had severe body aches and a headache. I believed she wanted to monitor our conversation. Shuborna mentioned she wasn't close to her mother. She glanced sideways at her grandmother, and explained she was much closer to her grandmother who had brought her up. When asked about the foreign benefactor, Shuborna mentioned that she had met him by chance, while selling towels and begging on the streets of Gulshan 1, in March 2022. His name was Jonas, and he was from Germany. Jonas had rolled down his car window and gave her some cash but did not take the towel. Instead, his driver told her, "Sir does not need a towel. He has given you money, so you can buy something to eat. Sir wants to know why you sell towels at such a young age." She explained to the driver that she was poor, and this was how she earned her income. Later that afternoon, the foreigner returned to Gulshan 1 with his driver, gave her a gift of clothes and asked to speak to her grandmother. The driver explained to Shuborna that his boss "felt affection for her and wanted to take responsibility for her future."

On Jonas's insistence, Shuborna enrolled at a nearby school in March; he paid for the costs of admission, books, and materials. Initially, Jonas had insisted to Shuborna's grandmother that Shuborna could not sell on the streets anymore, but the grandmother negotiated that Shuborna would continue to work in the afternoons, while she attended school in the mornings. She was fully dependent on Shuborna and Jihad's income to manage her household, including having to feed her adult son and his wife. Jonas agreed to the compromise. He also hired a tutor to visit Shuborna daily in her home since the accident, so she could continue studying and learn English. Shuborna explained that she spoke with Jonas "two or three times a week on video … he wants me to learn English so I can talk to him." He had bought her a smart phone, and she was the only one who had his phone number. She was strictly forbidden to share his number with anyone else. Her grandmother had Jonas's driver's number for any emergencies. Shuborna described Jonas as "an old man who wasn't married … he asked me to call him by his name. He said he wants to take me to his country when I am older ... when I am 18. He sees me like his daughter." Jonas visited Shuborna twice after the accident, bringing food for her. He also covered some of the costs incurred at the hospital for her treatment; other costs were covered by the person responsible for her accident.

Shuborna's grandmother seemed to be torn between what might seem like winning a lottery ticket, since Jonas entered their lives, and his intentions: "He is not married, and he has no children of his own. He wants to take her (Shuborna) to Germany later, when she is older. I don't know if he has any other plans or not ... but I am close to some of the police in Gulshan 1. I will not send my girl abroad on Jonas' request ... I will have the police check him out." For the grandmother, a very poor, illiterate woman, the police are her only recourse to ensure her granddaughter's safety. Although being poor also meant she had little power over this situation. She didn't seem to have any other means of managing this 'powerful, white, wealthy, foreigner,' and responded with false bravado. Jonas had recently become an important figure in their lives and was supporting their material needs. Her voice trailed off as she became aware that Shuborna was sitting nearby. She seemed to change her attitude, and quickly added, "Well if Shuborna wants to go abroad ... then, why not? He wants something good in her life." Shuborna seemed mature for her age, but she was oblivious to our conversation and was busy on her phone, listening to some music.

I do not know whether Jonas was genuinely compassionate of Shuborna's plight, or whether he had less than noble intentions, and if she had fallen prey to a relationship that would later lead to sexual exploitation and abuse. Shuborna's status and power had been elevated in the family since Jonas had singled her out for attention. Jonas recently had his driver purchase 1kg of rice and *rui* fish, an expensive fish eaten on special occasions, just for Shuborna to enjoy. The grandmother was unhappy because she felt Suborna's younger brother was overlooked and continued to work on the streets, while Jonas only spoilt her granddaughter. Shuborna explained to me that his driver had told her that Jonas had said that her face and behaviour was not like someone who lives in a slum. She smiled. She was pleased she was seen as 'different' from other poor children, living life on the margins. Shuborna, had two options: to carry on working on the streets, day after day, to support her grandmother, and replicate her mother's and grandmother's life, or to remain in contact with Jonas, hopefully get an education, learn English, gain some other material advantages, and better opportunities. The promise of going abroad was a miracle for Shuborna, given her life circumstances, and she wasn't going to easily let go of her dreams for a better future for herself.

Child sexual abuse and sex trafficking are common in Bangladesh (Islam & Akhter, 2015). The reality is that poor young children are at risk of sexual exploitation, and desperation for cash can compel families to sell their children for a price. Children who lead harsh lives end up in arrangements knowingly or unknowingly, which can be abusive, but with few alternatives mean taking decisions which may be the lesser evil of the two. Their very lives are embedded in the cruel reality of poverty and precariousness, and what we may consider as less desirable option, is often seen as the only alternative available for 'cash, opportunities or a better life,' to those left on the fringes of society.

Fatema: Banking on the Future

It was June 2022, and Fatema was sharing her aspirations for her children. She was determined to offer her children a better life, so they did not end up selling towels on the streets, as she did: "My elder daughter is three years old, and I am planning to enrol her in a school nearby when she is four years old." She smiled with pride: "My daughter can say A, B, C, D, some names of animals and birds. I want to educate my two daughters. I work but my father has agreed to pick her up and drop her to school, and my mother will help me out." An education, she hoped, would allow entry into more formal and better paying jobs in the garment sector, for instance, or in an office, as an entry level assistant. This option was not available to her or her husband, Riaz, as they had very little education. She was worried as she often spotted young boys and some girls, around on the corner of the alleyway inside Gulshan 1, sniffing glue (called dandy). Some of these young boys and some older hawkers sold marijuana and other drugs to young college students, who were their primary customers. But, Fatema commented, the boys are often bare bodied, only wearing pants or shorts, they look dirty, and their hair is messy and unwashed. Some were orphans, sleeping alone on the footpath.

Fatema continued, "There are also children whose parents who don't care and force their children to earn money." One of her close childhood friends, Rasel, had been beaten to death at the age of 14 by a rich man in Gulshan, when he was caught stealing inside their apartment in early 2020 (pre-Covid-19). He was forced to steal and engage in other illicit activities from a very young age, because his parents pressured him for cash. His parents were "bribed TK2 lacs (approximately US$2,547 in 2016)," an enormous amount of money for them, to not press charges. Fatema was 12 years old at the time. The memory of his death and burial stayed with her. She promised herself, that no matter how her life turned out, she would not abuse her children and instead, save money and try and educate them. She said, "My father did nothing with his life and my mother worked, so I started working at an early age to support my mother. I was selling toys and pens on the streets from a very young age. If my mother didn't have enough cash, my father would beat her."

Fatema had started taking the pill because she didn't want to fall pregnant again. "I have two children and I don't need anymore. Bringing up a child is expensive. What Allah has blessed me with, I am happy; now I just pray my sister-in-law is able to conceive. This would make my brother very happy." Riaz purchased the packet of pills for her every month. Now they felt that after a long time, they were in a less stressful place financially. Riaz had recently found some work on a construction site, and combined with her 'decent' towel sales, they were bringing in a combined income of TK8,000 (approximately US$81) for the past two months. Fatema usually kept her savings with Faruk, as he had a bank account. Riaz agreed. His wife was pragmatic, he explained, and this strategy allowed them to only access her savings from her brother during emergencies. Last month, Faruk had finally convinced Fatema to open a bank account, after asking her repeatedly to do so for a year. Fatema had kept avoiding taking that step: "I didn't feel the need and then I didn't know how to do it on my own. I just kept giving my brother money and he would keep it for me.' Faruk wanted a more stable future for his sister, Fatema and her children.

He took the day off work and took her to the Agrani (government) bank to assist her to open an account in her name. He already had his own account at this bank, located at Mohakhali, 25 to 30 minutes away from Gulshan 1. Faruk explained this to me:

> She (Fatema) has two children, and they are growing up and she needs to save for their future. My sister suffers a lot and every day she goes to sell towels in Gulshan. She runs the family with the money she earns, as my brother-in-law doesn't always find work. The children have demands and Fatema buys coke and chips for her eldest daughter daily … but she must stop spending like this. Children want snacks and she can buy them sometimes, but she needs to put away money.
>
> She wants to put her girl in school … so where will the money come from?

Fatema opened an account with an initial deposit of TK2,000 (approximately US$20). She was extremely pleased and planned to try and keep saving as much as possible, given that her income flow was satisfactory presently.

Faruk told me that Fatema had several loans and debts because the police arrested her husband earlier, because of the pregnancy and delivery and the recent road accident that left her unable to work for almost two weeks. He bemoaned that before Covid-19, his sister's life was stable, as her husband had found a job in a company and was earning regular wages. He blamed 'corona disease' for his brother-in-law's unemployment, forcing Fatema to get back on the streets to sell towels. Their lives had changed yet remained the same in terms of continued unpredictability and precariousness. Work is erratic and cash is required to survive, and family support and networks are critical.

What is the future for all these young women and their families? In June 2022, Meena revealed that she had been offered sex work on two occasions. She reported that she chooses not to take that route. But who knows what will push Meena to eventually take up this 'option?' How many more days of unemployment will force her to rethink the unthinkable to earn cash? Her adolescent daughter is being forced to drop out from school as cash is required while Liton remains comfortable with his wife and even his daughter supporting him and the household and shows little remorse. Shuli is alone, navigating life on the streets and in the slums. She may remarry, which means her mother-in-law will most likely return to the village. Shuli may not have another child with a potential suitor, but a child is perceived to strengthen one's marriage and relationship. Marriages can be unstable and men unreliable: Shuli's first husband abandoned her and remarried several times. But other men like Shumon and Faruk earned incomes and supported their wives and family members. Shuli's daughter, Shuborna had found a patron, but the future and risks are uncertain. Fatema is struggling but has a tightknit, supportive family, which creates a buffer for her, during times of extreme stress and crisis situations. For all the young women, there are multiple risks – personal, economic, physical, mental, and social. Given the extreme scarcity in their lives, it is difficult to judge any of their decisions.

References

Beaubien, J. (2016). Child laborers in Bangladesh are working 64 hours a week. www.npr.org/sections/goatsandsoda/2016/12/07/504681046/study-child-laborers-in-bangladesh-are-working-64-hours-a-week.

Hawkins, K., Cornwall, A., & Lewin, T. (2011). Sexuality and empowerment: An intimate connection. Pathways Policy Paper, Brighton: Pathways of Women's Empowerment.

Islam, F., & Akhter, G. A. (2015). Child abuse in Bangladesh. *Ibrahim Medical College Journal*, 9(1), 18–21.

Bangladesh Bureau of Statistics (BBS). (2015). *Census of slum areas and floating population programe 2014*. Bangladesh Bureau of Statistics; Ministry of Planning. http://203.112.218.65:8008/WebTestApplication/userfiles/Image/Slum/FloatingPopulation2014.pdf

Bangladesh Bureau of Statistics (BBS). (2020). *Statistical Yearbook Bangladesh 2019* (39th ed.). Bangladesh Bureau of Statistics;Statistics and Informatics Division (SID); Ministry of Planning.

12 Dead End

Nowhere to Turn!

Characterizing life as precarious for Monsura, Roshonara, and Sayeeda, along with their families in Phulbari back in 2002, and for Meena, Shuli, and Fatema, along with their families in Baniganj in the present day, would be an understatement. These young women and their families exhibited a quiet but unyielding determination as they grappled with limited opportunities, consistently seeking ways to navigate, confront, and manage their lives under the most challenging circumstances. Their experiences align with the 84 case studies I compiled during two distinct time periods: 50 from 2002 to early 2003 and 34 from 2020 to 2022. The life narratives presented in this book, while diverse, broadly represent this vulnerable group.

Improvements in their lives remain uncertain, marked by recurring cycles of harassment, abuse, debts, loans, and the continual barrage of minor and major shocks. Family support, social connections, and networks, both within and beyond the slum, played a pivotal role in managing calamities and emergencies. Marital instability was prevalent, with many young women marrying at a young age, some even experiencing second marriages while raising young children. These households residing in the slums and working in the city had to grapple with varying degrees of exploitation from influential residents, slum leaders, the police, employers, and other powerful entities.

Their lives unfolded in anticipated and unexpected ways, with interventions from social networks, strangers, employers, and others helping during challenging times, thereby providing glimpses of hope. Nevertheless, the persistent fear of falling into deeper poverty or destitution remained a constant source of concern. The prospects for leading healthy lives remain grim.

Tumultuous Lives

Living on the margins, the three young women and their families in Phulbari in 2002 battled local politics, national policies and gatekeepers, and relied on family when they could, as well as stable and temporary social relationships and networks, all of which was disrupted by the eviction in 2002, creating

DOI: 10.4324/9781003467472-12

adverse consequences on their lives. Similarly, the second group of three young women in Baniganj in 2022 are still reeling and trying to recover from the shocks of the pandemic, critically highlighting how endemic poverty, lack of rights and powerlessness drive multiple levels of vulnerability and health risks. Ross aptly captures the situation for these marginalised young women and their families in Dhaka slums as she writes of the struggles of shantytown residents in South Africa: "hunger and want shapes bodies, capabilities, relationships, and possibilities, as poverty and desire rub against one another, producing inflammatory and corrosive contexts in which life itself is at stake" (Ross, 2015).

The young women's case studies in 2020 demonstrate that not much has changed in the past twenty years. Their daily existence is a juggling act of gut-wrenching choices, and the larger social, economic, and political landscape continues to weigh heavily against them. All of the young women and their family members had little to fall back on, yet were resourceful and intelligent as they explored multiple ways to earn cash, selling watermelons, renting a tea shop, as Roshonara did while living in Phulbari; 'offering massages to men' as Ratna alleged Monsura did, Sayeeda selling saris; and; Fatema toiling away, selling towels even while heavily pregnant; and Shuli and her children begging on Dhaka streets, pre and post Covid period. Meena worked as a maid but was not always employed. For most of them, there were weeks and months when they earned less than what was needed to keep their households running. This often pushed them to the brink of despair and created a lot of mental anguish.

Without land or other assets in the rural villages, the young women and their families who live in Dhaka city, and work in the informal economy need cash to rent a home, buy food, and pay for access to basic services and other living costs. They live in rooms in units/compounds made of semi-brick with tin walls or roofs, sharing latrines, kitchen, and a water tap with 15 or more households. Daily life is often a frenetic juggling act, as individuals skilfully navigate their routines, hurriedly trying to prepare meals within the allotted time, visit the latrine, and take a bath while waiting in line for access to water. The water supply is erratic, requiring them to fill buckets and large drums only when water became available for storage and future use. The water can be dirty, smelly, while clean water is purchased for drinking purposes.[1] The latrines are often decrepit and filthy and shared by many tenants.

Where some of the young women lived, there was little to no drainage, and during the monsoon season, alleyways and dirt paths overflowed with waste, sludge, and sewage. Arjun Appadurai (Appadurai, 2001) mentions how residents in Mumbai slums in India use latrines without running water and without sewage systems and have little privacy. This is both humiliating and removes any dignity for residents, and such unhygienic conditions are also ripe for waterborne and water-washed diseases, some of which can be life-threatening. The daily degradation of living in such spaces, infested with mosquitoes, cockroaches, insects, and rats and the smell of garbage and other waste, permeating the air, is cruel and inhuman. Poor families have little choice and cannot afford anything else. Millions of people live in such environments around the world.

Life Insecurities and in Limbo

Risks are frequent and hard to anticipate, be it police raids and arrests, harassment by other powerful actors, the sudden demolition of Phulbari in 2002, and the more recent pandemic induced abrupt shutdown of the country in 2020 and 2021 resulting in the loss of wages. In general, the lack of stable income sources for these households, and the horrific limited options of backbreaking, unrewarding low paid work, is exhausting and depressing. Few options exist for the poorer groups, as they remain unskilled with little to no education. For men, there is rickshaw driving, construction work, breaking bricks, running small shops, and menial tasks, by and large, work that others will not do. One can argue that this can explain some of the frustration, outbursts of anger, and alcohol and drug use among men. Inertia with life and a disregard for their families was evident in both Sayyied, Monsura's husband and Liton, Meena's husband. One could argue that Sayyied's form of escape was to smoke, drink and gamble, and a perpetually sick and possibly disinterested Liton spent hours at a tea shop or slept for days on end.

It was a common sight to see men sitting around in the corners of the slum alleyways, chatting, sipping tea during the day, and some gambling and drinking in the evenings; a few seemingly disillusioned with their circumstances. For both groups of young women, those from twenty years ago, and for those who experienced the recent Covid-19 pandemic, the repetitive cycle of scarcity, taking on the burdens of trying to manage their households, manifested in physical ailments. They regularly complained of 'worry illness (*chinta roge*)', sleepless nights, tension, and worries, palpitations, a lack of appetite, headaches, coughs, colds, body aches, and other more serious diseases, as a bleak future awaited them. Monsura in Phulbari spent hours lying on her bed, day after day, staring at the tin roofed ceiling, or stood outside the compound, bored, gazing at strangers as they walked past.

Chinta roge (tensions) serve as an idiom of distress through which these young women spoke about their living conditions and expressed their physical and social suffering – a consequence of political, economic, and institutional oppression (Kleinman et al., 1997). During the post-lockdown period in 2021, Meena overwhelmed by financial worries, would come home and lie down, often turning to face the wall, unable to speak to anyone in her household. The despair is akin to what Wool and Livingstone write of individuals who led precarious and uncertain lives, which was often one of "unproductive dead ends of a toxic or melancholic present" (Wool & Livingston, 2017). The daily experiences of these young women and their husbands to make ends meet in a hostile city, literally a battleground, has them living a life that often seems to go nowhere, notwithstanding their best attempts to improve their situation.

Despite these conditions, Meena who was a maid, and Fatema who sold towels on the streets, shared aspirations especially for their children; what Berlant would refer to as "cruel optimism", as they had a narrow life, tightly bound by structurally unequal systems and policies, with the future greatly uncertain (Berlant, 2011). As Wool and Livingstone write, the fantasies of a good life are hard to achieve and costly, and yet investments and the hope for them continues and propels people's lives along, even if they often seem to be at a dead end (Wool & Livingston, 2017). Intergenerational poverty persists amongst these very poor families in Dhaka, with many of them repeating the cycle of their poor parents, not having graduated to better life circumstances. It is unknown whether any of these young women, families and their children will ever be able to get out of the cycle of poverty. Meena's mother is a widow and begged for a living, and her daughter Meena eventually dropped out of school to start working, first on the streets selling flowers to support her mother, and then as a maid in 2019, to support her husband and children. Meena's daughter joined a garment factory and dropped out of school.

Fatema was better off in comparison and had close family relationships, with several members working and earning, and they often pooled their income together and helped each other out, during cash shortages or an emergency. Fatema had a television and fridge in her apartment and more recently in 2022, opened a bank account and was planning to enrol her daughter in school. She was, however, struggling because of the treatment expenses for her injury from the recent road accident, as well as the costs for releasing her husband from jail, as he was picked up by the police for an alleged violation. Whereas, in early 2022, Shuli lost her husband tragically in a motorcycle accident. Bereaved and now a single income earner, she was left saddled with a new baby and fallen on hard times financially. She was not close to her mother or her children from her first marriage. Like her, her daughter Shuborna also sold towels and occasionally begged on the streets. Shuborna supported her grandmother, but her life took an unexpected turn when an older male foreigner decided to support her financially and invest in her education. It is uncertain how this may turn out.

Alternatives remain few and unreliable for those positioned at the bottom of the social, political and economic hierarchy. Any crisis or a series of multiple crises can potentially have these families fall deeper into uncertainty and precariousness. With no social security, protection, or insurance, even those who are better off and more established in a slum can have their lives upended without notice, with unexpected consequences. This is evident in the case of Malek Master, once a powerful leader, who went into hiding and lost his rental income from the ten homes he 'owned,' after Phulbari was demolished. His wife, previously a high-status leader's wife in Phulbari, was allegedly looking for a job as a cook in early 2003. Similarly, Chachi, Roshonara's mother, was devastated when she was unexpectedly widowed, and lost her home a few weeks later because of the demolition of Phulbari slum. With no income, she had begun working as a maid at the end of 2002, and was staying in an unsafe, filthy, smaller slum on the outskirts of the city. She worried about her youngest daughter's safety and security. She was 50 years old but looked much older, her face lined with worries, crisscrossing her forehead. She was depleted. Life had been unexpectedly brutal to her and so many other residents who had been displaced overnight. A slum resident's fate, whether as a tenant or a slightly better off landlord or landlady, can be fickle, with instability a grim reality.

For many of the young women and their families, daily life moved between the mundane and the precarious, between the predictable and the unpredictable, such as the repeated police raids in Phulbari in 2002. Although not completely shocking for residents, it was still frightening, as they never knew who would be persecuted and jailed. Tenants such as Monsura, who had no networks, and Ratna the landlady, who had a few networks with leaders, remained petrified during these raids, and worried if their husbands would be jailed or if they would 'disappear' once picked up by the police. They were acutely aware that they belonged to the category of individuals who would go unnoticed and have limited access to justice if their husbands faced harm or arrest. Arrests also implied an immediate requirement for funds to secure their release. The balance of power rested entirely with law enforcement officials, who were widely distrusted by the majority of residents.

Similarly, unjust policies and the role of law enforcement officials was evident 20 years later, as street vendors like Fatema and Shuli had become accustomed to managing them and paying bribes to avoid harassment, to keep working. To add to their woes, the recent Dhaka City Corporation drive in 2021 to clean up the streets and arrest vendors led to further struggles and enormous stress as they were just recovering from lockdown and post-lockdown, having earned less cash during 2020.[2] The government policy to clean up the city streets was implemented almost a year and half after mandatory lockdown in 2020, with intermittent shorter periods of Covid-related lockdown and curfews well into 2021. In addition, in 2019, policies were implemented to restrict the movement of rickshaws and auto-rickshaws (battery run) off the main thoroughfare, as these particular types of auto-rickshaws are considered illegal. The ban on rickshaws was taken to improve traffic congestion (Anjum, 2019). Shuli was picked up by the police for selling on the streets and jailed for two weeks in early 2022. She had to go to court and paid a large sum of cash to a local 'clerk' for her case to be cleared, but the payments and the case stretched well into mid-2022.

Post Covid-19, Shuli and Fatema and their family members, and many thousands of families in slums who worked in the informal economy were continually playing catch up, recovering from fewer sales due to reduced cars on the streets and fewer clients in 2020. These families were still paying off debts and loans they had accrued in the previous two years to pay rent, buy food, medicines, and other costs required for everyday living. This was yet another discriminatory policy that disproportionately affected those with the fewest options, individuals who worked tirelessly to make ends meet.

Many of the residents in slums in different yet complex ways, actively, contest, negotiate to challenge their marginal position with more powerful actors (see Aceska et al., 2019). This was evident when many hundreds of residents protested the demolition of Phulbari in 2002, and post eviction began harassing ex-leader Malek Master for the cash they had invested to stave off eviction. Others more recently defied the lockdown restrictions in 2020, as they left the slums, despite law enforcement being on the streets, to search for income earning opportunities selling towels, begging, riding rickshaws, and 'even tricked the police by recruiting a disabled,' person to pose as the 'owner', to avoid losing the transport vehicle, and so on. In these cases, it evident that the poor "realise agency in their daily practices" in creative ways, when they can (Van Dijk et al., 2007). It is important to note that they are not simply passive recipients of structural violence, but at the same time, it is critical not to overstate or romanticise their agency, in the face of overwhelming obstacles. Their life was one of continual negotiation with powerful actors. As Cresswell writes, the poor try to "transform in whatever ways were possible, existing relationships of domination, oppression, and exploitation," but the cycle of powerlessness continues (Cresswell, 2004:29).

Young women and their families, in 2002 and 2022, had their lives enmeshed in struggles with powerful and diverse interest groups. Their narratives are a testimony to their continued resourcefulness to try to manage the relentless onslaught of multiple challenges. In Bangladesh, police as a law-enforcing institution, appears to be the least regulated, thereby creating a space for violation of human rights, and abuse of the law (Sen et al., 2004). The ambivalence of the State, and informal system of extortion and payment to local leaders (*mastaans*), police, gangs and other powerful intermediaries who regulate activities in the slums and fine and arrest the poor in the city, receive limited attention on the role they play on health in public health literature. The extensive curtailing of income generating opportunities, restricted movement, and economic insecurities and the numerous risks faced illustrating the profound marginalization experienced by these urban poor young women and their families. These agonising struggles are beyond their control and exert a considerable toll on them, affecting both their financial stability and psychological well-being and ultimately their daily lives.

Social Relationships, Networks, and Reputation

Social relationships in a household and networks can be both stable and unstable and shift, with no guarantees for enduring relations. Any major conflict or cash crisis may destabilise existing bonds. Young women tenaciously hold onto both long-term and short-term relationships, seizing and endeavouring to cultivate connections at every available opportunity. This is key to their survival. Relationships with their spouses, extended family members, neighbours, tenants, leaders, landlords/landladies, health providers, employers, co-workers on the streets, customers, and shopkeepers and others, can all provide some buffer and critical support in times of upheaval.

The eviction of residents in Phulbari in 2002 demonstrate how quickly networks built over the years can be destroyed by this single act and disappear over time as people are forced to relocate to different parts of the city. Ratna, the landlady at Phulbari lent cash when her tenant Monsura's son Joy was sick, so she could rush him to a hospital. Post-eviction, and relocating to a new slum, Monsura and Sayyied lived with a new landlady, who did not appear to be as supportive, as trust and relationships and mutual support are built over time. There were also devasting consequences for landlords and landladies, those who once had their own homes, such as Malek Master and Roshonara's mother, lost their steady source of rental income. They were reduced to being tenants and having to generate cash to pay rent. Eviction of slum residents, which is a recurring situation in the country, illustrates how poverty status is fluid for those who live in slums, as previously 'well-off' landlords and even some leaders, can also lose key material gains and supportive networks in a demolition, and become displaced and vulnerable.

During the Covid-19 lockdown in early 2020, the urgency to bring cash to manage a household also led to unrelated and related household members leaning on each other. During this period and post lockdown, Meena, and Fatema shared stories of long term residents who are tenants in Baniganj (referring to them as aunts/*chachis*) who helped them and each other out with meals, including sharing chillis, onions, rice and even potatoes, and small amounts of cash to buy food. However, these relationships could also be quickly disrupted if money became tight and conflicts arose. The fights could be temporary or longer term, depending on the relationships. There were incidences of Fatema and Shuli screaming at each other, with accusations of stealing from each other's customers, when selling on the streets in 2021 and 2022. Just as quickly, other sellers stepped in to resolve the conflict. When things cooled off, one would find Shuli and Fatema hours later sitting together on the sidewalk, discussing animatedly the money they earned that day. Fatema told me that they warned each other and other sellers if new police were arriving to harass them. Shuli and her mother also had very public verbal and physical fights, from 'shoving, punching and kicking' over cash not being shared, yet after these exchanges, one would regularly find Shuli and her mother chatting and laughing together. On the other hand, Meena's relationship with her last landlord and landlady was permanently damaged, when she delayed rent payments and her children were accused of theft. Humiliated and furious, she relocated with her family to another room in Baniganj.

In Phulbari in 2002, during difficult times, Razia (Roshonara's sister) stopped contributing her garment worker's salary to her mother and the household. For this she was punished, with her mother not cooking her afternoon meals. One afternoon when she found that no afternoon meal had been prepared for her yet again, Razia had a huge public shouting match, and left her mother's home, enraged. However, following mediation by some close neighbours, she moved back home after a few days.

The narratives of the young women and their families reveal that relationships within a household and with others are complex, dynamic, and changeable. Some husbands and wives and external family members may pool resources, strategise together or independently, and take decisions, turning to family and others, while some of them extracted money from each other. Despite the chaos and conflicts, this is a shared world, where they seem to understand each other's struggles, along with the momentary ruptures in relationships. Banerjee and Duflo (Banerjee & Duflo, 2011), argue that economists tend to oversimplify the family unit, conflating one individual for all individuals in the household. One can argue that this over-simplification overlooks the varied interests, and multiple dynamics, including individual desires, power, conflicts, and collaborative nature of relationships, which tend to fluctuate in a household and with others.

If there was a cash crisis in the household, in Phulbari (2002), it was Monsura, Ratna and Roshonara who actively borrowed or pooled money from family members, took small loans from fellow tenants, or borrowed from local organisations and landlords to sustain their households. Monsura was always pushed by her husband to ask for money from Ratna the landlady, and his brother, as he was not comfortable and ashamed to ask for loans. Likewise, Meena, Shuli, and Fatema, during the Covid-19 lockdown and post lockdown, preferred to seek loans from a range of individuals, family members, known acquaintances and non-kin close relationships, as well as employers, as these loans came with no or low interest rates, compared to the often-usurious rates charged by money lenders. Shopkeepers familiar with individuals who had been living in the slum for a long time, provided food on credit. Borrowing from networks they knew could also be fraught with tension, and young women worried about not being able to repay various loans on time. There was a reluctance to turn to money lenders for loans because they worried about the high interest rates. However, most of them did reach out to known moneylenders, when they were in dire need of large amounts of cash.

None of the young women I interviewed, in 2002–2003 and in 2020–2022, nor their families reported belonging to any formal micro-credit organization, although other residents did so and were able to use this when in need. Banerjee and Duflo (2011) argue that some of the poorer households, such as fruit sellers or other vendors, with highly unstable work and persistent precarity in developing countries, may choose to exclude or self-select themselves out by not becoming members of micro-finance organizations.

The young women explained they turned to money lenders for larger sums of cash, because of social familiarity, ease of access, and their ability to lend them cash immediately, which were all important considerations. Despite the interest charged and the abuse faced, as was Meena's experience over delayed repayments, money lenders were still viewed as quite flexible with repayments. In addition, the relationship with a money lender was not always simply transactional, but was also personal and social, as those seeking loans knew them from within the slum and the local area. Banerjee and Duflo (2011) argue that moneylenders had to know and assess the resident's capacity to repay, if they were employed, and the kind of employment, and if they were long term residents in the slum. Similarly, during my fieldwork, I found that a temporary migrant with fewer connections would struggle to secure a loan, and someone who was unemployed even if he or she was a longer-term resident, such as Meena's husband, Liton, was considered a 'bad candidate' and viewed as unreliable. In this case, this meant that the entire burden for borrowing, and repayment fell on Meena. In other households, men also borrowed, although they were far more reluctant than their wives to do so. This was the case of Shumon, Shuli's late husband. He shared that he felt humiliated to ask for money from others, and believed that as a man, he should be able to support his wife. However, Covid-19 led to him losing his job in a small shop in 2020. There is anxiety tied to not being able to repay, which often led to estranged relationships with family, friends, and others.

Monsura, a tenant in Phulbari (2002), began to detest Ratna, her landlady. Ratna lent Monsura cash occasionally, but continually reminded her of her 'kindness in helping her out' and at times belittled her for 'being a daughter of a beggar,' and not repaying loans on time. Over time their relationship deteriorated beyond repair, and post-eviction they did not stay in contact with each other. In 2021/22, Meena began to avoid Alam, who ran a pharmacy (often referred to as drug-seller shops, unlicensed), until she was able to repay him. She was embarrassed because she owed him money for the medicines she had received on credit. Shuli also took great pains to explain how she was repaying the owner of the pharmacy in Gulshan 1, a small amount every few days, so he would not have any reason to be annoyed. She was hoping this would ensure he trusted her and ensured future loans. Rumours spread quickly if a person was persistently unreliable or defaulted on a loan. This was a deeply shameful and vulnerable position to be in. This was a reputation none of them could afford to have, given loans and other kinds of support was a critical lifeline for all of them (see Walker & Bantebya-Kyomuhendo, 2014).

Repayment or at least attempts to pay back small amounts over time to money lenders, relatives, and other individuals in one's networks, requires work and continuing relationships, no matter how fraught they may become. The young women were savvy enough to calculate all expenditures for food, rent and other costs incurred, while also setting aside small amounts of money to repay various individuals. It was a struggle and often food intake was reduced to manage this. They often cajoled and pleaded for more time from money lenders, which was very taxing on them[3] (see Kabir et al., 2023).

Social relationships and reputation were important for young women and their families. Maintaining their dignity and social standing with family members and others in the community was critical for their self- worth and belonging. Inside a slum, micro-level distinctions emerge, primarily driven by factors such as education, income, housing size, household possessions, social status, connections, and the perceived level of wealth and accessibility. Within this community, residents distinguish between those considered very poor, who may be subject to condescension or sympathy, and those from relatively prosperous households who are perceived as doing well and being better off. Despite the widespread insecurity, drug trade and other forms of violence in the slums, social and moral codes dictate that residents and tenants did not engage in less than desirable work, such as begging, sex work, selling drugs, and menial jobs. This is frowned upon and poorer residents found to be engaged in these 'less than desirable jobs,' are seen as inferior. Fear of ostracism was of paramount concern for many, as they were poor, less powerful and not well-connected, and judged quickly, compared to their landlords and better off residents. For example, on several occasions, Shuli and Shumon remained anxious that their landlady would find out that Shuli and her children begged to earn money. Meena was very emotional about the rumours being circulated that she was engaging in sex work to pay for household expenses and was lying about her job as a maid. Fatema worried about the nasty rumours being spread when her father was nearly arrested by the police for 'selling drugs,' and when her husband was jailed briefly by the police for alleged burglary, both of which she vehemently denied to her neighbours and landlord. As gossip or accusations were made, mortified young women sought to 'clear their own or their family's name.'

Giorgio Agamben's analysis of power in shantytowns of Africa reveals the distinction made among residents between a bare (raw) life and a qualified life (better decent life) and argues that the trope of decency becomes the central norm, by which people imagine themselves and their lives, and desire to be respected and accepted in their communities (Agamben, 1998). Fiona Ross (2015) also found despite the fragility of life and poverty, people in shantytowns in South Africa worked hard to be perceived as upright and reputable for their own dignity, and for residents, amongst other things, it was important to emphasise that they lived in proper homes, and not just in shacks occupied by those at the bottom of the social ladder living in informal settlements.

Another major concern for young women and their families during the two different time periods (2002 and 2020) was their struggles to pay their rent on time. These young women mainly needed cash to pay rent as landlords and landladies were mainly concerned about their rental payments. Given this was the top-most priority, any gossip about the character of the individual could also take a backseat if a resident was seen to be paying on time. On the other hand, when rental payments became overdue and were coupled with gossip, or when someone less well connected, openly defied the 'social norms' in the community, it could lead to a family being forcibly evicted from their rented homes. Socially and economically, it was not in the best interest of the landlord or landlady to continue supporting a tenant or family who were rapidly turning into a burden.

For tenants, having a room (home) in a slum, despite the occasional hostility of landlords and landladies and other challenges, offered some stability and security in a seemingly uncaring sprawling Dhaka city. For those who had already established relationships with neighbours and other tenants, and had lived for several years in the slum, it was easier to put up with some of the mistreatment than relocate. A bigger fear was being forced to join the ranks of the millions of homeless residents who live and sleep on Dhaka streets, under threadbare blankets, or without, on hard cemented sidewalks and lanes. These pavement dwellers are a visible and powerful reminder of what could happen if a family lost everything. For many residents who had been living for a long time in the area, slums are 'their locality', a place despite the challenges, where they belonged, a familiar space and micro-world, with its own rules, norms, and conduct.

Unpacking Health – How the Social and Biological Entwine

The narratives, both from two decades ago and from the present, are remarkably similar, shedding light on the experiences of young women and their husbands from vulnerable households. They grapple with various health issues, including recurrent fevers, coughs, colds, as well as acidity, chest pains, chronic body aches, palpitations, insomnia, 'worry illnesses and tensions,' and other chronic health conditions. Some of them required medical interventions, such as Sayyied, Monsura's husband from Phulbari, who suffered from a hernia and needed surgery. Additionally, Monsura underwent an unsafe abortion post-eviction, which could have been fatal. The decision was not made by her but was forced on her, due to poverty. After being evicted from Phulbari, Sayyied was not working, and her mother was harassing her for money that was owed to her. They had relocated to a new slum, and she had little choice when she took this decision. Similarly, Liton, Meena's husband, had tuberculosis which required ongoing treatment and was costly. Post Covid, work was unstable. Meena was perpetually exhausted and suffered from bouts of illnesses from 2021–2022, and she was the single income earner for their household. Liton and the children survived on her earnings.

To address the various ailments of poor young women and their families living in slums and in the city, pharmaceutical companies have been offering a plethora of medicines, syrups, and tonics since the 1980s. Public and private hospitals and health facilities offer an array of treatment options but have long wait times, can be very costly due to various diagnostic tests that are recommended and doctors' visit fees. In contrast, drug shop sellers are easy to access, provide medicines on credit and offer temporary solutions to alleviate chronic health symptoms. Therefore, young women and families visit trusted, local drug shop sellers who are quick to provide a diagnosis and prescribe medicines, provide advice and counsel, and allow for delayed payments. Alam, for Meena and Fatema and their families, was not simply a provider, but was viewed as a family member and a 'life saver.' It is critical to recognise and acknowledge the local social worlds of young women who seek care and receive advise from those with whom they are most comfortable with and respect, who provide medicines on credit and are sympathetic to their plight.

Drug shop sellers running small (unlicensed) pharmacy shops, are largely embedded in the communities they serve, communicate in a familiar language, and are empathetic to the plight of residents and are neither rude nor dismissive. While in public health systems they are relegated to the category of unlicensed practitioners, for many residents in slums they are an anchor and often a trusted guide, who treat them well and refer suffering individuals to specific doctors and clinics for further investigation. Often these referrals can assist with facilitating quicker access and services from clinic staff and doctors, which is usually out of reach for very poor people.

Young women and their husbands preferred to avoid further investigations, unless it was an emergency, and preferred taking various medicines to manage. They remained hopeful that the symptoms would be kept under control, and not worsen. This was the approach taken by Shumon, Shuli, and even Meena. They admitted that their present circumstances did not allow them to invest time and money on their chronic health problems, as they had much bigger challenges to manage – to keep working for basic survival. Falling sick and not being able to work had multiple negative effects, such as loss of daily wages, termination of employment, or reduced pay. Any of these led to further anxiety and panic about the disastrous consequences this would lead to.

In Phulbari (2002), Abdul, Ratna's husband, was petrified of losing his stable job from the spectacle shop where he was employed, if his illness continued to linger. Unlike many other men, he didn't pull a rickshaw or engage in daily labour work, and his job gave him status and a fixed monthly salary, unusual for many men living in slums. Meena worked as a maid and, post-lockdown in 2021, she feared that taking sick leave when she was terribly ill would lead to her being fired. This would be especially traumatic for her as she had been struggling for almost a year and a half to find work as a maid, which ensured a steady income. When she was very ill, and missed work, she had her salary cut, not an insignificant amount for her. Fatema lost 15 days of selling towels on the streets when she was injured in a road accident and explained how much money she lost when she was recovering in a hospital. She received no financial compensation, was left badly injured, and had to pay for costly treatment. This set her and her family back financially for months.

Studies have found that leaving the labour force because of ill health is already known to be associated with poorer financial conditions and a major driver of poverty (Brazenor, 2002; Schofield et al., 2011; 2013). Evidence points to workers in the informal economy suffering from a range of illnesses, colds, fever, skin disease, respiratory problems, eye problems, electric shock, malnutrition, parasitic diseases, asthma, skin allergies, chemical poisoning, food poisoning, musculoskeletal disorders, traumatic injury, musculoskeletal problems, backaches, etc. (Loewenson, 1998; Sumon, 2007; Sutarjo, 2007). Illnesses in addition to loss of one's ability to work, can also cause large levels of out-of-pocket healthcare expenditure, which reduces current and any accumulated household savings and pushes individuals and their families into impoverishment and poverty (Huq et al., 2014; Sarker et al., 2016).

Health challenges are very real dilemmas and a crisis. Decisions on what to do next are not taken lightly but are weighed up and carefully thought through. It is not always ignorance or a lack of awareness that deterred these young women and their husbands to seek appropriate care. There were deliberate delays and postponing treatment from a facility or a hospital, given the costs involved and the shortage of cash available. Other factors also affected their behaviour and decisions – including their social relationships, trust, behaviour of providers, ease of access, and the perceived seriousness of the health condition. If they could manage their health, they continued working, given the limited options available and took the most pragmatic decision available to them, given their life circumstances.

Their health causes are much deeper rooted and structural as much as they are biological. Their health experiences highlight the importance of paying attention to the interconnected nature of the environment in which people live, and the multiple social factors and oppressions which produce inequalities and bad health. The pandemic revealed how millions of vulnerable populations' lives were deeply rooted in inequalities, powerlessness, and uneven co-morbidities, and health and health care access were severely compromised due to their low socio-economic status. The circumstances of their lives, placed them at risk, not only from malnutrition and persistent illnesses and diseases, but at risk of catastrophic economic losses with long lasting repercussions that continued to multiply (Wahlberg et al., 2021). Covid-19 is a reminder, once again, that any disease, "is a social and political as well as a biological fact, grinding against the lived realities of everyday life" (Wahlberg et al, 2021:3).

Baer, Singer, Farmer, and other scholars have pointed out that we need to recognise that structural and social factors may be of far greater importance than the nature of pathogens that infect bodies (Baer et al., 1997; Farmer, 2004; Singer & Clair, 2003). There needs to be a shift in the way we conceptualise disease as inside the body, to a more holistic approach which emphasises the links between macro and micro forces, social conditions, and inequalities. That is, we need to "make social of disease" (Frankenberg, 1980; Singer & Clair, 2003). Similarly, the syndemic theory argues that disease and health conditions do not exist in isolation from one another, and intersectional factors and conditions of everyday life are critical in influencing health outcomes (Singer & Clair, 2003).

There is an argument that the conventional, disease-centric understanding of public health needs a thorough re-evaluation. It's crucial to recognise its limitations and to present an alternative vision for the future of global and public health. This means integrating, "decolonised approaches – advanced by individuals and institutions from diverse settings, to recognise and address the complex interdependence between history, colonization, health, economic development, governance, and human rights". (Buyum et al, 2020:1). Cash and Patel (2020) delved into the difficulties associated with adhering to a universal global strategy of extensive Covid-19 lockdowns, mandatory physical distancing, and a heavy reliance on advanced tertiary hospital care and technological solutions. This approach was ill-suited for less affluent countries with distinct populations, divergent needs, different healthcare systems, and fewer resources. The challenges of copy and pasting global lockdown approaches in Bangladesh was evident, where poorer households' predominant fear was impending starvation, rather than dying from Covid-19 (Rashid et al., 2020). Afifi and authors interrogate what public health risks means for those who live in disadvantaged environments in diverse settings. There continues to be a neglect of the "fundamental social causes" of disease, which worsened the situation for millions during the pandemic, who were affected in multidimensional ways, including erratic water supply in informal settlements, no income as economies shut down, reduced food intake with rising inflation, and other multiple challenges of living with such deprivations (Afifi et al., 2020).

Fault in our Methods

Knowledge is power and there is an explicit value placed, and a hierarchy that exists in public health research. There is a need to unpack the kinds of research evidence that are solely legitimised. For example, the way in which public health is predominantly defined influences the tools and methodologies used to measure and report health outcomes. Public health research can tend to generalise populations who become nameless beings with *diseases*, boxed in and labelled, existing as 'data sets.' The urgent need for social science research was evident during the peak of Covid-19 in 2020, where global strategies and policies, mainly relied on clinical knowledge of infection transmission and responses which was adopted across the world – with lockdown, mandatory distancing, wearing masks and washing hands as the main prevention efforts (Rashid et al., 2020). There was little to no critical reflection as to how 'health was lived and experienced' among marginalised populations in different contexts during the pandemic, with hard sciences dominating the landscape.

One of the challenges is the trend of relying on large scale surveys and increasingly on randomised clinical trials (RCTs) and its claims to methodological superiority in evaluating designed interventions in global health, across diverse settings. This is encouraged and even pushed by large scale international funders and agencies. While surveys and RCTs are extremely useful, it does not answer the how and why of what occurs in communities, the variations that exist and the complexity of social environments and local contexts. It fails to capture the nuances and messy entanglements that exist in peoples' lives, which is critical to understanding social drivers and vulnerabilities that shape poor peoples' lives, constraints, their choices, decisions, and health outcomes (Adams et al., 2015). Naila Kabeer further argues that

RCTs tend to generalise about a larger population, but the methodology doesn't allow for human agency which can disrupt, and challenge assumed behaviours and effects (Kabeer, 2020). Therefore, any intervention and policy analysis must be grounded in an appreciation of the interaction between the realities of lived experiences and the larger historical, social and economic and political contexts in which they unravel.

Current research leans towards certain methodologies and policy approaches, which are typically segmented, sector-specific, and often informed by Northern-led priorities and paradigms. An understanding of the lives and health of young urban poor women living in Dhaka slums cross disciplinary and policy silos and requires inclusive, integrated, interdisciplinary research responses. Responses to health, education, and livelihood needs are usually the focus of separate research efforts and policy responses, yet they are deeply connected and conditioned by the political environment and power structures. There also needs to be a recognition of how intersectional factors, such as poverty, gender, age, sex, religion, caste, class, location, etc., impact on health, and the ways in which structural and social systems continue to reproduce inequities, inequalities, and deprivations. For instance, social science research, anthropological methods, community based participatory approaches, can be designed to allow for collaborative research engagement with directly affected communities, which leads to co-designing and learning from heterogenous groups/communities and their life experiences, leading to the localised co-production of evidence (Desai & Rashid, 2023). An example is the ARISE[4] project which has developed tools and methodologies to involve a wide range of community members as co-researchers alongside researchers from institutions. This approach ensures that tools, methodologies, and research questions are not only relevant but also aligned with the priorities of the communities needs in specific settings.

Adams and colleagues (Adams et al., 2015) argue that the most complex health problems require careful reflection and a commitment to incorporating rich and nuanced understandings of how health unfolds for those who are most marginalised, thereby allowing for a greater recognition of the influence of multiple and concurrent risks. Considering the realities on the ground, they raise questions about the definition of evidence and advocate for the establishment of room for "alternative accounting." This approach seeks to reconceptualise our understanding of what qualifies as evidence. This implies more than just an effort to change how we collect evidence; it also entails a critical and conceptual re-evaluation of what qualifies as evidence. I would argue that there needs to be an epistemic shift in the way public health is defined, allowing for more inclusive research methodologies and diverse disciplinary approaches, with recognition and investments by funding bodies and institutions. Now, more than ever, it's essential to engage in discussions about the dominance of particular research methods in the field of public health. These approaches can lack the necessary contextual understanding of the diversity and complexity of local settings. A transformation as to what constitutes evidence is urgently required, and will lead to richer insights, which is meaningful and allow for ethical and appropriate policies and interventions for those who are on the margins.

Fundamental Values

Why do some peoples' lives improve, "while it leads to exclusions for others, as they slip deeper into poverty or continue to persist at the margins as outcasts without the power to claim, protest or even speak of their maladies?". (Sen et al, 2004:1). Duffield (2001) defines exclusion of the poor, particularly those living on the fringes, within the framework of global governance politics. This exclusion is characterised by a system that assigns greater importance and support to certain human beings over others, perceiving those dwelling in poverty-stricken conditions as strategically inconsequential. Consequently, they are often overlooked, forgotten, and their experiences, including the unnoticed deaths of millions, remain unaddressed (Duffield, 2001). In an interview on the plight of the marginalised in America, Professor Desmond, argues that poverty extends beyond mere material scarcity and the absence of income. It encompasses the absence of choices, the anguish, and the overwhelming fear associated with abuse, discrimination and the overall unpredictability of life. He described it as "this exhausting collection of social maladies that overwhelm and burden them in unimaginable ways." (Desmond, 2023). This also aptly describes the lives of the very vulnerable young women and their families living in slums in Dhaka city. Their persistent material hardships create a messy and chaotic life at the margins: excluded from social and economic gains. This keeps a large segment of this population in limbo, stuck in an endless cycle of poverty, despite decades of economic progress in Bangladesh.

Abdullah Shibli in a newspaper article, (2023) argues that Bangladesh's fixation on GDP growth rate is causing "collateral damage," and the country should instead be focussing on strengthening "social safety net and health care services," for poorer populations, and social protection (See also Devereux & Sabates-Wheeler, 2004).[5] Insurance for the poor is critical to counter multiple crises facing vulnerable families, so they do not spiral into deeper poverty (Shibli, 2023). I briefly refer to two models[6] which are noteworthy in their attempts to address the formidable gaps[7] faced by those who are marginalised, such as BRAC's Ultra-Poor Graduation, in Bangladesh, which began in 2002 (World Health Organization, 2018). The programme has served over 2.1 million ultra-poor households in Bangladesh as of December 2020. The programme addresses poverty multi-dimensionally, mitigating context-specific and people-specific challenges, based on principles of the four pillars of the Graduation approach – livelihoods promotion, financial inclusion, social protection, and social empowerment[8] – with intensive holistic approaches which target the most vulnerable groups. For instance, the extreme poor targeted earn some cash, and are provided with income generating assets (e.g., livestock, poultry, shop, van), followed by two years of training, geared towards developing and managing the asset. Other components include a food subsidy, education, social and legal support. This model has been adapted and tested through 10 pilot projects in eight countries in Asia, Africa, and Latin America between 2006 and 2014. While the evidence is extremely positive, the question of how to operate this approach at scale remain, given the resources needed, time and labour involved (Hashemi & De Montesquiou, 2011).

Another model worth mentioning is SEWA (the Self- Employed Women's Association), which is a membership organization in India, founded in 1972 by labour lawyer and organiser Ela Bhatt. It is a movement rather than a program, for informal workers, who have organised into a labour union to struggle for their rights, with more than 100 cooperatives to improve their economic security. Large numbers of members have increased their incomes through both the collective pressure, and gained access to markets through information campaigns, assistance with product improvement, and SEWA-run marketing services and access to banking facilities (Nanavaty & Baug, 2004). Both these models remain difficult to replicate at a national scale, without state commitment, investment and support.

Global accountability also seems to be lagging. In 2008 the WHO Commission on the Social Determinants of Health set out an agenda for change by 2040, yet a forthcoming report[9] by WHO, finds that progress has been slow and disappointing, with inequities being unacceptably high. Disadvantaged populations, with lower incomes, education levels, and socioeconomic status, as well as marginalised groups are the most affected, experiencing shorter and unhealthier lives. The report highlights that the world has not taken adequate action based on the Commission's recommendations, which call for addressing the uneven distribution of power, wealth, and resources, enhancing everyday living conditions, and implementing more effective monitoring of the social determinants of health and health equity. Progress in addressing the structural determinants of health, such as unjust economic systems, systemic discrimination, and fragile societal infrastructure, has been lacking. It is imperative to recognise the urgency of the global challenges confronting the world during a time of poly-crises, including the repercussions of a weakened global economy, climate change, the Russian invasion of Ukraine, the after effects of the Covid-19 pandemic, and the recent Middle East conflict between Israel and Palestine in October 2023. This prompts questions about responsibility and accountability, and the ongoing failures of national and global actors, structures, systems, and policies.

Where people are born, how they live, work, fall sick and how they die are affected by the environments they live in. We must ask ourselves again, what is the value we place on human life? This requires critical reflection on how power, privilege, politics operate, and our own individual and collective values, as lives continue to unravel and disappear into oblivion. We need a firm commitment to acknowledge and tackle the underlying root causes of *bad* health, which requires transformative action, from reallocation of resources, radically changing current global and national policies and holding to account multiple powerful actors, or we will continue to have an endless cycle of poverty and worsening inequalities. To bring about any *real* change, there needs to be a profound shift in our values, structures, and systems, for an equitable, socially just, and healthy world for all. This means acknowledging our shared humanity and envisioning a better world and future for all human beings who can live in dignity. I end with a quote from Sir Fazle Hasan Abed, founder of BRAC and BRAC University, Bangladesh, when he was awarded the Ramon Magsaysay in 1980: "Poverty is not the absence of resources, it is the unequal sharing of them."[10]

Notes

1 A study of residents living three slums in Dhaka city, found water to be undrinkable, having a foul smell and poor residents purchased water from nearby places (unpublished study of JPGSPH, BRAC School of Public Health, 2023, ARISE).

2 A recent national level Covid-19 survey, which collected multiple rounds of data, reveals that due to the lockdown in 2020, continued economic fallout, and subsequent smaller periods of lockdown in 2021, there was an emerging 'new poor' – vulnerable people made poor by the pandemic in the country. In addition to those who were already poor, in March 2021, 15% of the national population was estimated to be the 'new poor', a total of 32.4 million people when extrapolated to the entire population of the country (see Rahman et al, 2022).

3 The distressing experiences of Meena, Shuli, Fatema, and their families during the pandemic are reflected more generally in a survey by PPRC and BIGD during that period, covering 4,872 households, 54% from urban slums across city corporations and municipalities in districts, 45% from rural areas, and 1% from the Chittagong Hill Tracts region. Everywhere, poverty had increased, and outstanding loans had more than doubled. The survey found that most of the urban poor reported borrowing from shopkeepers (61%), NGOs (49%), and neighbours or relatives (38%) to survive. Another 11% borrowed from moneylenders. Most families borrowed to cover basic living costs, food, and health related bills, and a fifth were borrowing to invest in (small) businesses, and a similar proportion were repaying loans. Slum residents compared to their rural counterparts were far more worse off, because of the pandemic and lockdown (see Rahman et al., 2022).

4 https://www.ariseconsortium.org/

5 There are ongoing debates about which interventions constitute social protection, and which category they fit under. Social protection is commonly understood as "all public and private initiatives that provide income or consumption transfers to the poor, protect the vulnerable against livelihood risks and enhance the social status and rights of the marginalised; with the overall objective of reducing the economic and social vulnerability of poor, vulnerable and marginalised groups" (Devereux & Sabates-Wheeler, 2004, p. i)

6 There are other models that exist to address those who live in extreme poverty, be it small or at a larger scale, but that is not the aim of this chapter, but just to refer to these examples of attempts by some institutions to address these overwhelming challenges for the poor.

7 The Shanghai Declaration on Promoting Health in the 2030 Agenda for Sustainable Development in 2016, highlighted that health and wellbeing for people at all ages be only achieved by promoting health through all the SDGs – through

commitment to Health in All Policies (Shanghai Declaration. Geneva: World Health, 2017). These approaches have proved to be a useful entry point for identifying integrated action across SDGs, such as linking SDGs in urban and transport-planning, environmental exposure, behavioural and health outcomes, concluding that at least 38 SDG targets are relevant to urban health, corresponding to 15 SDGs (Ramirez-Rubio et al., 2019).

8 www.brac.net/program/wp-content/uploads/2021/09/UPG-programme-Bangladesh-overview.pdf

9 I was an Advisory Member of the WHO Commission of the forthcoming report (*Progress on the social determinants of health and health equity*, draft, August, 2023).

10 www.brac.net/latest-news/item/271-brac-founder-fazle-abed-receives-entrepreneur-for-the-world-award

References

Abboud, O. (2022). Recognition and respect could change street vendors' lives. www.wiego.org/blog/recognition-and-respect-could-change-street-vendors

Aceska, A., Heer, B., & Kaiser-Grolimund, A. (2019). *Doing the City from the Margins: Critical Perspectives on Urban Marginality*. Anthropological Forum.

Adams, A. M., Islam, R., & Ahmed, T. (2015). Who serves the urban poor? A geospatial and descriptive analysis of health services in slum settlements in Dhaka, Bangladesh. *Health Policy Plan, 30*(1), 32–45. https://doi.org/10.1093/heapol/czu094

Adams, V., Craig, S. R., & Samen, A. (2016). Alternative accounting in maternal and infant global health. *Glob Public Health*, 11(3), 276–294. https://doi.org/10.1080/17441692.2015.1021364

Afifi, R. A., Novak, N., Gilbert, P. A., Pauly, B., Abdulrahim, S., Rashid, S. F., Ortega, F., & Ferrand, R. A. (2020). 'Most at risk' for COVID19? The imperative to expand the definition from biological to social factors for equity. *Prev Med*, 139, 106229. https://doi.org/10.1016/j.ypmed.2020.106229

Afsar, R. (1996). *Onus of Poverty on Women in the Poorer Settlements of Dhaka City*. Dhaka: Women for Women Research and Study Group.

Agamben, G. (1998). *Homo Sacer: Sovereign Power and Bare Life*. Stanford University Press.

Ahamad, R. (2021). Slum dwellers pay more rent per sq ft than posh areas. *The Business Post*.

Ahmad, A. (2007). *Provision of Primary Healthcare Services in Urban areas of Bangladesh: The Case of Urban Primary Health Care Project*. Working Papers 2007:9, Lund University, Department of Economics.

Ahmed, K., & Islam, R. (2021). The making of a megacity: How Dhaka transformed in 50 years of Bangladesh. *The Guardian*.

Ahmed, M. (2022). Learning loss from Covid-19: Can a generational threat be averted. *The Daily Star*, 13.

Ahmed, N., & Ahmmed, F. (2015). Problems and challenges of deserted women in Bangladesh: An observational study. *Journal of International Social Issues*, 3(1), 1–11.

Ahmed, S. (2013). Civic environmentalism and the politics of marginalized people: A case study from megacity Dhaka, Bangladesh. *Environmental Justice*, 6(2), 56–61.

Ahmed, S. M., & Hossain, M. A. (2007). Knowledge and practice of unqualified and semi-qualified allopathic providers in rural Bangladesh: Implications for the HRH problem. *Health Policy*, 84(2–3),332–343.

Ahmed, S. M., Naher, N., Hossain, T., & Rawal, L. B. (2017). Exploring the status of retail private drug shops in Bangladesh and action points for developing an accredited drug shop model: A facility based cross-sectional study. *Journal of pharmaceutical policy and practice*, 10, 1–12.

Ahsan, A. (2019). Dhaka-centric growth: At what cost. *Policy Insights. Policy Research Institute, Dhaka.*

Ali, A. (2013). Informal labour force. Dhaka, Bangladesh. https://unnayan.org/wp-content/uploads/2021/05/INFORMAL-LABOUR-FORCE.pdf

Amis, P. (1995). Making sense of urban poverty. *Environment and Urbanization*, 7(1), 145–158.

Anam, S. (2020). What about workers in the informal sector. *The Daily Star.*

Anjum, S. (2019). In Bangladesh, a rickshaw ban for major Dhaka city roads spurs protests and debate. *Global Voices.*

Appadurai, A. (2001). Deep democracy: Urban governmentality and the horizon of politics. *Environment and Urbanization*, 13(2), 23–43.

Arefin, S., & Rashid, T. (2021). The urban poor in Dhaka: Perspectives on the right to the city. *Journal of Urban & Regional Analysis*, 13(1).

ARISE: https://www.ariseconsortium.org. downloaded October, 2023

Atkinson-Sheppard, S. (2016). The gangs of Bangladesh: Exploring organized crime, street gangs and 'illicit child labourers' in Dhaka. *Criminology & Criminal Justice*, 16(2), 233–249.

Baer, H. A., Singer, M., & Susser, I. (1997). *Medical Anthropology and the World System: Critical Perspectives*. Bloomsbury Publishing.

Baker, J. L. (2005). Dhaka: Improving living conditions for the urban poor. https://documents.worldbank.org/en/publication/documents-reports/documentdetail/938981468013830990/dhaka-improving-living-conditions-for-the-urban-poor

Banerjee, A. V., & Duflo, E. (2011). *Poor Economics: Rethinking Poverty & the Ways to End It*. Random House India.

Bangladesh Bureau of Statistics (BBS). (2015). *Census of slum areas and floating population programe 2014*. Bangladesh Bureau of Statistics; Ministry of Planning. http://203.112.218.65:8008/WebTestApplication/userfiles/Image/Slum/FloatingPopulation2014.pdf

Bangladesh Bureau of Statistics (2016). Bangladesh education statistics. https://lib.banbeis.gov.bd/BANBEIS_PDF/Bangledesh%20Education%20Statist ics%202016.pdf

Bangladesh Bureau of Statistics (BBS). (2020). *Statistical Yearbook Bangladesh 2019* (39th ed.). Bangladesh Bureau of Statistics;Statistics and Informatics Division (SID); Ministry of Planning.

Banks, N. (2013). Female employment in Dhaka, Bangladesh: Participation, perceptions and pressures. *Environment and Urbanization*, 25(1), 95–109.

Banks, N. (2016). Livelihoods limitations: The political economy of urban poverty in Dhaka, Bangladesh. *Development and Change*, 47(2), 266–292.

Bashar, T. (2022). Residential stability of the urban poor in Bangladesh: The roles of social capital. *Cities*, 126, 103695.

Beaubien, J. (2016). Child laborers in Bangladesh are working 64 hours a week. www.npr.org/sections/goatsandsoda/2016/12/07/504681046/study-child-laborers-in-bangladesh-are-working-64-hours-a-week

Berlant, L. (2011). Introduction: Affect in the present. In *Cruel Optimism* (p. 0). Duke University Press. https://doi.org/10.1215/9780822394716-001

Biehl, J., & Locke, P. (2017). *Unfinished: The Anthropology of Becoming*. Duke University Press. www.dukeupress.edu/unfinished.

Blaxall, J. G. N. (2004). *India's Self-Employed Women's Association (SEWA) – Empowerment through Mobilization of Poor Women on a Large Scale*. World Bank. http://docum ents.worldbank.org/curated/en/692491468771277275/Indias-self-employed-womens- asso ciation-SEWA-empowerment-through-mobilization-of-poor-women-on-a-large-scale

Bourdieu, P. (1986). Forms of capital. In *Handbook of Theory for the Sociology of Education*. Greenwood Press.

Brazenor, R. (2002). Disabilities and labour market earnings in Australia. *Australian Journal of Labour Economics*, 5(3), 319–334.

Büyüm, A. M., Kenney, C., Koris, A., Mkumba, L., & Raveendran, Y. (2020). Decolonising global health: if not now, when? *BMJ Global Health*, 5(8), e003394.

Cash, R., & Patel, V. (2020). Has COVID-19 subverted global health? *The Lancet*, 395 (10238), 1687–1688.

Cassell, J. (2002). Perturbing the system: "Hard science," "soft science," and social science, the anxiety and madness of method. *Human Organization*, 61(2), 177–185.

Chattopadhyay, S. (2021). Much more to do to tackle inequality. https://thewire.in/ south-asia/bangladesh-much-more-to-do-to-tackle-inequality

Chowdhury, A. M. R., Bhuiya, A., Chowdhury, M. E., Rasheed, S., Hussain, Z., & Chen, L. C. (2013). The Bangladesh paradox: exceptional health achievement despite economic poverty. *The Lancet*, 382(9906), 1734–1745.

Coleman, J. S. (1994). *Foundations of Social Theory*. Harvard University Press.

Committee, I. D. (2022). Extreme poverty and the sustainable development goals: Fifth report of session 2022–23. House of Commons. https://publications.parliam ent.uk/pa/cm5803/cmselect/cmintdev/147/summary.html

Cresswell, T. (2004). *Place: A Short Introduction*. Blackwell.

Cross, J. C., & Karides, M. (2007). Capitalism, modernity, and the "appropriate" use of space. In *Street Entrepreneurs* (pp. 41–57). Routledge.

Crouthamel, B., Pearson, E., Tilford, S., Hurst, S., Paul, D., Aqtar, F., Silverman, J., & Averbach, S. (2021). Out-of-clinic and self-managed abortion in Bangladesh: menstrual regulation provider perspectives. *Reproductive Health*, 18(1), 1–12.

Daily Star (1998, April 28). Two Stroke auto-rickshaws should be phased out. *Daily Star*.

Daily Star (2002, August 3). Two-Stroke ban firm on track. *Daily Star*.

Das, V., & Randeria, S. (2015). Politics of the urban poor: aesthetics, ethics, volatility, precarity: an introduction to supplement 11. *Current Anthropology*, 56(11), S3–S14.

Davis, M. (2006). Planet of slums. *Open House Int*, 8(5).

Desai, S., & Rashid, S. (2023). Group think? Questioning the persistent myth of the individual expert in global health. *The Lancet*, 11.

Desmond, M. [YouTube]. (2023). *The Privileged are Complicit in America's Poverty Crisis. Amanpour and Company*.

Devereux, S., & Sabates-Wheeler, R. (2004). *Transformative Social Protection*. Brighton: IDS.

Center for Policy Dialogue (2023). Reducing out-of-pocket expenditure to improve the quality and affordability of national health care system (Draft Policy Brief 2023).

Duffield, M. (2001). *Global Governance and the New Wars*. Zed Books.

Etzold, B. (2013). The politics of street food. Contested governance and vulnerabilities. In *Dhaka's Field of Street Vending*. Franz Steiner Verlag.

Etzold, B., Hossain, M. A., & Rahman, S. (2013). Street food vending in Dhaka: Livelihoods of the urban poor and the encroachment of public space. *Dhaka*

Metropolitan Development Area and Its Planning: Problems, Issues and Policies. *Bangladesh Institute of Planners (BIP) Dhaka.* www.bip.org.bd/SharingFiles/journa l_book/20140427160

Financial Express (2021, August 3). Growing income inequality in Bangladesh causes concern. https://thefinancialexpress.com.bd/views/reviews/growing-income-inequa lity-in-bangladesh-causes-concern-1627918086

Farid, C. (2013). New paths to justice: A tale of social justice lawyering in Bangladesh. *Wis. Int'l LJ*, 31, 421.

Farmer, P. (2004). *Pathologies of Power: Health, Human Rights, and the New War on the Poor* (Vol. 4). University of California Press.

For their outstanding record of promotion of health and human development (2023). *Right Livelihood.* https://rightlivelihood.org/the-change-makers/find-a-laureate/za frullah-chowdhury-gonoshasthaya-kendra/

Frankenberg, R. (1980). Medical anthropology and development: A theoretical per-spective. *Social Science & Medicine. Part B: Medical Anthropology*, 14(4), 197–207.

Giménez, L., Jolliffe, D., & Sharif, I. (2014). Bangladesh, a middle income country by 2021: What will it take in terms of poverty reduction? *The Bangladesh Development Studies*, 37(1 & 2), 1–19.

Haque, K. N. H. (2012). *The Political Economy of Urban Space: Land and Real Estate in Dhaka City.* https://bigd.bracu.ac.bd/publications/the-political-economy-of-urban-space/

Haque, S. S., Yanez-Pagans, M., Arias-Granada, Y., & Joseph, G. (2020). Water and sanitation in Dhaka slums: Access, quality, and informality in service provision. *Water International*, 45(7–8), 791–811.

Hashemi, S. M., & De Montesquiou, A. (2011). Reaching the poorest: Lessons from the graduation model. *Focus Note*, 69(1), 1–15.

Hawkins, K., Cornwall, A., & Lewin, T. (2011). Sexuality and empowerment: An intimate connection. *Pathways Policy Paper, Brighton: Pathways of Women's Empowerment.*

Heinrich Boll Stiftung (2020). Double repression: Lockdown measures in Bangladesh and its impact on informal sector workers. https://th.boell.org/en/2020/05/13/dou ble-repression-lockdown-measures-bangladesh-and-its-impact-informal-sector-workers

Hossain, I. (2021, July 26). Breaching lockdown rules: Poor arrestees struggling to pay fines. *Dhaka Tribune.* www.dhakatribune.com/bangladesh/253381/breaching-lock down-rules-poor-arrestees

Hossain, M., Khan, M., Haque, M. A., Roy, S., & Hasan, M. (2015). *Changing Pat-terns of Urbanization in Bangladesh: An Analysis of Census Data.* Bangladesh Bureau of Statistics.

Hossain, M. J., Soma, M. A., Bari, M. S., Emran, T. B., & Islam, M. R. (2021). COVID-19 and child marriage in Bangladesh: Emergency call to action. *BMJ Paediatrics Open*, 5(1).

Hossain, M. S. (2006). *Urban Poverty and Adaptations of the Poor to Urban Life in Dhaka City, Bangladesh.* UNSW Sydney.

Huda, M. N. (2014). Food security among pavement dwellers in Dhaka City. *World Vision*, 8(1), 46–59.

Huq, M. N., Howlader, S. R., & Kabir, M. (2014). The impact of health on pro-ductivity in Bangladesh. *Global Journal of Quantitative Science*, 1(2), 24–31.

Institute for Development Policy (2007). *Accountability Arrangements to Combat Corruption in the Delivery of Infrastructure Services in Bangladesh: A Case Study.* Loughborough University Press. https://hdl.handle.net/2134/9578

Islam, F., & Akhter, G. A. (2015). Child abuse in Bangladesh. *Ibrahim Medical College Journal*, 9(1), 18–21.

Islam, N., Mahbub, A., Nazem, N., Angeles, G. L., & Lance, P. (2006). *Slums of Urban Bangladesh: Mapping and Census, 2005*. www.measureevaluation.org/resources/publications/tr-06-35.html

Jackman, D. (2019). The decline of gangsters and politicization of violence in urban Bangladesh. *Development and Change*, 50(5), 1214–1238.

Jahan, N. (2019). Pulling the weight of the world. *The Daily Star*. www.thedailystar.net/star-weekend/labour-rights/news/pulling-the-weight-the-world-1698940

Jesmin, S., & Salway, S. (2000). Marriage among the urban poor of Dhaka: instability and uncertainty. *Journal of International Development*, 12(5), 689–705.

Jianxin, Y., Rabbi, F., Siraj, M. B., & Zhenzhen, L. (2021). Road traffic accident situation in Dhaka City, Bangladesh. *Journal of Transportation Systems*, 6(3), 23–34.

Kabeer, N. (2020). 'Misbehaving' RCTs: The confounding problem of human agency. *World Development*, 127, 104809.

Kabir, S. S., Chowdhury, A., Smith, J., Morgan, R., Wenham, C., & Rashid, S. F. (2023). A social cure for COVID-19: Importance of networks in combatting socio-economic and emotional health challenges in informal settlements in Dhaka, Bangladesh. *Social Sciences*, 12(3), 127.

Khan, M. (2010). *Impact of Climate Change on the Livelihood of the Urban Poor: A Case of Dhaka City*. Master of Public Policy and Governance Program thesis, North South University, Dhaka, Bangladesh.

Kleinman, A., Das, V., & Lock, M. M. (1997). *Social Suffering*. University of California Press.

Koonings, K., & Kruijt, D. E. (2007). *Fractured Cities: Social Exclusion, Urban Violence and Contested Spaces in Latin America*. Zed Books. https://doi.org/http://dx.doi.org/10.5040/9781350220225

Loewenson, R. H. (1998). Health impact of occupational risks in the informal sector in Zimbabwe. *International Journal of Occupational and Environmental Health*, 4(4), 264–274.

Logan, K. (1983). Part 5: The role of pharmacists and over the counter medications in the health care system of a Mexican city. *Medical Anthropology*, 7(3), 68–89.

MacMillan, S. (2022). *Hope Over Fate, Fazle Hasan Abed and the Science of Ending Global Poverty*. Rowman & Littlefield Publishers. https://bracusa.org/hope-over-fate/

Mamun, A. A. (2019, September 7). The menace of teenage gangs. *The Business Post*. www.tbsnews.net/bangladesh/crime/menace-teenage-gangs

Misha, F., Imtiaz, S. H., McConnell, M., Cash, R., & Rashid, S. F. (2023). Using mobile financial services to improve community health workers' efficiency during the COVID-19 pandemic in Dhaka, Bangladesh. In *Inoculating Cities* (pp. 167–185). Elsevier.

Mitlin, D., & Satterthwaite, D. (2012). *Urban Poverty in the Global South: Scale and Nature*. Routledge.

Mpanje, D., Gibbons, P., & McDermott, R. (2018). Social capital in vulnerable urban settings: An analytical framework. *Journal of International Humanitarian Action*, 3(1), 1–14.

Mridha, M. K., Hossain, A., Alam, B., Sarker, B. K., Wahed, T., Khan, R., & Roy, S. (2009). The perceptions of community groups to improve MNCH in urban slums: An exploratory case study of Korail slum in Dhaka. MANOSHI Working Paper Series No 9.

Muggah, R. (2012). *Researching the Urban Dilemma: Urbanization, Poverty and Violence*. IDRC; CRDI; UKaid.

Nahar, P. (2021). *Childlessness in Bangladesh: Intersectionality, Suffering and Resilience*. Routledge. https://doi.org/10.4324/9781003050285

Nargis, N., Thompson, M. E., Fong, G. T., Driezen, P., Hussain, A. G., Ruthbah, U. H., Quah, A. C., & Abdullah, A. S. (2015). Prevalence and patterns of tobacco use in Bangladesh from 2009 to 2012: Evidence from International Tobacco Control (ITC) Study. *PloS one*, 10(11), e0141135.

Nastiti, A., Prabaharyaka, I., Roosmini, D., & Kunaefi, T. D. (2012). Health-associated cost of urban informal industrial sector: An assessment tool. *Procedia-Social and Behavioral Sciences*, 36, 112–122.

National Housing Policy [Draft of 2008]. (2008). www.nha.gov.bd/pdf/national_hou sing_policy_(rough).pdf

Naziha, S. (2013, June 25). Female Bangladeshi migrant workers face abuse: IOM study. *News Global*. www.iom.int/news/female-bangladeshi-migrant-workers-face-a buse-iom-study

Nichter, M., & Vuckovic, N. (1994). Agenda for an anthropology of pharmaceutical practice. *Social Science & Medicine*, 39(11), 1509–1525.

Paul, S., Afzal Aftab, M. R., Nazneen, S., Azmi, R., & Hossain, S. (2019). Subjective experiences of stigma related to tuberculosis: A qualitative exploration at Peri-urban, Bangladesh. *Am. J. Prev. Med. Public Health*, 4(2), 27–36.

Pereira, F. (2004). When the will is far from the way: Rising concern over the non-implementation of court judgements. *Daily Star*.

Perlman, J. E. (1975). Rio's favelas and the myth of marginality. *Politics & Society*, 5 (2), 131–160.

Podder, V., Morita, T., & Tanimoto, T. (2019). Reducing road traffic accidents in Bangladesh. *The Lancet*, 393(10169), 315.

Preetha, S. S., & Islam, Z. (2020). 1931 brands have delayed & cancelled $3.7bn worth of orders from garment factories during COVID-19. *Business & Human Rights Resource Centre*. www.business-humanrights.org/en/latest-news/bangladesh-1931-brands-ha ve-delayed-cancelled-37bn-worth-of-orders-from-garment-factories-during-covid-19/

Putnam, R. D. (2000). *Bowling Alone: The Collapse and Revival of American Community*. Simon and Schuster.

Rahman, H. Z., Rahman, A., Faruk, M. S., Avinno, I., Matin, I., Wazed, M. A., & Zillur, U. (2022). *Recovery with Distress: Unpacking COVID-19 Impact on Livelihoods and Poverty in Bangladesh*. UNU-WIDER. https://doi.org/10.35188/UNU-WIDER/2022/144-0

Ramirez-Rubio, O., Daher, C., Fanjul, G., Gascon, M., Mueller, N., Pajín, L., Plasencia, A., Rojas-Rueda, D., Thondoo, M., & Nieuwenhuijsen, M. J. (2019). Urban health: An example of a "health in all policies" approach in the context of SDGs implementation. *Globalization and health*, 15, 1–21.

Rashid, S. F. (2004). *Worried Lives: Poverty, Gender and Reproductive Health of Married Adolescent Women Living in an Urban Slum in Bangladesh*. PhD thesis. Australian National University.

Rashid, S. F., & Islam, M. I. (2019). The invisible illness of life: Women's health narratives in a Dhaka informal settlement. https://blogs.lse.ac.uk/southasia/2019/05/20/ lse-uc-berkeley-bangladesh-summit-2-the-invisible-illness-of-life-womens-health-nar ratives-in-a-dhaka-inform

Rashid, S. F., Theobald, S., & Ozano, K. (2020). Towards a socially just model: Balancing hunger and response to the COVID-19 pandemic in Bangladesh. *BMJ Global Health*, 5(6), e002715.

Ross, F. C. (2015). Raw life and respectability: Poverty and everyday life in a post-apartheid community. *Current Anthropology*, 56(11), S97–S107.

Roy, S., Sowgat, T., Ahmed, M. U., Islam, S. M. T., Anjum, N., Mondal, J., & Rahman, M. M. (2018). *National Urban Policies and City Profiles for Dhaka and Khulna*. Bangladesh: GCRF Centre for Sustainable, Healthy and Learning Cities and Neighbourhoods.

Sarker, A. R., Sultana, M., Mahumud, R. A., Ahmed, S., Ahmed, M. W., Hoque, M. E., Islam, Z., Gazi, R., & Khan, J. A. (2016). Effects of occupational illness on labor productivity: A socioeconomic aspect of informal sector workers in urban Bangladesh. *journal of Occupational Health*, 58(2), 209–215.

Satterthwaite, D. (1997). Urban poverty: Reconsidering its scale and nature. *IDS Bulletin*, 28(2), 9–23.

Satterthwaite, D., & Mitlin, D. (2013). *Reducing Urban Poverty in the Global South*. Routledge.

Scheper-Hughes, N. (1992). *Death without Weeping: The Violence of Everyday Life in Brazil*. University of California Press.

Schofield, D., Passey, M., Percival, R., Shrestha, R., Callander, E., & Kelly, S. (2011). Retiring early with cardiovascular disease: Impact on individual's financial assets. *International journal of cardiology*, 146(1), 125–126.

Schofield, D. J., Callander, E. J., Shrestha, R. N., Percival, R., Kelly, S. J., & Passey, M. E. (2013). Premature retirement due to ill health and income poverty: A cross-sectional study of older workers. *BMJ open*, 3(5), e002683.

Scoones, I. (2013). Livelihoods perspectives and rural development. In *Critical Perspectives in Rural Development Studies* (pp. 159–184). Routledge.

Sen, B., Hulme, D., Ahmad, I., Kabeer, N., Ali, Z., Khan, I., Begum, S., Matin, I., Haider, O., Sen, C., & Shahabuddin, Q. (2004). *Chronic Poverty in Bangladesh: Tales of ascent, Descent, Marginality and Persistence: The State of the Poorest 2004/2005*. Bangladesh: Bangladesh Institute of Development Studies Dhaka.

Shamim, I. (2006). The feminisation of migration: Gender, the state and migrant strategies in Bangladesh. In *Mobility, Labour Migration and Border Controls in Asia* (pp. 155–171). Springer.

Shibli, A. (2023, February 4). What is holding Bangladesh's GDP growth rate down? *The Daily Star*. www.thedailystar.net/opinion/views/open-dialogue/news/what-holding-bangladeshs-gdp-growth-rate-down-3238926

Shupto, N. A. (2019, July 21). Rickshaw restrictions: Is it justified?. *New Age*. www.newagebd.net/article/79103/rickshaw-restrictions-is-it-justified

Singer, M., & Clair, S. (2003). Syndemics and public health: Reconceptualizing disease in bio-social context. *Medical Anthropology Quarterly*, 17(4), 423–441.

Sinthia, S. A. (2020). Analysis of urban slum: Case study of Korail Slum, Dhaka. *International Journal of Urban and Civil Engineering*, 14(11), 416–430.

Sowgat, T., & Roy, S. (2013). Pro-poor development: An assessment of the national level policies and programs in Bangladesh. *Plan Plus*, 6, 43–61.

Streatfield, P. K., & Karar, Z. A. (2008). Population challenges for Bangladesh in the coming decades. *J Health Popul Nutr*, 26(3), 261–272.

Sultana, H., & Fatima, A. (2017). Factors influencing migration of female workers: a case of Bangladesh. *IZA Journal of Development and Migration*, 7, 1–17.

Sumon, A. (2007). Informal economy in Dhaka City-Automobile Workshop and Hazardous Child Labor. *Pakistan Journal of Sociel Science*, 4(6), 711.

Sutarjo, U. S. (2007). Ergonomics policy in Indonesia. *Journal of Human Ergology*, 36 (2), 57–61.

van der Heijden, J., Gray, N., Stringer, B., Rahman, A., Akhter, S., Kalon, S., Dada, M., & Biswas, A. (2019). 'Working to stay healthy', health-seeking behaviour in Bangladesh's urban slums: a qualitative study. *BMC Public Health*, 19(1), 1–13.

Van Dijk, R., De Bruijn, M., & Gewald, J.-B. (2007). Social and historical trajectories of agency in Africa: An introduction. In *Strength beyond Structure* (pp. 1–15). Brill.

Wahlberg, A., Burke, N., & Manderson, L. (2021). Introduction: Stratified liveability and pandemic effects. In In A. Wahlberg, N. J. Burke, & L. Manderson (Eds), *Viral Loads* (pp. 1–24). UCL Press. https://doi.org/10.2307/j.ctv1j13zb3.7

Walker, R., & Bantebya-Kyomuhendo, G. (2014). *The Shame of Poverty*. Oxford University Press.

William, S. K. (2022). We need to recognise the diversity of the urban poor. *The Daily Star*. www.thedailystar.net/opinion/views/news/we-need-recognise-the-diversity-the-urban-poor-3121506

Wood, G. D. (2005). Poverty, capabilities and perverse social capital: The antidote to Sen and Putnam. In *Making a Living: The Livelihoods of the Rural Poor in Bangladesh*. UPL.

World Bank (2019). Bangladesh poverty assessment: Facing old and new frontiers in poverty reduction.

World Bank (2015). World Bank leveraging urbanization in Bangladesh. www.worldbank.org/en/country/bangladesh/brief/leveraging-urbanization-bangladesh

World Bank (2020). COVID-19 to add as many as 150 million extreme poor by 2021. www.worldbank.org/en/news/press-release/2020/10/07/covid-19-to-add-as-many-as-150-million-extreme-poor-by-2021

World Bank (2022). Out-of-pocket expenditure in Bangladesh. https://data.worldbank.org/indicator/SH.XPD.OOPC.CH.ZS?locations5BD

World Food Programme (2020). WFP Bangladesh Country Brief. www.wfp.org/countries/bangladesh

World Health Organization (2018). *Promoting Health: Guide to National Implementation of the Shanghai Declaration*.

Wool, Z. H., & Livingston, J. (2017). Collateral afterworlds: An introduction. *Social Text*, 35(1), 1–15.

Yunus, M. (2023). The Nobel Peace Prize 2006. *NobelPrize.Org*. www.nobelprize.org/prizes/peace/2006/yunus/biographical/

Index

Abed, Sir Fazle Hasan 9, 163
Abortion(s): 53–54, 56, 104, 128, 133,
  166; clandestine 129; unsafe 2, 156
Africa 155, 162, 171
Agamben, Giorgio 155
Agrani (government) bank 144
ailments: physical 148; stress related 156
anthropological methods 160
Appadurai, Arjun 147
ARISE project 160
Asia 73, 95, 162, 170
Atkinson-Sheppard, Sally 79, 83

Badda 37, 40, 135, 140
Baganbari 127–128, 134
Banani 34, 135
Bangladesh 2, 4, 6, 8–13, 16, 24–27, 30,
  34, 42, 56, 59, 73–74, 79, 83, 107–110,
  113, 117, 122, 125, 134, 137, 140, 142,
  145, 151, 159, 161, 163–171
Bangladesh Bureau Statistics 13
Bangladesh Worker Welfare Foundation
  Act 2006 41
Baniganj 34–35, 38, 40, 64, 70, 86, 139,
  146–147, 152; slum 34, 70, 139
basti 21, 81
Beaubien, J. 42, 73, 145, 165
beggar 44, 47, 85, 100, 154
begging 38, 41, 63, 65–68, 76, 84, 92–93,
  113, 118, 141, 147, 151, 155
Bhatt, Ela 162
BRAC 9, 24, 161, 163
BRAC University 24, 163
bribes 13, 45, 88, 91, 122, 150
bureaucratic court system 122

Center for Urban Studies (CUS) 15
child: labour 137; marriage 26, 30, 42, 167;
  sexual abuse 142; mortality rates 9

chinta roge (worry illness) 98–99, 148
Chittagong Hill Tracts 16, 163
Chowdhury, Zafrullah 9, 24
city corporation 16, 88–89, 91, 139
climate: change 162; disasters 11
community(ies) 1, 9, 13, 17, 26, 54, 64,
  91, 95, 109, 111, 113, 119–120, 129,
  146, 154–155, 160, 168, 170;
  heterogenous 124
Constitution of Bangladesh 127
Coronavirus Disease (COVID-19) 2, 4,
  10, 16–17, 22, 25–27, 30, 36–37, 42,
  60, 65, 70–71, 84, 87, 119, 137, 144,
  147–148, 150, 152–154, 156, 158–159,
  162–164, 166, 168–169, 171; lockdown
  (s) 16, 84, 159; pandemic 2–4, 9,
  16–17, 22–23, 26–27, 147–148, 158,
  162–163, 168–169, 171; post 19, 150;
  pre-Covid 37, 62, 65, 119, 143; State
  Mandated Covid Guidelines 85
court 7, 24, 35, 87–89, 121, 125, 134,
  139, 150, 169
credit 7, 12, 43–44, 51, 57, 61, 67, 71, 73,
  114, 129, 153–154, 156; provide
  medicines on 99, 156

debts 2, 16, 61–62, 67, 72–73, 83, 99,
  119, 144, 146, 150
Department of Telegraph and Telephone
  Board of Bangladesh (T&T) 34
Desmond, M. 161, 166
Dhaka 2–8, 10, 11–13, 15, 17, 19–20,
  24–27, 30, 32, 34, 36, 42–45, 48–49,
  56, 59–60, 66, 72, 78–79, 83, 86–87,
  89, 94–96, 99, 103, 109–110, 118, 120,
  122–123, 127, 133–134, 137–140, 147,
  149–150, 156, 160–161, 163–170;
  district 137
Dhaka City Corporation 95, 150

discrimination 3, 4, 17, 18, 21–22, 95
displacement 7, 127
divorce 46, 55, 104, 112
dowry 32, 52, 100, 104, 108
Drug Ordinance of 1982 99
drug: seller(s) 37, 49, 57, 64, 98–99, 102, 106, 108, 115, 119, 156–157; selling 155; trade 14, 20–21, 31, 77–78, 81, 123, 155

economic: advancement 11; class 76; growth 10; security 162; shop 7, 16, 35, 65, 99–100, 109, 115–116, 128, 165; situation 19, 55; support 46, 133, 140; trade 14, 20–21, 31, 77–78, 81, 83, 123, 155; unjust economic systems 162
education 5, 9–11, 13, 21, 40, 55, 57, 136, 142–143, 148–149, 154, 160, 162, 165; dropout rate 137
Environment Protection Index (EPI) 10
ethnographic: data 5; evidence 17; research 24
Etzold, B. 15, 25, 91, 94–96, 166
evicted 1, 8, 28, 43, 116, 129, 155–156
eviction(s) 2–3, 7–8, 12–13, 15, 17–24, 35, 73, 123, 125, 127–132, 134, 146, 151–152, 154, 156, 161; forced 8, 127; high eviction risks 12; of residents in Phulbari 152; of the slum 13, 24
excessive use of state violence 95
extortion 13, 79, 83, 85, 88, 131, 134, 151; money 79

female: employment 20; migrants 59; headed households 104
fertility rate 9
formal: micro-credit organization 153; services 12
fundamental principles of state policies (FPSP) 127

gang(s) 53, 77–79, 83, 151, 165, 168; criminal 123; violence 29; and crime 29; rival 76, 78–79
garment(s): factory(ies) 11, 26, 30, 34, 41, 52, 104, 129, 132–133, 137, 149, 169; industry 137; sector 16, 143; worker 152
gatekeepers 4, 13–14, 83–84, 91, 124, 146
Gazipur 95, 117
GDP 8–10, 27, 161, 170; growth rate 27, 161, 170

gender: inequality 30; related vulnerabilities 104; gendered nature of migration 59
global regulations 44
Gonoshashto founder 9
Bangladesh Government: agendas 44; hospital 117; land 15, 28; policies 11, 59
Grameen Bank 9, 24
Gulshan 34, 39–40, 60, 64–71, 84–87, 90, 92, 116, 121, 135–139, 141–144, 154

harassment 4, 7, 18, 20, 71, 85, 95, 102, 138, 146, 150
hawker(s) 37–38, 41, 64–65, 67, 84–85, 87–88, 90, 92–94, 116, 121, 143
health 1–7, 9, 12, 15–21, 24–26, 27, 29, 33–34, 41–42, 53–56, 58, 64, 75–76, 80, 97–104, 106, 108–122, 124, 128–129, 133, 147, 151, 156–158, 160–164, 166–171; bad 4, 108, 158, 163; care 15–16, 25, 99, 109, 124, 158, 161, 166, 168; challenges 158; clinic 7, 18, 29, 80; crises 100, 119; facilities 56, 116, 156; issues 115, 156; provider(s) 2, 33, 41, 53– 55, 76, 80, 106, 128–129, 133, 151; risks 147; worker(s) 19– 21, 26, 29, 34, 54–55, 100, 112, 129, 168
healthcare: expenditure 158; systems 159
heroin addicts 75
homeless residents 156
Household Income and Expenditure Survey (HIES) 9
housing insecurities 151
Human Development Index report 10
human rights 83, 125, 159; violation of 151; lawyers 125

illicit activities 14, 20, 49, 79, 91, 143
income 3–5, 8–10, 12–13, 16–17, 19–20, 22, 25–26, 31, 34–38, 41, 43, 45, 49, 51, 54–58, 65, 67–70, 72, 85– 87, 102, 105, 113–115, 118, 124, 129, 132–134, 137–141, 144, 149, 151, 154, 156–157, 159, 161, 163, 166–167, 170; distribution 9–10; inequality 9, 25, 166; lack of stable 148; limited 131; opportunities 13; source(s) 3–4, 19, 35, 45, 134; rental 124, 149, 152
infection: clinical knowledge of transmission 159; urinary tract 116
informal: economy 13–14, 16, 19, 40–41, 77, 87, 147, 150, 157; job(s) 7, 136; judge-jury system 46; sector 12–13, 20,

41–42, 77, 104, 165, 167–168, 170;
sector workers 41, 167, 170; work 2–3,
15, 35, 85, 95, 162; work economy 15;
worker(s) 2–3, 35, 44, 85, 95, 162
INGO clinic 106–107
interest 10, 19, 61–63, 67, 127, 137, 151,
153, 155
international health organization 29

job opportunities 64–65, 113
Jordan 58, 60

Kabeer, Naila 159
Kashimpur Jail 95
Konabari Police Station 84

Labour Law of 2006, 41
land: holding numbers 31; ownership
structures 127
landlady 2, 19, 29, 43, 45, 47, 51, 55,
63–64, 68, 72, 104, 116–117, 128, 136,
138, 150, 152, 154–155
landlord(s)18, 28, 39–40, 43–44, 51, 55,
57, 60–61, 63–65, 68–69, 71, 73, 80,
91, 93, 102, 116, 124–125, 128, 131,
139, 150–153, 155
large scale international funders 159
Latin America 26, 79, 83, 96, 162, 168
law(s): abuse of the 151; enforcement 20,
23, 79, 86–87, 122, 150–151; internal
77; road safety 122
legal: frameworks 94; services 77;
termination 105
literacy requirements 137
livelihoods promotion 161
loan(s) 10, 12–13, 32, 45, 48–49, 51–52,
62, 65, 67–68, 73, 87, 90, 98–99,
101–103, 109, 113, 119, 123, 126, 144,
146, 150, 153–154, 163
local: (unlicensed) pharmacies 16; clinic
18, 53, 105; gangs 49, 83; illegal
violence 79; leader(s) 12–14, 18–20,
31, 33– 35, 41, 51, 77–78, 80, 102,
124–126, 151; political networks 13;
politicians 78, 126; politics 146
lockdown 2–3, 16, 19, 26, 60–61, 63–67,
70–71, 84, 86–88, 90, 93, 96, 119,
150–152, 157, 159, 163, 167; national 2;
partial 86; post 19, 64–66, 148,
152–153; *see also* COVID-19; pandemic
loss of wages 88, 148
low: legal status 91; socio-economic
status 158; income area 129; income

households 17; income housing 32, 37,
77–78, 140

marginal: people 4; status 122
marginalised populations 5, 159, 162
marginality 6, 26–27, 164, 170
marijuana 71, 91, 93, 141, 143
mastaans 13–14, 20–21, 31, 34, 77–80,
124, 151
Mastanocracy 14
maternal: and child health 103; mortality
rate 9
medical practitioners 99
menstrual: problems 111; regulation 54,
56, 128, 134, 166
Mia, Barek 85, 88
Migrant(s) 8, 11–12, 34, 43, 46, 73, 75,
169, 170; female 59; men 46; new 8,
48; rural 8 temporary 5, 154
migration 59, 73–74, 170
Mirpur 28, 123–124, 131
Misoprostol 56, 128
money: borrowing 43, 58, 63, 67;
extortion 79; lender(s) 48, 57, 62, 67,
109, 153–154

National Board of Revenue (NBR) 9
National Housing Policy (1993) 127
National: lockdown 2; policies 4, 146,
163; political leadership 13
networks 2–4, 14, 17, 19–20, 43, 49, 55,
59, 64, 66–67, 72–73, 89– 91, 104, 124,
126–127, 134, 136, 138, 144, 146,
150–154, 168; social 48, 55, 61, 146
non-governmental organisations (NGO)
9, 11, 15, 29, 105, 124, 133, 137, 151;
clinic 105, 133; school(s) 29, 137;
worker 151
Nobel Peace Prize 9, 27, 171
nutrition interventions 9

organized crime 83, 165

paramedic 29, 81; *see also* COVID-19;
lockdown
party politics 15, 125
pavement dweller(s) 43, 56, 156, 167
pharmaceutical: companies 156;
industry 99
Phulbari 1–2, 7, 18– 21, 28–34, 40, 43,
47–52, 54–55, 72, 75–78, 80–83, 101,
108, 123, 125–126, 128–131, 133–134,
146–150, 152–154, 156–157; slum 1,

28, 47, 75–76, 80–81; sudden demolition of 125–126, 128, 148–149, 151
police 2–3, 13–14, 18, 21, 31, 37, 40, 48, 51, 59–60, 66, 71–72, 77–91, 94–95, 117, 121–122, 124, 127, 139, 142, 144, 146, 148–152, 155; raid(s) 21, 78, 81, 83, 90–91, 148, 150; policemen 18, 81, 85, 90, 125–126; policewoman 88–89
Policies 25, 27, 163, 166, 170
Political: environment 140, 160; leaders 127; muscle 79
pollution 45, 56, 102
poverty 3–5, 8–11, 14, 16–17, 22, 25–27, 30, 41, 47–48, 55, 59, 79, 84, 98, 133, 143, 146–147, 149, 152, 155– 158, 160–161, 163, 166–167, 170–171; global 9; intergenerational 3, 149; rural 11; urban 5, 6, 11–12, 25, 42, 134, 165
power brokers 91
pregnancy 55–56, 70, 101, 105–107, 119–120, 128, 133–134, 144; terminations 55, 107
private: clinic 54, 105, 129; health care facilities 15
psychological well-being 151
Public Works Division (PWD) 34
public: clinics and hospitals 103; doctors 103; health 5, 9, 15, 24, 99, 118–119, 151, 157–160, 170; health literature 151; health research 159; health risks 159; health services 99; health systems 157; toilets 116

randomized clinical trials (RCTs) 17, 159, 168
Rapid Action Battalion (RAB) 78
real estate developer 126
rent 3–4, 7, 12–13, 16, 18–19, 21–22, 34–35, 38, 43–44, 47–49, 51, 57–58, 60–65, 68, 70, 72–73, 89, 93–94, 99–100, 111, 116–117, 124, 126, 128–130, 132–133, 137–139, 147, 150, 152, 154–155, 164; debt 72
reproductive health 133
revenge murders 77
rickshaw 30–39, 41, 43, 48, 51, 54, 64, 66, 71–72, 74, 90, 105, 111, 117, 136, 148, 157, 165, 170; pullers 41, 66
road accidents 118
Ross, Fiona 155
Russian invasion 162

samity 45, 49, 51, 102, 109
Sanitation facilities 12
scarcity 11, 19, 53, 62, 99, 128, 134, 145, 148, 161
second-class citizens 14
self-medication 100
Self-Employed Women's Association (SEWA) 162, 165
semi-government school 29, 36
several high-rise apartment complexes 126
sewage systems 147
sex work 94, 136, 144, 147, 155
sexual: assault 134; exploitation 59, 142; exploitation and abuse 142
shalishes 46
Shamim, Ishrat 59
shared facilities 132
Shibli, Abdullah 161
shontrashis (thugs) 14
slum(s) 2–5, 7–8, 11–23, 28, 31, 33–34, 36, 38, 42–43, 46–48, 51, 53–55, 60, 64–67, 69, 72, 75–79, 81–83, 90, 95–96, 98–99, 101–105, 107–108, 114–116, 118, 123–127, 134, 136–138, 140, 142, 144, 146–157, 163–164, 166, 168, 170; clearing 127; demolitions of 126–127; Dhaka 4, 20, 137, 147, 160, 167; displaced slum residents 127; elite 33; established 12, 132; leaders 13, 79, 125, 127, 146; of Dhaka 5, 12; power and politics within 13; residents 3, 8, 14–16, 55, 77, 79, 99, 103–104, 127, 134, 152–153; settlement, 7; urban 11, 15–16, 46, 56, 79, 108, 110, 163, 168, 171
social: acceptance 46, 54, 101, 140; and economic hierarchy 149; and political resources 5; conditions 158; connections 7, 19, 78, 146; costs 157; dominant social system 4; empowerment 161; hierarchy 47, 136; inequalities 3, 100; mobilization 126; networks 48, 55, 61, 146; protection 10, 161, 163; relationships 1, 4, 14, 61, 67, 73, 91, 116, 120, 146, 151, 154, 158; safety net 161; scale 4; science research 5, 159–160; security 3, 149; standing 61, 154
socio-cultural: beliefs 30; norm 109
socioeconomic status 162
South Africa 147, 155
South Asia 9, 30

Special Programme of Research, Development and Research Training in Human Reproduction 20
Spivak, Gayatri 5
street vendors 34, 42, 85, 88, 150, 164
structural: and social inequalities 4; violence 3, 18, 151
Supreme Court 8, 127
syndemic theory 158
systematic: exclusion 3; discrimination 162

tenant(s) 12, 19, 21, 31, 33, 35–37, 39, 43–45, 47, 49, 51, 55, 57, 61–63, 70–72, 75, 80, 90–91, 104, 107, 117, 124, 126, 129, 131–132, 136, 147, 150–156
termination(s) *see* abortion(s)
territorial warfare 78
textile industry 137
The Lancet 9, 25, 122, 166, 169
tobacco consumption 108
trained doctors 119
tuberculosis 36, 57, 111–113, 156, 169

unemployment 59, 61, 70, 144
unhygienic conditions 147
unlicensed pharmacist 119
urban: development in Bangladesh 11; economies 94; health system 15; informal economy 13; land administration in Bangladesh 127; political economic culture 14; poor 3, 5–6, 8, 11–12, 15–17, 25, 27, 45, 56, 73, 79, 83, 86, 95, 127, 134, 151, 160 161, 163 166, 168, 171
urbanization 7, 8, 10– 12, 27, 47, 171

vacuum aspiration procedure 105
violating health guidelines 87

water: collection 131; irregular availability 98; piped 12; running 147; supply 147, 159
waterborne: and water-washed diseases 147; diseases 132
WHO Commission on the Social Determinants of Health 162
widowed 37, 104, 138, 140, 149
women 2– 5, 9, 12, 17–23, 28–29, 32–34, 40–41, 45–47, 49–50, 54–55, 58–59, 72–73, 75–76, 78, 80–83, 88–89, 91–94, 98–99, 101, 103–105, 107–109, 113, 123–125, 129, 132, 140, 145–149, 151, 153–158, 160, 164–165; adolescent 21, 33, 99, 101, 112; and their families 1, 3–5, 17–19, 21–24, 53, 57, 73, 91, 144, 146–147, 150–151, 153–156, 161; divorced 55
worker(s): agriculture 41; child 41; construction 41; domestic 41, 59; garment 152; health 19– 21, 26, 29, 34, 54–55, 100, 112, 129, 168; informal 2–3, 35, 44, 85, 95, 162; NGO 151; transport 41
World Bank 8, 10, 11, 15–16, 27, 44, 56, 165, 171
World Health Organization 20, 134, 171

Yale Environmental Protection Index 10
young women's: case studies 18, 147; sexual lives 140
Yunus, Muhammad 9, 24